Intermediate
LEISURE & TOURISM

CAMBRIDGE
TRAINING AND

CTAD

DEVELOPMENT
LTD

Oxford University Press

Oxford University Press, Walton Street, Oxford OX2 6DP

Oxford New York

Athens Auckland Bangkok Bombay Calcutta Cape Town Dar es Salaam Delhi Florence Hong Kong Istanbul
Karachi Kuala Lumpur Madras Madrid Melbourne Mexico City Nairobi Paris Singapore Taipei Tokyo Toronto

and associated companies in
Berlin Ibadan

Oxford is a trademark of the Oxford University Press

© Cambridge Training and Development Ltd 1996

First published 1996

A CIP catalogue record for this book is available from the British Library.

ISBN 0 19 832798 6

Typeset and designed by Design Study, Bury St Edmunds and Chris Lord Information Design, Brighton, East Sussex

Printed and bound in Italy by Canale & C. S.p.A. - Turin

Contributors include:
Pamela Beaves, Robert Manning School
Josephine Walton, Robert Manning School
Debra Howard
Thanks go to:
Caroline Horrigan, The Travel Training Company Ltd

Thanks for permission to reproduce
photographs/extracts go to:
The Sports Council (Sports Council logo, p.7,
Sports graph, p.13); English Heritage (English
Heritage Brochure, p.8); Wicksteed Leisure Ltd
(Children's playground, p.9); Ragdale Hall Health
Hydro (Ragdale Hall, p.9); The Minack Theatre,
photographer: Murray King (Minack Theatre,
p.10); Museum of the Moving Image (MOMI
display, p.10); The Dome, Doncaster Leisure Park
(The Dome, p.12); Plas y Brenin National
Mountain Centre (Potentially dangerous activity,
p.13, Climbing Instructor, p.68); The Independent,
writer: Glenda Cooper (Eating out graph, p.14);
Lake District National Park (National Parks map,
p.15); Cambridge Arts Theatre (Lottery payout,
p.16); National Trust Photographic Library
(Volunteer warden, p.19, Conservation project,
p.48, National Trust Shop, p.147); National Trust
(National Trust logo, p.47); Moyses Hall Museum,
photographer: Graham Portlock (Moyses Hall
Museum, p.20); Northumbrian Water (Kielder
Reservoir, p.22); Forte PLC (Waiter, p.23, Chef,
p.43, Chefs, p.94, Diners, p.94, Business
package, p.104, Girl in restaurant, p.168, Friendly
bar, p.169, Staff on computer, p.176, Office
scene, p.191, Bar person, p.209, Young waiter,
p.209, Young receptionist, p.210, Salesperson,
p.216, Student in B&B, p.230, Bridal fayre,
p.237); McDonald's Restaurants Ltd (Fast food
server, p.23, McDonald's logo p.95); The
Ironbridge Gorge Museum (Ironbridge Living
History, p.26, Ironbridge map, p.26); South
Kesteven District Council (FFDD Festival, p.27);
Thorpe Park, Leisure Sport Ltd (Thorpe Park,
p.29, Thorpe Park, p.189); Eurotunnel (Le Shuttle
& Eurotunnel logos, p.33); London Tourist Board
and Convention Bureau (London Attractions,

p.35); British Tourist Authority (Information symbol
p.36, Visitor pie chart, p.40, Japanese Tourists,
p.38, BWJ logo, p.38, BTA logo, p.46, BWJ Front
pages, p.140, Japanese visitors, p.197); Pizza
Hut (UK) Ltd (Pizza Hut logo, p.36); Snowdonia
Tourist Services (Regional leaflet, p.36); British
Rail Customer Services (Rail leaflets, p.41); Peter
Ballingall International Golf Schools (Specialist
holiday, p.42); St. Edmundsbury Borough Council
Leisure Services (Pakenham Mill, p.43, Rompers,
p.88, Good cheap leaflets, p.145, Disabled sport,
p.198, Sports receptionist, p.210, Kids being
coached p.223, Kids funday, p.242, Street
festival, p.275); Thomas Knowles, Transport
Consultant (Oxford Tour Bus, p.45); English
Tourist Board (ETB logo, p.46); Wales Tourist
Board (WTB logo, p.46); Wales Tourist Board
Photographic Library (Deserted beach, p.92,
Crowded beach, p.92); Scottish Tourist Board
(STB logo, p.46); Norwich Area Tourism Agency
(Town Centre, p.49); Kirklees Metropolitan Council
(Holmfirth town centre, p.50); White Rose Line
(York Riverboat, p.54); York Barbican Centre
(Barbican Centre, p.55); The Swan, Lavenham
(Female chef, p.58, Restaurant telephone
booking, p.218); ADIA UK Ltd (Employment
agency window, p.60); Employment Department
Group (Job Centre logo, p.60); Butterfly Hotel,
Bury St Edmunds (News headline, p.62);
Hobsons Publishing PLC (Hobsons Titles, p.63);
National Extension College (NEC logo, p.72); Club
Med (Children at Club Med, p.85); The Sanctuary
(Glossy Brochure, p.88, Exclusive club photo,
p.113); Metro-Goldwyn-Mayer Cinemas Ltd
(Cinema Listing, p.89, Multiplex photo, p.90);
Booker Foods (Wholesaler, p.94); Adidas (UK) Ltd
(Adidas logo p.95); Bordeaux Direct (Wine club
ad, p.96); Saturday Guardian (Travelogue, p.97);

Leeds United Association Football Club Ltd (Gary
Speed, p.99); Thistle Hotels & Mount Charlotte
Hotels (Leeds United Sponsorship p.99); The
National Motor Museum, Beaulieu (National Motor
Museum, p.103); Saga Holidays (Saga logo,
p.108); The Ritz Hotel (Racial orientation, p.109);
Trailfinders (Lifestyle phrase, p.111); Windmill
Ways, Jonathan Markson Tennis (Target markets,
p.114); Orange service from Hutchinson Telecom
(Mobile phone man, p.115); New Angle
Productions (Asian family, p.115, Team leader,
p.253 and p.290); Aldeburgh Foundation (Music
festival, p.121); First Choice (Travel brochure,
p.124); Guerba Expeditions Ltd, Simply Ionian,
Simply Crete (Brochure front covers, p.145);
Ashford Luxury Coaches (Coach p.158); Wimpy
International Limited (Good service, p.164); The
National Maritime Museum, Greenwich (Tour
guide, p.178, Maritime Museum, p.224); Lunn
Poly (Travel agent's window, p.188, Travel agent,
p.208); Bury St Edmunds Sports and Leisure
Centre (Map, p.196); London Toy and Model
Museum, Keith Hurst Associates (Museum shop,
p.208); Sunsail); photographer, Ian Booth (Resort
representative, p.211); The Angel Hotel, Bury St
Edmunds (Hotel receptionist, p.216); Bury Bowl
(Bowling alley receptionist, p.225); London
Transport Museum (LTM logo, p.227); Theatre
Royal, Bury St Edmunds (Theatre ticket, p.229,
Packed venue, p.247); The Natural Theatre
Company, Bath (Street theatre, p.238); Cambus
Ltd (Bus timetable, p.247); Bradford Telegraph
& Argus (Bradford headlines, p.250); Patrick
Eagar, photographer (Rained-off event, p.251);
Stephen Lazarides, photographer (House party
venue, p.268); Norfolk Constabulary (Policing
football, p.269).

Contents

ABOUT THE BOOK

This book contains the information you need to complete the four mandatory units of your Intermediate Leisure and Tourism GNVQ.

How it's organised

This book is organised in units and elements, like the GNVQ, so it's easy to find the information you need at any point in your course. Each element has several sections. They cover all the topics in the element, using the same headings as the GNVQ specifications. At the end of each element there are some key questions, so you can check your knowledge and prepare for the unit tests. There are also suggestions for an assignment, which will help you produce the evidence you need for your portfolio.

What's in it

The book presents information in several different ways so it's interesting to read and easy to understand. Some information is given in the words of people who actually work in leisure or tourism jobs – for example, a ranger in a National Park, a travel consultant in a travel agency or the manager of a hotel in a seaside resort. There are definitions of important words like 'heritage' or 'tourism'. Maps show you things like the main transport networks in the UK, the location of facilities in a major attraction or airline routes to Australia. There are illustrations and diagrams, extracts from people's diaries, examples of brochures and leaflets. Case studies go into the details of organisations like the Sports Council, major attractions like theme parks and campaigns such as the 'Britain Welcomes Japan' promotion. And there are around 200 photographs showing all sorts of attractions, facilities and people working in them.

How to use the book

Decide which part you want to read. For example, you can go straight to any element and read through the relevant sections. You can find the information about any topic by looking at the list of contents at the front of the book and seeing which section looks most useful. Or you can use the index at the back to find a specific topic or organisation.

As well as information, the book has suggestions for things you can do to help you learn about leisure and tourism in a practical way. Discussion points suggest topics that you can think about and discuss with other people – other students on your course, your tutor or teacher, friends, family, people who work in leisure and tourism. Activity boxes ask you to do things like write a memo about a promotional campaign, collect examples of leaflets or brochures and see what they contain, visit two similar facilities to compare the prices they charge, and so on. They will help you to get a real life picture of leisure and tourism organisations and what it's like to work in them.

When you've finished an element, try answering the key questions at the end. You may want to make notes of your answers and use them when you're preparing for the unit tests. The assignment at the end of each element suggests what you can do to produce evidence for your portfolio. You might want to make an action plan for each assignment to help you plan and carry out the work.

Other resources

By itself this book is an important and valuable source of information for your GNVQ studies. It should also help you use other resources effectively. For example, it suggests that you should find out more information about some topics, such as the different types of recreation facilities in an area or how facilities keep records about their customers. You might be able to get this extra information in a local library or tourist office, or from other books about leisure and tourism. It also asks you to investigate facilities yourself, by visiting them, reading about them in magazines or watching relevant programmes on television.

Over to you

It's your GNVQ and your job to make the best of the opportunity to learn about leisure and tourism. Use this book in whatever way helps you most. For example, you could:

■ look at the contents page to give you the whole picture
■ use the index to find out specific bits of information
■ read a section at a time to help you understand a topic
■ look at the assignment before starting an element so you know what you have to do
■ turn things on their head and start with the key questions to see how much you already know about an element.

It's over to you now. Good luck.

UNIT 1

Element 1.1
The leisure and recreation industry

Element 1.2
The travel and tourism industry

Element 1.3
Preparing for employment

The leisure and tourism industries

ELEMENT **1.1**

The leisure and recreation industry

The aim of this element is to help you get an overview of the leisure and recreation industry, nationally and in your local area. You will already have your own impressions of what leisure activities are. But what else comes into the category of leisure and recreation? What facilities are there to meet the growing demand for activities to fill people's leisure time? Who owns and runs them? You'll be looking at questions like these, and coming up with some answers based on your own investigations.

66 *I think the reason my business has grown is because people now have more leisure time. Horse riding has increased as a hobby since the 1960s when it was too expensive for the average person to afford. We complement what people do as their hobby – they enjoy riding at the weekends and then they think about coming on a holiday.* **99**

owner of a riding school which also provides holidays

66 *We contribute to the local community by creating employment and running workshops alongside the shows we put on. We also have a variety of concessions for different special needs groups. We want to make our venue as accessible as possible for everyone.* **99**

press and publicity officer at an entertainments venue

66 *My job is to manage the play team. There are five employees in the team and we provide play opportunities for children in the city. Our brief is to develop, support and provide opportunities for school age children in the city, particularly in the areas where there is no provision and for children who do not get many opportunities. We organise a summer programme and one-off events as and when required.* **99**

community play officer working for a city council

66 *There has been an increase in pool use in recent years because people are more interested in health and fitness nowadays. It's a non-weight-bearing activity and so it's good for people with any kind of injury. It's also a very cheap sport – you don't need any kind of fancy equipment. All you need is your costume!* **99**

development manager, swimming pool

What are the components of the leisure and recreation industry?

Leisure and recreation play an important part in people's day-to-day lives, helping them to relax, socialise and keep fit. People choose what they want to do in their leisure time. Some people's idea of relaxing is sitting in front of the television or visiting friends, others would rather go to the cinema or play a game of football. Often, how people choose to spend their leisure time changes as they grow older. Few ten-year-olds enjoy gardening or playing bowls, and how many 60-year-olds do you know who spend hours glued to a Gameboy?

Leisure is time people have to enjoy themselves, when they are free to choose what they want to do. It is usually time left over once they have finished activities they have to do, like working, studying and sleeping.

Recreation is the activities people enjoy doing in their leisure time, like watching television, playing a sport, or going out with friends.

To meet the different interests and needs of everybody in society, a large and profitable leisure and recreation industry has developed in the UK. The industry can be divided into six main sections or 'components'.

Components of leisure and recreation

- arts and entertainment
- sports and physical activities
- outdoor activities
- heritage
- play
- catering and accommodation

Arts and entertainment

The arts and entertainment industry provides leisure activities based on people's creativity – for example, painting, music, acting, writing and dancing. Common activities include:

- watching television (the most popular pastime in the UK)
- listening to the radio, CDs or tapes
- reading books
- visiting a museum or gallery
- going to the cinema
- going to night-clubs
- going to the theatre
- going to concerts
- taking part in dramatic or musical performances.

Between them, they offer something for all age groups and interests. You can choose to be entertained in the home (by watching TV, reading or listening to music), or go out to a cinema, theatre or night-club. You can either watch others taking part in arts and entertainment activities (be passive), or take part yourself by joining a local theatre or music group (be active).

If you and your friends kept a record of how much time you spend on different leisure activities, you would soon start to see the importance of the arts and entertainment industry in its different forms. This is how one 18-year-old student spent a typical Saturday.

Saturday 30 September	
8.00–8.30	watched children's TV while getting ready to go out
8.30–9.00	travelled to town, listening to a personal stereo
9.00–1.00	part-time shop work (half-day only)
1.00–2.00	had lunch with friends
2.00–4.30	went to the cinema to see a new film
4.30–5.00	shopped for CDs and books
5.00–5.30	travelled home, listening to music again
5.30–6.30	played computer games and watched TV
6.30–7.00	ate tea, watching TV at the same time
7.00–7.30	read a magazine
7.30–8.00	played new CDs while getting ready to go out
8.00–10.00	met friends in the pub
10.00–1.00	went to a new night-club in town
1.00–3.00	watched late night TV in bed

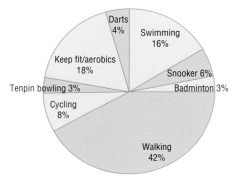

Figure 1 Percentage participation in the eight most popular sports (female) – 1990

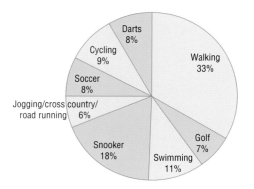

Figure 2 Percentage participation in the eight most popular sports (male) – 1990

Sports and physical activities

Sporting and physical activities have always been popular pastimes – the first Olympic Games took place back in 776 BC. People enjoy sports in two different ways:

- as spectators – they are passive
- as participants – they are active.

Spectator sports like football, cricket and rugby attract large crowds throughout the year. Major sporting events – like the FA Cup and Wimbledon – are watched by thousands of people live, and by millions more on television. Recognising the value of this captive audience, British industry spends about £200 million each year on sponsorship.

Many people in the UK also take part in sporting and physical activities for enjoyment and health reasons. The 1990 General Household Survey found that almost two-thirds of those interviewed had participated in at least one sporting activity in the previous four weeks. The most popular sports and physical activities include walking, swimming, snooker, aerobics and yoga, and cycling.

Some sporting activities are free – you don't have to pay to go jogging with a group of friends or kick a football around the local recreation ground. But some sport has become big business. The sports industry has recognised the potential to build on the current fitness boom and is developing larger arenas and sports centres, providing better equipment, and offering a wider range of services.

THE SPORTS COUNCIL

The Sports Council was set up in 1972 to:

- increase participation in sport and physical recreation
- increase the quality and quantity of sports facilities
- raise standards of performance
- provide information for and about sport.

To achieve its aim of increasing participation in sport, it:

- gives grants to the national governing bodies of sports
- gives grants to help local organisations involve local people in sport
- runs campaigns to persuade people to take part in sport
- tries to increase sporting opportunities for the people who are least likely to participate in sport – including young people, women, ethnic minorities and the disabled.

Outdoor activities

Outdoor activities are popular in the UK. The countryside and coastline offer opportunities for rambling, hiking, mountaineering, rock climbing, orienteering, diving . . . and many more.

The Countryside Commission (in England), the Countryside Council for Wales and Scottish Natural Heritage are responsible for conserving the natural landscape and improving the facilities it offers for open-air recreation. They aim to keep a balance between meeting the public's needs for parks, picnic sites, paths and signage, and protecting the environment from the pollution and erosion visitors can cause.

A National Park ranger explains these two aspects of his job:

❝ *I work for the National Park authority in a beautiful National Park in the north of England. The authority is responsible for protecting this environment and making sure the general public is able to enjoy it to its full. We help to organise public access to land and encourage farmers to manage their land in the traditional way. We plant trees and look after footpaths, stiles and signage. We also provide car parks and picnic sites, and set up information centres where the public can come for information on what to see and do in the area. Although conserving the natural environment is the main part of my job, I get a real sense of satisfaction from seeing people of all ages making the most of the countryside.* ❞

Heritage

Heritage is a country's historic buildings, monuments, countryside, traditions and culture. The UK has a particularly strong heritage which attracts many visitors from other countries.

The heritage component of the leisure and recreation industry in the UK consists of two types of attractions:

- old buildings, monuments and gardens which preserve the past – for example, the Tower of London, Caernarvon Castle and Edinburgh Castle
- museums and exhibitions that bring history to life – for example, the Ironbridge Gorge Museum in Telford, Shropshire.

English Heritage is the organisation responsible for conserving heritage in England. It protects buildings of special architectural or historical interest and ancient monuments and looks after over 400 historic properties. Many of these are open to the public – across the UK there are hundreds of stately homes, castles, palaces and parks to visit.

DISCUSSION POINT

Heritage sites and museums have to move with the times. Visitors today aren't happy just to look at roped off rooms and objects behind glass.

How do you think history should be presented to make it interesting? What do you think would attract:

- children?
- young people?
- older visitors?

1	Tower of London	2,235,199
2	St Paul's Cathedral	1,400,000 (estimated)
3	Edinburgh Castle	986,305
4	Roman Baths and Pump Room, Bath	895,948
5	Windsor Castle, State Apartments	769,298
6	Warwick Castle	690,000
7	Stonehenge, Wiltshire	649,442
8	Shakespeare's Birthplace, Stratford	577,704
9	Hampton Court Palace	580,440
10	Blenheim Palace, Oxfordshire	486,100

Table 1   Number of people who visited the top ten historic properties in the UK in 1991–2

Play

Play is the main way that children choose to spend their leisure time. It's an important part of their learning and development – socially, physically and imaginatively.

The play component of the leisure and recreation industry has particular concerns and priorities, including:

- ensuring children's safety
- providing equipment that they enjoy using and which gives them opportunities to develop physically and socially
- providing the right equipment in terms of size, shape, materials used
- supervising play.

Catering and accommodation

The catering and accommodation industries are closely linked to other components of leisure and recreation. A catering manager who organises food for major sporting events explains the role of catering:

66 *Catering can mean anything from a stall selling sweets, crisps and cans of drink, to self-service cafés and gourmet restaurants. Eating out has become more and more popular in recent years, and now people expect to be able to buy food and drink when they're visiting a museum or after swimming. So facilities have to provide catering services to meet these customer expectations. As well as keeping visitors happy, well-planned catering services can also make a lot of money. Walk around a theme park and you'll find everything from popcorn and hot dog stands to restaurants and coffee shops. I read somewhere that Alton Towers sells over a million doughnuts a year!* **99**

Accommodation plays a similar role to catering, providing a base from which people can enjoy leisure and recreation activities. As with catering, there is a wide range on offer, from camping and caravans to five star hotels.

RAGDALE HALL

Good catering might not be the first thing which comes to mind when you think of health farms. But Ragdale Hall is a health resort combining a traditional Victorian house and grounds with up-to-date facilities and excellent food all set in beautiful Leicestershire countryside. For people who need time to relax, unwind, pamper themselves, get fit or lose weight, Ragdale Hall offers shared and single rooms of varying degrees of luxury together with well planned, calorie-controlled meals catering for all tastes and dietary needs. Food is beautifully presented in an elegant dining room and belies the stereotypical health-farm image of lettuce leaves and carrot juice. A snack bar offers hot and cold drinks together with healthy – and tasty – cakes and biscuits, providing additional sustenance between meals if necessary.

Leisure and recreation facilities

> **Facilities** are the resources which people use for leisure and recreation. They can be buildings and equipment, like a sports centre or exhibition space, or they can be part of the natural environment like a lake or mountain.

Each component of the leisure industry has different facilities which the public visits, uses and enjoys – from long distance footpaths and parks to museums and venues. Many facilities cover more than one component of the industry – for example, a public park will probably provide opportunities for sport and physical activities, outdoor activities and play, and may also provide catering.

DISCUSSION POINT

In 1992 almost 11 million people went to the theatre in London's West End, the UK's centre for theatre. But to some people, theatre still has the reputation of being an expensive, inaccessible leisure activity.

■ Is there a theatre in your area?

■ How well do you think it is used by the local community?

■ How could you attract people to the theatre who usually stay at home watching television?

Theatres

Component: arts and entertainment

The UK is one of the world's major centres for theatre. There are about 300 professional theatres around the country and many more small venues which stage amateur and fringe productions. Some theatres are privately owned, but most are owned either by the local authority or non-profit-making organisations. In the summer, open-air theatres are popular, including one in London's Regent's Park and the Minack Theatre on an open cliffside in Cornwall.

'34 8951;
ad ⊖)
al comedy
ree Tony
music by
'win, the
indards
overed
id Helen
7.45pm;
).

39 5987;

le, one of
and star of
e musicals,
spectacular
any of 23
Mon-Sat at
. £20-£30.

attitude to things romantic. Last peri...
Nov 10/11,15/16 at 7.15pm; last mats **Nov 11,16** at 2pm.

Savoy Theatre

Strand, WC2. (0171-836 8888; Charing Cross ⊖)
DEAD FUNNY The death of Benny Hill provides the impetus for Terry Johnson's smash hit comedy about sex therapy and the English sense of humour, which now returns to the West End with a cast that features Belinda Lang and Kevin McNally. Mon-Fri at 8pm; Sat at 5pm & 8.15pm; Wed mat at 2.30pm. £10-£22.50.

Shaftesbury Theatre

Shaftesbury Avenue, WC2. (0171-379 5399; cc 379 4444; Tottenham Court Road/Holborn ⊖)
EDDIE IZZARD This multi-faceted comedian returns to the West End with a brand new stand-up show to follow the sell out success of his last two seasons at the Ambassadors in 1993 and at the Albery in 1994. Tue-Sat at 8pm; Sun at 7.30pm. £5-£17.50. Until **Dec 16**.

Moe, Les Miserables, miss Saigon, Phantom of the Opera and other sold out shows. Price (twice actual ticket value) includes contribution towards AIDS relief in the UK. Tickets **071 976 6751**. Information **0171 976 8100.**

FRINGE

Included here are shows at suburban and edge-of-town theatres, plus those in the smaller venues in Central London. Please note that some are theatre clubs and may charge a small membership fee up to £1 and may require 24 hours notice for membership

Almeida

Almeida Street, N1. (0171-359 4404; Angel/Highbury & Islington ⊖)
VENICE PRESERVED Ian McDiarmid directs a rare London production of Thomas Otway's "Shakespearean" tragedy of love and friend-ship. In beautiful decaying 17th century Venice, the hopes and dreams of four young people are in conflict with the demands of a stagnant government and a cynical revolution. Mon-Sat at 8pm; Sat mat at 4pm. £6.50-£16.50. Until **Dec 2**.

Bridge Lane, Battersea, :
8828; Clapham Junction ≠
170, 245, 319, 344, 349, I
ANGELA HITLER Hailed a
the Brighton Festival in M
proud to announce the Lor
Eliza Wyatt's ground-bre
£8.50,£6.50 concs (not Fri

The Brixton Shaw Theatr

The Brix, Brixton Hill, ::
4443; Brixton ⊖/≠)
HAMLET Nicholas Pegg ;
intelligent and gimmick-fre
Shakespeare's most hurr
incest, adultery, murder
Dec 2 Mon-Sat at 7.30
(£5 Mon).

Bush Theatre

Shepherds Bush Green,
3388; Shepherds Bush ⊖)
ONE FLEA SPARE by Nao
London during the Great Pl
people are boarded up in th
and Darcy Snelgrave. At the :

Halls

Components: arts and entertainment, sports and physical activities, play

Halls – like those attached to churches, schools and community centres – are an excellent facility for local people's leisure and recreation. The public can hire them quite cheaply for meetings, parties, sports events, play groups, concerts and amateur dramatics. Some facilities also hire equipment like stage blocks, lighting and sports nets.

Halls are often run by volunteers. Sometimes there's a manager employed by the local authority, who makes sure that bookings run smoothly and the space is kept clean.

ACTIVITY

Arrange to talk to the person responsible for a hall near you. Find out:

■ what it was used for last week

■ the different groups who hired it.

Then produce a timetable for the week. Colour-code different sessions depending on which component of leisure and recreation they belong to.

MUSEUM OF THE MOVING IMAGE, LONDON

The award-winning Museum of the Moving Image (MOMI) describes itself as 'the most exciting cinema and TV museum in the world'. Since it was opened in 1988 over 2.5 million people have visited.

MOMI charts the history of cinema, TV and video through cameras, costumes and hundreds of favourite film clips. Over 1,000 video sequences are shown continuously under computer control. The Museum's different areas include a Hollywood film studio, a TV studio and a cinema. Visitors are able to try early optical toys, read the news, be interviewed by Barry Norman and fly like Superman. A complete cast of actor-guides help explain exhibits and encourage active participation.

Museums

Components: heritage, arts and entertainment

There are over 2,000 museums and galleries in the UK open to the public. About 100 million people a year, of all ages and backgrounds, visit them. Most cities and towns have museums for art, archaeology and local history. A visitor to a local history museum describes some of the changes he has seen in museums in recent years:

66 *Since I started going to museums ten years ago, they have really shaken off their old dusty image. If you go to a museum nowadays, you can often see new interactive displays, special events and workshops. Many use new technology – from video to virtual reality – to bring history to life. Others have become living museums, where actors and actresses play the roles of people who lived in the past. Outdoor museums which recreate the way we used to live have also become popular. Some of them are almost like theme parks.* 99

Parks and play areas

Components: outdoor activities, play, sports and physical activities

Public parks with play areas have always been an important facility for local leisure and recreation. The whole community uses parks – children clamber on the equipment, young people play football, the elderly enjoy a stroll. Most provide open space, some sporting facilities (such as bowling greens or tennis courts) and a playground for young children.

A member of the ground staff at a local park explains his job:

66 *I'm part of a team employed by the local authority to look after the park in a small town. We work together to make sure the plants and grass in the park are well kept and maintain the football pitches, tennis courts and bowling greens. I get a lot of satisfaction from watching people enjoying the park – old people walking their dogs, children in the playground, our local team's football matches. Working in it every day, I see how important the park is to the community. I think that's what keeps me going when it's freezing cold and I'm clearing leaves off the football pitch.* 99

Local authorities have provided and maintained children's play areas with swings, slides and climbing equipment for many years. Private facilities, such as stately homes, also provide play areas to encourage families to visit. This new interest, combined with growing safety concerns, has resulted in the development of better quality equipment, materials and play environments.

Sports centres, swimming pools and tracks

Component: sports and physical activities, play

Facilities for sport and physical activities can be indoor or outdoor and include sports centres (which offer a wide range of indoor activities), swimming pools, athletics tracks and arenas. Most sports facilities are provided by local authorities, sometimes with financial help from the Sports Council. As well as offering space and equipment for sport, many facilities also offer coaching, health and fitness programmes and events for different groups in the community.

More and more people are taking part in sport. Facilities are improving in line with demand. Your local swimming baths may well have become a leisure pool, with a wave machine, jacuzzis, saunas and waterslides. Many sports halls have been replaced by leisure centres, with full catering facilities and a wide range of amenities under one roof.

THE DOME, DONCASTER – 'THE CATHEDRAL OF LEISURE'

The Dome in Doncaster is a good example of how the sports component of the leisure and recreation industry has expanded in recent years, becoming a focal point for a range of other services and facilities.

The Dome is one of the most advanced leisure complexes in Europe. Sports and physical activities are at the centre of the facility. A two-tier ice rink is linked by rising and falling platforms with real trees and artificial snow. The swimming complex is in six sections with huge waterslides, waterfalls and fountains. There's a river ride that goes outside. There are also hydrotherapy jets, bubble beds and an outdoor sun terrace. On a more traditional note, people can join the bowls club, health club, snooker arcade or squash club.

Alongside the sports facilities there is a hall which seats 2,000, where a wide range of events and meetings are held. There are also bars and restaurants. Plans for the future include a lake and marina, a golf course, and cricket and tennis centres. A neighbouring complex also provides a cinema, ten-pin bowling alley and a supermarket.

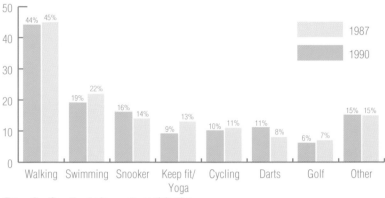

Figure 3   Growth rate in sports participation

Activity centres

Components: sports and physical activities, outdoor activities

Recently there has been a rapid growth in activity centres offering sporting and outdoor activities like pony-trekking, rock-climbing, water sports and sailing. Activity centres are often used by organised groups – such as school parties, youth clubs and Scouts – who either visit for the day to try activities, or stay for a longer holiday.

Heritage sites

Component: heritage

Heritage sites – places like the Tower of London and Edinburgh Castle – are among the most important visitor attractions in the UK. Maintaining old buildings and sites is extremely expensive, and heritage facilities often need high entry charges to cover their costs. Heritage sites have often lasted for hundreds or even thousands of years. It's a priority to make sure they last long into the future.

STONEHENGE

Stonehenge on Salisbury Plain in Wiltshire is one of the UK's World Heritage Sites. The ring of stones dates back to as early as 3000 BC. Millions of people a year visit the site, including New Age travellers and Druids celebrating the summer solstice. In efforts to protect Stonehenge from the damage caused by touching hands and tramping feet, a wire fence has been erected to keep people away from the stones. Although some visitors complain, preserving history has been put before modern demands on the site. Plans for a new access route and visitor centre may help to solve the problem.

The UK's cultural and architectural heritage is well known. Recently people have also become more aware of its important industrial heritage. Many breakthroughs in transport and industry came from Britain and these are being celebrated at heritage sites like the Ironbridge Gorge Museum in Shropshire.

Catering provision

Component: catering and accommodation

People in the UK spend more money than ever before on eating out. For many it has become a favourite way to spend leisure time, turning a necessity (eating) into a recreation activity.

ACTIVITY

What catering provision is there in your local area? Choose two or three streets in the town centre and list the complete range of catering outlets, including catering in other leisure and recreation facilities. Draw a map marking their location.

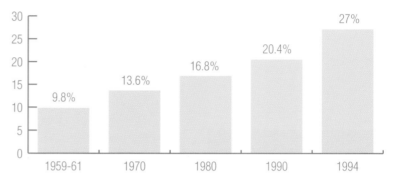

Figure 4   The increased rate in eating out as a percentage of food expenditure in the UK, 1959–94

To meet this new demand, the number and range of catering facilities is growing quickly. If you live in a big town or city, you can choose to eat food from almost anywhere in the world. You can eat in roadside cafés or fish and chip shops, enjoy pub food and drink, or go to an expensive à la carte restaurant for a special occasion.

Accommodation provision

Component: catering and accommodation

As with catering, there is a wide range of accommodation facilities in the UK. These can be divided into two main groups:

- serviced accommodation – where guests are given services they need during their stay (such as meals and cleaning). Examples are hotels, guest houses, youth hostels and motels
- self-catering accommodation – where visitors rent a self-contained space and prepare their own meals. Examples are cottages, villas, camping and caravan sites.

DISCUSSION POINT

Think about the different types of accommodation for people visiting your area.

- Are they related to the leisure and recreation opportunities nearby?
- Or is the accommodation used for another reason?

Self-catering accommodation is particularly popular with families, who like the freedom and flexibility it offers. As there are often catering facilities nearby or on site, visitors can choose how independent to be.

The location of accommodation can be closely linked to opportunities for leisure and recreation. People want to stay in areas where they can enjoy outdoor activities, heritage, and arts and entertainment. So hotels, guest houses, cottages and campsites have grown up to meet their needs.

Natural environment features

Component: outdoor activities, sports and physical activities

The UK has a varied natural environment which offers a range of natural facilities for leisure opportunities.

Natural facilities

- rights of way for walking – local councils are responsible for keeping public paths open and signposted; in England and Wales there are 140,000 miles of footpaths
- National Parks – ten National Parks have been established to preserve the natural beauty of the countryside and to promote its enjoyment by the public
- Areas of Outstanding Natural Beauty (AONB) – over 35 parts of England protected for public enjoyment
- heritage coasts – these are maintained for visitors by creating footpaths, removing litter, and ensuring clean water for swimming
- national trails – long-distance routes for walkers and riders
- nature reserves – there are 245 national nature reserves and two marine nature reserves to protect wildlife and plantlife.

DISCUSSION POINT

Is there a National Park or national trail in your area? If there is, what leisure opportunities does it offer for the general public?

If there isn't a National Park or trail in your area, are there any features of the nearby natural environment which you think should be preserved as a facility for the public's enjoyment? What leisure and recreation activities could take place there?

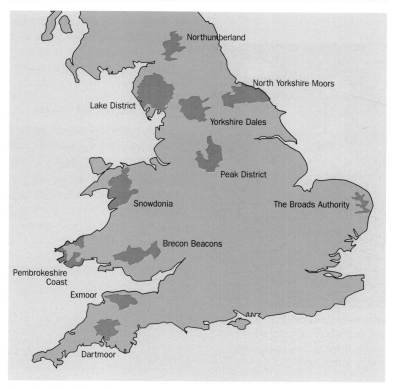

Figure 5   The National Parks in England and Wales

15

The public, private and voluntary sectors

All leisure and recreation facilities need to earn money (income) to pay wages, buy equipment, and maintain amenities. Where this money comes from depends on whether the facility is in:

- the public sector
- the private sector
- the voluntary sector.

Public-sector facilities

The State – national and local government – uses money from taxes to provide leisure and recreation facilities for communities. Adult education classes, parks, community centres and libraries are funded in this way. Sports centres also often belong to the public sector. But some facilities are part publicly and part privately funded.

> **Public-sector** facilities are funded and controlled primarily by government or local authorities. They aim to provide a service for everyone and are not run for profit – but they do have to make enough money to survive.

National or local?

Facilities funded by government are organised on a local basis. The aim is to provide a service or amenities for the community and jobs for local people. For example, in the area of arts and entertainment, local authorities maintain over 1,000 museums and art galleries. They also support many arts buildings, organisations and events in their areas.

Who does the work?

A combination of paid staff and volunteers. Local people are employed by the council to work in facilities as librarians, receptionists, sports coaches, cleaners and so on. The running of facilities is overseen by local council officials, who are elected by people living in the area and work for the community on a voluntary basis.

How is the sector funded?

By local authorities who get money through direct grants and loans from central government, local and national lotteries, local taxes, and income from facilities – admission fees, equipment hire and car parking charges.

Some facilities are also funded through grants from government-sponsored organisations such as the Arts Council, the Sports Council, the Countryside Commission and English Heritage. The National Lottery is providing a new source of funding on a national basis.

Members of Cambridge Arts Theatre staff and building team celebrate the first birthday of the National Lottery whilst building work goes on

DISCUSSION POINT

Spend a few minutes talking about the different methods of public-sector funding. Which do you think are the best ways of providing funds to public-sector facilities? What difference is the National Lottery making to funds for leisure and recreation facilities?

Private-sector facilities

Business organisations can be owned by individuals or groups of people. They fund and run private-sector leisure facilities with the aim of making a profit. This means that the money they make from selling products and services must be more than they spend on buying stock, providing services and paying wages.

Facilities which are usually provided by the private sector include cinemas, theatres, hotels, restaurants, pubs and theme parks – as well as sports and leisure centres.

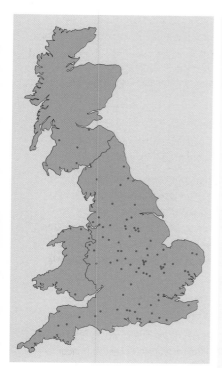

Figure 6   Little Chef facilities in Great Britain

National or local?

Both. National facilities include roadside restaurant chains such as Little Chef and Happy Eater and cinemas like Odeon or MGM. Many of the large companies behind national leisure and recreation facilities are household names, such as Trusthouse Forte and Ladbrokes.

Some private-sector leisure facilities are one-offs, run on a local basis. Many of these are small businesses only known to the people who use them – family-run cafés, bed and breakfast accommodation. Others are based in just one locality, but are known nationwide, such as Alton Towers.

Who does the work?

Private-sector facilities pay staff to maintain amenities and provide services.

How is the sector funded?

By private capital – money from individuals or organisations backing the business – and when the business is in profit, by reinvestment. Once a facility is established, it aims to make a profit out of leisure by charging fees for entrance, parking and so on, selling food and other products, and offering services such as coaching and guided tours. The income has to cover running costs and pay back the capital investment.

ACTIVITY

Make a list showing three leisure facilities which are part of the public sector and three which belong to the private sector.

■ What are the similarities and differences between the facilities in the two lists?

■ What differences does it make that they are funded in different ways?

Arrange to visit two facilities on your list, one in the public sector and the other in the private sector. Choose similar facilities – for example, two sports centres or two play areas.

■ Can you tell that they are funded in different ways?

■ How can you tell?

Voluntary-sector facilities use volunteer workers – people who offer their time and skills for free – to keep costs low. They don't aim to make a profit – any money they make is used to develop and improve amenities.

Voluntary-sector facilities

Voluntary-sector facilities are not provided by the State and not run for profit. They are usually formed to:

- meet a particular interest or need in the community, for example, a sport
- raise interest in a particular problem such as a conservation issue
- encourage constructive use of leisure time, for example, Scouts and Guides.

Leisure and recreational clubs, associations and societies – such as sports clubs, amateur dramatic societies, Women's Institute and leisure groups for the elderly – are run on a voluntary basis.

National or local?

Either, ranging from the weekly whist drive run in a village hall, a sports club in a large town and a national organisation like Brownies or Townswomen.

Who does the work?

Mostly volunteers, although large organisations employ some paid staff. A worker for a local council of voluntary organisations explains:

66 *Small facilities, such as village coffee mornings, are usually run very informally. Volunteers help out as and when they can, perhaps following a rota. Larger facilities, such as sports clubs and youth clubs, are more structured. Most have committees, made up of club members who are elected to roles such as chairperson, secretary and treasurer. Committee members often volunteer a large amount of time and effort to ensure the club is well managed.*

Large voluntary facilities – for example, the guiding organisations, the National Trust, and large sports clubs – rely on a combination of volunteers and paid staff. Paid staff with specialist skills like accountants, catering staff and event coordinators are sometimes employed on a full- or part-time basis. They work alongside volunteers. 99

How is the sector funded?

From membership fees, selling equipment and providing services such as catering. Extra money is sometimes raised by organising fund-raising events such as discos and through sponsorship. Some facilities also receive financial support from companies, charities and government grants.

THE NATIONAL TRUST

The National Trust is a charity which preserves buildings, gardens and other sites of historic and architectural importance. It protects over 600,000 acres of land and over 400 buildings and gardens in England, Wales and Northern Ireland. The National Trust depends on voluntary funding, including subscription fees from its two million members, entrance fees to properties, gifts, legacies, commercial sponsorship and public appeals. To make extra money, it also runs enterprises such as gift shops and tea shops. The National Trust employs full-time staff to manage and run it, but may also depend on members to work as voluntary wardens, stewards and lecturers.

ACTIVITY

Produce a chart comparing public-, private- and voluntary-sector leisure facilities. Your chart should show:

- whether the facilities in each sector are national or local
- who is responsible for carrying out the work – paid staff, volunteers, or a combination of both
- how facilities are funded – by grants, membership fees and so on
- whether they aim to make a profit.

Section 1.1.4

Leisure and recreation products and services

Products and services are what a facility offers to its customers. For example, a hotel may sell a weekend break package as a **product**, which also contains several **services** (meals, accommodation and entertainment).

Leisure and recreation is a big industry in the UK. In 1992 about 15 per cent of total household expenditure went on leisure goods and services. Millions of pounds are spent on sport alone.

So what's the money spent on?

Arts and entertainment

Facilities like cinemas, theatres, galleries and night clubs tend to offer straightforward products – for example, a film, a play, an exhibition, a particular type of music or themed club night. People buy a ticket, which gives them access to the product. Facilities like these usually change their products regularly, so they offer something for everyone.

Alongside their products, most arts and entertainment facilities offer catering services to meet people's need for refreshment as they enjoy themselves. Museums and galleries also provide information services – booklets and tour guides – to help visitors make the most of their product.

Moyse's Hall Museum

Why not take a glimpse into the lives of West Suffolk people from the distant past to recent years? **You will find...**

Ancient jewellery,

fascinating objects associated with local characters,

along with more gruesome items!

Moyse's Hall Museum

The collections are housed in one of England's rare surviving Norman houses where the original features are still clearly visible. In its long history Moyse's Hall has been used as a gaol, fire station and railway parcels office before opening as a museum in 1899.

The nationally important archaeological collections and local history artifacts are complemented by a lively programme of changing exhibitions.

Manor House Museum

The museum is a Georgian mansion which has been restored to its 18th century glory. The collections are displayed in superb surroundings and interpreted through computer screens bringing a wealth of knowledge to your fingertips.

There is a "hands-on" gallery and a changing exhibitions programme.

The museum has a tearoom serving light refreshments and a shop with a wide range of gifts and souvenirs.

Abbey Visitor Centre

The Abbey Visitor Centre is housed in Samson's Tower, part of the West Front of the now ruined Abbey of St Edmund. The centre has displays reflecting major aspects of the abbey's history including objects found on the site. "Hands-on" activities ensure there is something to interest all the family.

Sports participation

People in the UK take part in an enormous range of sports, from angling and athletics to tennis and tenpin bowling. Some sports are informal and don't involve buying products or services – for example, a game of football on the local recreation ground. Many others need special equipment and space.

People buy sports products and services from clubs, parks and leisure centres. Examples are an hour's hire of a tennis court, a course of swimming lessons or enrolment on a health and fitness programme. Many facilities also offer special products for different groups in the community, such as courses for children and young people, activities for disabled people, and classes for the elderly.

Like arts and entertainment facilities, sports facilities usually provide catering services so people can buy refreshments. Many also offer equipment hire and sell sports clothing and equipment.

The manager of a squash and badminton club explains why it's important to offer a range of products and services:

66 *We're always reviewing the products and services we offer to make sure we meet our club members' expectations. Members pay a fee for the year – we give deals for families and special membership packages at particular times of the year. Once they've joined, people can hire courts, get coaching, play in tournaments, and join graded sessions. We talk to people about what they'd like, and try to provide products to meet their needs. Services we offer include equipment hire, a small shop selling equipment and clothes, a bar which sells simple food, and satellite TV. Although people join the club to play squash and badminton, they also like to wind down after a hard game, and it's important we give them the opportunity to do this.* **99**

Sports spectating

Sports spectating – watching on the TV or actually attending an event – is one of the most popular pastimes in the UK. The number of sports programmes on TV reflect the interest in products such as Wimbledon, golf tournaments, boxing, horse racing and football matches.

Going to an event live involves buying a ticket to get access to the product. Once there, catering services are usually on offer along with shops selling sports kit and souvenirs. Many facilities now provide entertainment before and after events – half-time music, play areas – and have large video screens so spectators get a bird's-eye view throughout the event.

DISCUSSION POINT

Going to a baseball match in America is an outing for the whole family, in which food and entertainment often play as important a part as the sport. How do you think football clubs in the UK could attract families to football matches? What products and services would they need to offer?

Some of the products and services offered at Kielder Water in

Outdoor activities

Many outdoor activities are simple and free, like going for a walk in the park or swimming in the sea. Facilities such as National Parks and activity centres also organise products to make sure visitors make the most of the environment. Examples are guided walks, cycle rides, birdwatching days and rock-climbing coaching.

Facilities such as parks and nature reserves usually provide basic catering services and information points suggesting activities and explaining the local environment. Some also hire out equipment for sporting activities.

Heritage sites

The main product of a heritage site is the site itself – that's what visitors come to see. As with museums and galleries, visitors buy a ticket to gain entrance to the site.

Many heritage sites now offer extra products and services to attract visitors. Some have outdoor theatres, exhibition areas, and organise dance and music festivals. Others run nature trails in their grounds. Most provide catering services and a gift shop selling books and crafts.

Play schemes

Play schemes are organised by local authorities, private-sector organisations and individuals to provide activities and entertainment for children while their parents are at work. The main product of a play scheme is the activities it offers children. Its most important service is childminding.

A worker in a private play scheme explains:

66 *I work in a holiday play scheme for seven- to ten-year-old children whose parents are at work all day. Parents pay for their children to attend the play scheme for a certain number of days or weeks and in return we offer a child minding service. The basic package includes a range of indoor play activities such as painting, games and music, outdoor sporting and fitness activities and refreshments during the day. Parents can also choose to pay extra for their children to go on outings and courses which we organise. Some children spend a week on a special drama and dance course. Others go riding once a week or go on trips to theme parks. Basically we offer a range of different activities, so parents and children can choose what they want.* 99

Catering

Whether they are running hotdog stands or gourmet restaurants, catering services all provide the same basic product: food and drink. Customers can choose to buy a take-away product or eat their meal in-house. The variety and cost of the product varies a lot. A fish and chip shop offers a simple menu consisting of different combinations of meat and fish with chips; an expensive restaurant's menu will include a wide range of starters, main courses, desserts and drinks.

The level of service customers receive depends on the type of food and drink they are buying. People buying a take-away meal ask for what they want, pay for the product, and expect to be given their food quickly. Customers sitting down to eat in a restaurant expect waiters and waitresses to take their order and serve their food efficiently and politely.

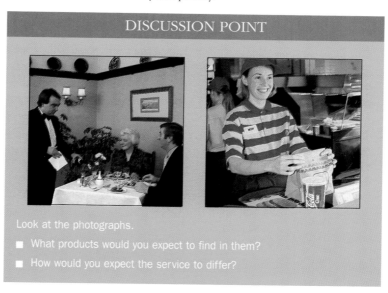

DISCUSSION POINT

Look at the photographs.
- What products would you expect to find in them?
- How would you expect the service to differ?

ACTIVITY

Produce a database of different leisure and recreation products and services. You might find it helpful to break the information down into the different components of the leisure industry. If you've done the activity on page 12, you may get some ideas for products and services from the activities you listed.

Accommodation

People visiting need somewhere to stay – a room in a bed and breakfast, a self-catering cottage or a suite in a hotel. The products they offer may be packaged to appeal to particular customers. For example, hotels offer theatre breaks, activity holidays and sporting weekends which combine accommodation with services such as food and entertainment.

The level of service varies: self-catering facilities get a weekly clean, five-star hotels aim to provide comfort and luxury every minute of the day – room service for meals, laundry, luggage-carrying, newspaper delivery and many more.

What facilities are of national significance?

Unique means that something is the only one of its kind. It's usually remarkable and unequalled in some way.

THE LAKE DISTRICT NATIONAL PARK

Surveys have shown that lakes and mountains attract most visitors to Cumbria, where the Lake District National Park is located. The park is 866 square miles in area and its beautiful scenery has made it a popular leisure spot since the eighteenth century. Today, the Countryside Commission aims to preserve the park's landscape, woods, buildings and traditional farming, while providing facilities for the twenty million people who visit each year.

Over 80 per cent of these visitors arrive by car or coach, mostly between April and September. They use and enjoy the area in many ways, but bring with them many problems for the park's rangers to tackle.

There are many leisure and recreational facilities in the UK. Only a few are of national significance, attracting visitors from far and wide. They are unique in terms of:

- natural landscape features
- size
- historical significance
- cultural significance.

Natural landscape features

The UK's varied natural landscape of fields, lakes, hills and coastline attracts many visitors. You can set out from most country villages and find good walks and pleasant views. A few areas are nationally significant because of their natural landscape. Some of these are remarkable because of their location – for example, Lands End at the very bottom of the country, and John O' Groats at its tip. Others attract visitors because of their spectacular scenery or the opportunities they offer for outdoor activities. Many of these facilities are designated as National Parks, Areas of Oustanding Natural Beauty and heritage coasts.

DISCUSSION POINT

Imagine you are managing the Lake District National Park.

- How would you tackle the problems highlighted in Figure 7?
- How would you provide the facilities people want for sports, walking and refreshment without damaging the natural landscape?

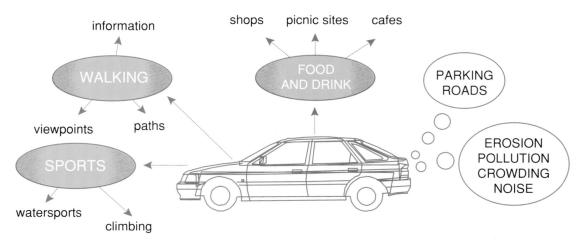

Figure 7   The impact of visitors on the Lake District National Park

Size

Facilities can be unique in terms of size in three ways:

- scale of the event
- level of attendance
- physical size of the facility.

Top-level leisure and recreation facilities in the UK attract visitors from across the country, and in many cases from across the world. People will travel to Stratford-upon-Avon, where Shakespeare was born, especially to see plays at the Royal Shakespeare Company's theatre. Many world-class sporting events are held each year at nationally significant facilities such as Wembley Stadium, Crystal Palace athletics track and Twickenham rugby ground. Each year thousands of people flock to the All England Lawn Tennis Club in Wimbledon, to watch the world's best tennis players in competition.

Facilities which are unique because of the number of people who visit them may also be remarkable in terms of their physical size. An example is the British Museum, which attracted over six million visitors in 1993 to see its six and a half million objects. A museum warden explains why the museum is so significant to the UK:

66 *The British Museum was the first public museum in the world, set up in 1759. Over the years we have built up a collection of art and artefacts which is famous world-wide. Today, millions of people visit every year – it's one of the UK's top ten visitor attractions. The museum is packed with treasures from around the world, from small pieces of stone to enormous statues. Each year we have special exhibitions and events which concentrate on a particular period of history or a country. The museum is also a centre of research and learning – over 8,000 students visited in 1993 and we publish many books. Working in such an important place can be daunting – the museum has such an enormous collection that I'm always being asked questions I can't answer! But it's fascinating spending every day surrounded by history.* 99

Historical significance

The UK has a long history. Many monuments, buildings and heritage sites survive which are historically significant to the nation. Some of these are important because of what they show about the way people lived in the past, like Hampton Court Palace outside London and the Jorvik Viking Centre in York. Others have played an important part in the country's history, such as The Tower of London and Hadrian's Wall.

Recently, people have recognised the national importance of the UK's industrial heritage. In 1986 Ironbridge Gorge was made a World Heritage Site, joining the Pyramids, the Grand Canyon and the Taj Mahal. It was the first British site on the world heritage list.

ACTIVITY

Make a list of leisure and recreation facilities which are of national significance because of:

- the scale of event held there
- the number of people who visit
- their physical size.

Choose three facilities, one from each list. Prepare a short talk explaining why they are of national importance, and persuading your audience that they should visit.

IRONBRIDGE GORGE MUSEUM

Ironbridge Gorge's central role in the birth of the Industrial Revolution has made it one of Britain's 14 World Heritage Sites. At Ironbridge, cast iron was used to make the first iron wheels, rails, boat, high pressure steam railway locomotive, steam engine cylinders and the famous Iron Bridge.

Today, the area's important industrial history is preserved in a group of museums, including:

■ Museum of Iron, Darby Furnace and Elton Gallery – celebrating the history and achievements of the ironmakers

■ Iron Bridge and Tollhouse – the first cast iron bridge in the world, made in 1779

■ Blists Hill Open Air Museum – a 'living history' site following a working industrial community in the 1890s

■ Jackfield Tile Museum – the history of the world centre for making decorative tiles

■ Coalport China Museum – the world-famous china works.

The Museum is an independent educational charity. Money raised through admission tickets and souvenir sales helps to protect the monuments and resources in the valley, once called 'the most extraordinary district in the world'.

Figure 8   The Ironbridge Gorge Museum sites

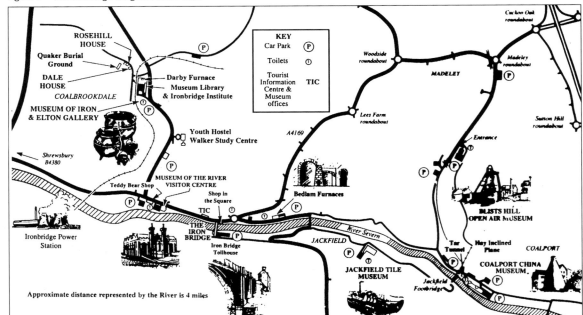

National museums and galleries

- The British Museum (see page 25)
- The Victoria and Albert Museum – the most important museum of decorative arts in the world, visited by one and a half million people a year
- The Tate Gallery – a collection of British paintings and modern art, visited by over two million people a year
- The National Portrait Gallery – culturally and historically significant, this displays the portraits of men and women who have played an important part in British history

DISCUSSION POINT

The National Gallery is visited by 4,300,000 people a year. It is one of the greatest art galleries in the world and undoubtedly unique in terms of cultural significance to the UK. How important do you think the National Gallery is to the average person in Britain? Could it play a more important role in bringing art to the whole of the nation?

Cultural significance

Leisure and recreation facilities of **cultural** significance show people's creative achievements (for example, art galleries), or look at the way other civilisations live.

National museums and art galleries contain some of the world's most important collections of artistic and cultural interest.

Other leisure and recreation facilities are of cultural significance to the UK because they give a unique insight into the way other civilisations live.

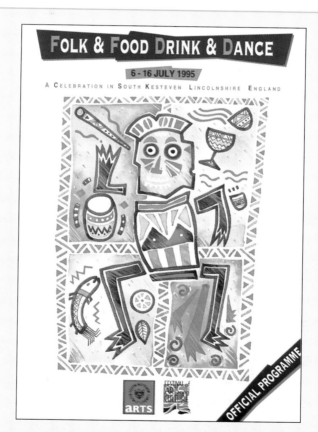

THE FOLK AND FOOD, DRINK AND DANCE FESTIVAL

This festival held in southwest Lincolnshire is a unique cultural event. It takes place over ten days in towns and villages around the district. These play host to a varied and exciting programme from many different cultures. There are traditional dance groups from the Ukraine, France, Ireland, America and Tibet. Food comes from America, India, Italy, with drinks on offer from around the world including real ale, whisky, wine and tea tasting.

Leisure and recreation in a locality

Deciding where to site a leisure and recreation facility involves several questions:

■ How will people travel to it?

■ Is there enough land available for building?

■ Do people live nearby who will use the facility?

■ Will the facility meet the needs of the community?

■ Are there natural features which make the site a good location?

■ Are there historical features which make the site a good location?

Accessibility

Leisure and recreation facilities need to be near to a good transport network so visitors can reach them easily.

In the past, most people travelled by rail, and it was important for facilities to be near railway stations. Over the last 40 years the number of people touring the country by train has fallen dramatically. Today, over 80 per cent of journeys to leisure and recreation facilities are made by car, with many more people choosing to travel by bus or coach. Because of this, the road network has become an important factor to bear in mind when deciding where to locate a new leisure facility. The theme park Alton Towers is in the middle of Staffordshire countryside, but is easily accessible from the M1 and M6 motorways. The nearest railway station is some distance away, but special bus transfers are available to bring train travellers to the theme park by road.

> **Accessibility** means how easy a place is to travel to, and how long it takes people to get there.

ACTIVITY

Using the map on the right and information you have collected on visitor attractions, advise drivers and non-drivers how to travel from London to:

■ Alton Towers, Staffordshire

■ Thorpe Park, Surrey

■ Blackpool Pleasure Beach

■ Eureka! The Museum for Children, Halifax

■ Strathclyde Country Park, Motherwell, Scotland.

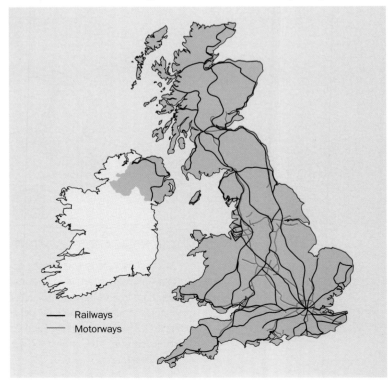

Figure 9   Motorway and main railway networks in the UK

Proximity to population centres means how close facilities are to places where people live, in particular towns and cities.

ACTIVITY

List three leisure and recreation facilities in your part of the country which aren't located in towns and cities.

- What are the main population centres people visit them from?
- How do they travel to the facilities?

DISCUSSION POINT

Which leisure and recreation facilities in your area do you think are located in a particular place to meet the needs of the community, or a section of the community? From the community's point of view, where in your area do you think it would be best to locate:

- a new old people's day centre
- a children's play scheme
- a cinema.

Availability of land

As well as a basic site for the facility, developers may need to make sure there is room for future expansion. Alton Towers is able to add new rides and build hotel accommodation because it is surrounded by open space and countryside. With more and more people travelling by car, there also needs to be plenty of space for car parking. Sometimes, facilities can turn the natural features of the land which is available to their favour. For example, Thorpe Park in Surrey was developed around the remains of a gravel pit – so the facility offers many water-based activities.

Proximity to population centres

In the past, leisure and recreation facilities had to be near to large towns and cities to attract day trippers. It's less important nowadays as transport systems have become quicker and more efficient – as long as a facility is accessible by road from major towns and cities it is able to attract visitors. Thorpe Park is too far away from London to attract non-driving visitors from the capital, but because it is close to the M25 it is easy to reach by car.

Meeting the needs of the community

Leisure and recreation facilities are often located in a particular place to meet the needs of the local community. For example, a leisure centre built by the local authority as part of a housing development is likely to be built close to the new estate so that people living there can use it easily. If a new housing estate attracts a lot of young families, a play area may be added to the local park to meet the children's need for play equipment.

Relationship to natural features

Some leisure and recreation facilities depend on natural features like hills, mountains, lakes, forests and the sea. These features can't be moved: their location is fixed by nature. So National Parks are located in parts of the UK with beautiful countryside, not in the most convenient spot for tourists.

Relationship to historical features

Historical features can also determine the location of leisure and recreation facilities in an area. Like natural features, the history already exists – leisure and tourism industries grow up around it.

Historical features can be a building or monument, such as Stonehenge in Wiltshire, or Leeds Castle in Kent. Both were built centuries ago and their location has nothing to do with their use today as leisure and recreation facilities. Some towns and cities are of such historical importance that they naturally become the site of facilities. The city of York has many old buildings and streets of historical importance, such as York Minster and The Shambles. These have been joined by modern facilities like The Jorvik Viking Centre, which is located in the city to explain the history of York to its many visitors.

ACTIVITY

Choose a leisure and recreation facility in your area. Using the case study of Rutland Water as a guide, produce a display about the facility and its location.

RUTLAND WATER

Rutland Water, completed in 1977, is the largest artificial reservoir in Western Europe. As the map shows, it is much more than just a reservoir. It has developed into an important leisure and recreation facility, incorporating watersports, outdoor activities, play areas, a museum, and accommodation and catering services. Its location has played an important part in its success.

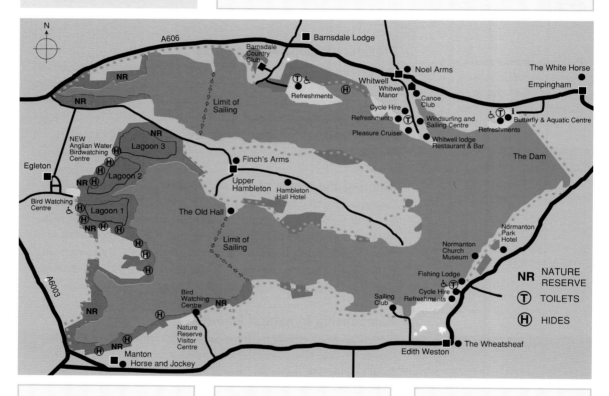

Meeting the needs of the community: the primary purpose of the reservoir is to meet the rising demand for water in expanding towns like Northampton, Peterborough and Corby. Its second purpose is to create a recreational facility and nature reserve for people living in the area.

Accessible: by road from all parts of the UK. The nearby towns of Stamford, Peterborough, Corby, Leicester, Melton Mowbray and Oakham all have railway stations.

Availability of land: plenty of land was available for the horseshoe-shaped reservoir with a shoreline over 20 miles long. Open space around the reservoir has been used for a string of leisure developments.

Natural features: although the reservoir is man-made, its design is sympathetic to the natural surroundings, needs of local residents, visitors and wildlife. It has made it possible for people to enjoy the lake without disturbing the wildlife.

Historical features: Normanton Church, built in 1826, would almost have been covered by the reservoir. Members of a local trust and Anglian Water raised the church's floor level and waterproofed the stone in order to save it, building a bank and causeway so visitors could reach it. It has now become an important feature of Rutland Water, housing a museum on the reservoir's history and fossils found while building it.

Proximity to population centres: Rutland Water is close to several large population centres, including Peterborough and Leicester.

Key questions

1 What is leisure and what is recreation? How are they different from one another?
2 What are the six components of leisure and recreation?
3 Can you name two facilities for each of these six components?
4 Some facilities can serve several components – why do you think this is?
5 What are the three sectors involved in the leisure and tourism industry?
6 How is each of these sectors funded?
7 What are some of the differences between the products and services that different facilities offer?
8 What are the four ways in which nationally significant facilities are unique?
9 Which six factors should be taken into account when deciding where a leisure and recreation facility is sited?

Assignment

Produce a folder on leisure and recreation in your area, for use in a local library or information centre.

Your folder should describe local opportunities for leisure and recreation in these six sections:
■ arts and entertainment
■ sports and physical activities
■ outdoor activities
■ heritage
■ play
■ catering and accommodation.

In each section, give an example of at least one facility, listing products and services it provides. Draw a map of the area showing where these facilities are located, and give reasons for their location.

Include a chart giving examples of public, private and voluntary sector facilities in your area. Explain whether they are national or local, who works there, and how they are funded.

Finally, suggest four leisure and recreation facilities of national significance which a visitor to your area could go to. Explain why they are important. Say how the facilities you choose are unique in terms of: natural landscape, size, historical significance, cultural significance.

ELEMENT **1.2**

The travel and tourism industry

Like Element 1.1, this element will help to give you an overview of an important part of the industry – travel and tourism. You will already have your own views about both. But what is tourism, exactly? And is travel separate from tourism, or part of it? You'll be answering questions like these by investigating different types of travel and tourism, nationally and locally. You'll also be looking at how travel and tourism affect the economy in a local area.

66 *The travel industry is changing as people become more adventurous. For example, getting married abroad used to be something just the rich could do but now it's an affordable choice for more people. Europe is becoming less popular and people are more prepared to travel worldwide.* 99

travel consultant in a travel agency

66 *Initially we provide local people and tourists with information on what is going on in the immediate area. Because we are linked with Tourist Information Centres throughout the UK, we also tell people what is going on elsewhere. We promote our area and services first, but we also provide information about other areas. We also have a holiday shop which provides free information for local people planning holidays in the UK.* 99

manager of a Tourist Information Centre

66 *Our job involves looking after guests, cooking breakfast and dinner, dealing with marketing, writing paperwork . . . In this day and age marketing skills are very important. Because we are fairly expensive we need to be able to target the right people. We find out what people want by talking to them – we know people are willing to pay more for the more interesting rooms we have, even though these are more expensive. And we can offer a range of prices.* 99

owner of a guest house in Bradford on Avon

66 *Some people now find it cheaper to hire a car than to buy one because they don't have to tax, insure and maintain the car – and in this part of the country people tend to use bikes rather than own cars. We do a small amount of tourist business as well but most of our customers are local.* 99

car rental manager in a car retail business

What are the components of the travel and tourism industry?

If you think the only purpose of the travel and tourism industry in the UK is to book package holidays to Spain, think again.

'Travel' in the tourism industry can be for leisure – for example, going on holiday by ferry or taking a coach on a sightseeing day trip. But it also covers flying to a business exhibition in another country or catching a train to visit friends and relatives in another part of the country.

'Tourism' can also be for leisure and business. Leisure tourism is any type of break or holiday – a fortnight in the Caribbean, a trip to stay with relatives in Scotland, or a weekend walking in the Lake District. Business tourism covers trips to conferences, exhibitions and meetings, in the UK and abroad.

To meet this range of needs for travel and tourism, the industry in the UK is divided into seven main components:

- travel services
- tours
- visitor attractions
- information services
- catering
- accommodation
- transport.

Travel services

> **Principals** in the travel and tourism industry are the main travel organisations, covering a range of modes of transport including airlines, rail companies, car hire companies and shipping companies.

Whenever people travel anywhere – families visiting relatives in another part of the country, a sales manager going to a conference in Barcelona – they have to plan their journeys. Organisations help people make these arrangements by providing travel services:

- retail travel agencies, like those you see in the high street
- travel agencies which provide a specialist service for businesses
- tour operators, which provide organised holidays
- principals, such as airlines, rail companies, car hire companies and shipping companies.

An assistant who deals with customer enquiries in a high-street travel agency explains the travel services she provides:

66 *Making travel arrangements is the most important part of my job. Whether a customer wants to book a day trip to Blackpool or a package holiday to the Caribbean, their booking involves travel. Our computer system is linked to the main tour operators, airlines, ferry operators and rail services, so we can advise customers what's available and sell them the services they need. I listen to what the customer is looking for, offer a range of possibilities – which means I have to*

Travel is the movement of people for a variety of reasons and in a variety of ways – such as for leisure, business, or to visit friends and relatives.

Tourism is when people move away from where they live and work for a short time and the activities they take part in while away. It can be a day trip, a longer holiday, or a business trip. Tourists always go away with the intention of returning home.

ACTIVITY

With the opening of the Channel Tunnel, people in the UK can now travel to mainland Europe in more ways than ever before.

A couple decide that they want to spend next Christmas staying with friends in Paris, travelling out on 21 December and returning on 27 December. Find out:

- the different ways they can choose to make the journey
- the disadvantages and advantages of each
- the costs.

Explain to the couple how you think they should travel to Paris, and why you recommend this particular route.

keep up to date with the best offers on the market – and make bookings. I also offer services such as insurance, foreign currency exchange and advice on visas. On the whole, it's quite exciting helping people plan their journeys. Sometimes on a quiet, rainy afternoon I wish I was jetting off with them! 🗪

Tours

Tour operators put together holiday packages or tours. They market them through brochures which they give to travel agents, who represent the tour operator to the public. Two types of tours are important to the UK travel and tourism industry:

- incoming tours – booked by people visiting the UK from other countries
- outgoing tours – booked by people living in the UK who want to travel abroad.

Incoming tours are important to the UK because visitors from overseas spend money in this country on accommodation, food, drink and entertainment. A tour operator explains how incoming tours are organised:

🗪 *Most visitors to the UK book their holiday through a travel agent in their own country. This travel agent contacts an incoming tour operator in Britain, who arranges travel services and plans any accommodation and entertainment required. Incoming tour operators like us are often asked to organise tours combining sightseeing with specialist interests like English language courses, or architecture. Most incoming tourists visit the UK from other parts of Europe or the United States, and they almost all spend time in London.* 🗪

Outgoing tours have come a long way since the late 1950s, when jet aircraft and package holidays first began to take off. In 1990, British residents went on over 15 million organised tours overseas, arranged by tour operators and booked through travel agents. The most popular destinations for outgoing tours are Spain, France, the Republic of Ireland, North America, Italy and Greece.

> ### DISCUSSION POINT
>
> Recently there has been a move away from package tours to independent holidays. More and more people are choosing to make their own travel and accommodation arrangements.
>
> - Why do you think this?
> - How are the tour operators changing to meet this new demand for independence?

Visitor attractions

Without visitor attractions, there wouldn't be a travel and tourism industry. Visitor attractions are the things that draw tourists to an area and then keep them entertained during their visit. Many people from overseas are attracted to the UK because of its strong cultural and historical heritage. Others want to explore the British countryside, while some come to see top-class sporting

---

> **Tours** are any holidays organised by tour operators – for example, package holidays, or coach tours. Many people choose to make their travel plans independently, rather than buying tours.

> ### Visitor attractions and entertainment
>
> - museums and galleries
> - historic houses, palaces, castles and heritage sites
> - natural attractions such as National Parks, Areas of Outstanding Natural Beauty and Heritage Coasts
> - sports facilities
> - theatres and cinemas
> - night clubs and restaurants
> - theme parks
> - play facilities
> - zoos, wildlife parks and nature reserves

events. Whatever the initial purpose of their visit, all can choose entertainment from a range of visitor attractions once they arrive.

An American student taking a month's vacation in England explains why she chose to visit the UK:

66 *I've been studying English literature at university this year, and I was longing to see where my favourite authors came from – I'd never been to the UK before. I did some research before I arrived. I've already been to Stratford-upon-Avon, Shakespeare's town, travelled up to Haworth in Yorkshire to see the home of the Brontes and then across to the Lake District to see what inspired Wordsworth. Now I'm planning to hit London – to see a bit of nightlife as well as theatre. I really love British music and fashion, so I'm going to do some serious shopping and maybe get to see some live bands too.* 99

DISCUSSION POINT

Think about the visitor attractions that drew this American tourist to England. If she had three days to spend in London, how would you suggest she spent her time? Can you suggest what should be on her itinerary?

Information services

Information services help tourists make the most of their time. Most overseas visitors arrive in the UK armed with some basic information from their travel agent and perhaps a guide book. The British Tourist Authority (BTA), which has offices world-wide, can also provide maps, city guides and event calendars to people planning visits. But in most cases, overseas visitors wait to find out the detailed information they need when they arrive in the UK.

England, Scotland and Wales each has its own national and regional tourist boards, which promote tourism and provide information services across the country. For local information tourists rely on Tourist Information Offices, which are found in almost all towns in the UK. They offer information and advice on accommodation, local transport, attractions and restaurants, as well as providing town and regional maps. If visitors want information on travel services, they can also contact travel operators such as the regional railways, the airlines, ferry operators and coach companies direct.

Catering

In the developed world, food and drink are part of people's social life and entertainment. In a country like the UK, domestic and overseas tourists expect to be able to eat what they want, when they want, where they want.

Food and drink on demand starts as soon as people board an aeroplane, ferry or train, where catering services are always on offer. When they arrive, they can choose to eat in an enormous range of outlets, ranging from cafés, pubs and bars to high-class restaurants and hotels. Many visitors choose bed and breakfast, half board or full board tour packages, in which some or all of their meals are provided by the place they are staying.

Since the 1970s, catering in the UK has become big business, with giant chains of restaurants and fast food outlets expanding fast.

PIZZA HUT (UK) LTD

From American origins, the UK Pizza Hut company was launched in 1973. Since then it has grown rapidly. There are now over 250 Pizza Hut outlets across the UK. In the early 1980s a joint venture company was formed between Whitbread and Pepsi Co, to manage and promote Pizza Hut. Tourists visit Pizza Hut because it offers efficient service, reliability and a reasonably priced meal. Because Pizza Hut is a world-wide chain it also offers the comfort of familiarity to overseas visitors. Like McDonald's or Burger King, you can walk into a Pizza Hut restaurant anywhere in the world and know what to expect.

Accommodation

Accommodation is one of the most important components of the UK travel and tourism industry. It employs 20 per cent of the total number of people working in tourism. Across the UK there are about 27,000 hotels and 20,000 guest houses, boarding houses and bed and breakfasts.

Almost all accommodation, from five star hotels to caravan parks, is run for profit by organisations and individuals in the private sector. Most smaller hotels and guest houses are run by owner-managers who live on site. Many larger hotels in the UK are run by international hotel groups such as Forte and Hilton.

Most accommodation is located in popular tourist areas: the major cities for overseas and business visitors and seaside resorts for domestic holidaymakers. Areas of natural beauty tend to have more self-catering than serviced accommodation, giving visitors freedom to go and explore the countryside in their own time.

UNIT

1

ELEMENT **1.2**

SEA & MOUNTAIN COTTAGES
in North and Mid Wales

WELSH HOLIDAYS
VERIFIED BY
SNOWDONIA TOURIST SERVICES

FOR BETTER VALUE SELF CATERING HOLIDAYS

INSTANT BOOKING SERVICE
(01766) 513829 or 512660

Nr. Criccieth - for sea, castle and wishing well. (11/C16)

Spacious farmhouse at Bryncir. (27/D58)

Porthmadog - sea, estuaries & mountains. (15/D55)

Harbour-side villas in Porthmadog. (14/D & 26/D57)

Snowdonia Tourist Services, Ynys Tywyn, High Street, Porthmadog LL49 9PG.

Transport

A good transport network is vital in order for a country or area to develop a strong travel and tourism industry. Transport in the UK can be divided into four main types:

- road
- rail
- sea
- air.

The use of cars for tourism has grown rapidly in recent years, at the expense of rail and coach or bus services. Traffic congestion and pollution now causes major problems in cities and the National Parks. Rail travel is more environmentally friendly but is generally less flexible and may be more expensive, particularly for families. The opening of the Channel Tunnel has made people aware of the potential speed of rail travel, with train journeys from Paris to London now taking just three hours.

Despite the Channel Tunnel, the vast majority of overseas visitors still arrive in the UK by sea or air. Many visitors from other parts of Europe bring their cars with them and travel by ferry or hovercraft. As an island, sea transport has always been important to the UK, and there are seaports around its coast. But about two-thirds of overseas visitors now arrive in Britain by air. London – the main point of arrival – is served by five airports.

DISCUSSION POINT

London is the largest city in Europe. Visitors often complain that it has one of the worst transport systems of any capital city in the world. How do you think transport could be improved in London? If nothing is done, how might the city's transport problems affect the UK's travel and tourism industry in the long term?

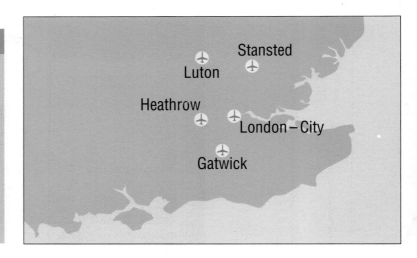

Travel and tourism products and services

The travel and tourism industry in the UK provides a wide range of products and services to people. Often, travel and tourism products and services are sold to clients as a complete package. For example, a hotel may sell a weekend break package as a product, but it will be made up of several services – meals, accommodation, entertainment and so on.

Travel and tourism products and services fall into five main categories:
- domestic (for UK residents staying within the UK)
- outgoing (for UK residents travelling to other countries)
- incoming (for people from other countries travelling to the UK)
- travel products and services
- tourism products and services.

Domestic products and services

Traditional UK domestic holiday products and services centred on the seaside. Before package holidays became popular in the 1970s, the vast majority of British people holidayed in the UK. Seaside hotels and guest houses sprung up to meet their needs, along with pier entertainment, amusement arcades, fairgrounds and restaurants. Each year the average family bought a fortnight's accommodation at a resort and enjoyed the traditional British holiday services of fish and chips, donkey rides and shows at the end of the pier.

All this has changed and the traditional domestic holiday product of a fortnight by the sea has been in decline for many years. Many people now take their long holidays abroad, choosing to take short breaks in the UK instead. The travel and tourism industry is responding by offering a variety of weekend and mid-week breaks throughout the year. These vary from packages catering for special interests, such as golf or walking, to reduced rates for short stays in self-catering accommodation. Many hotels now specialise in business packages, providing special deals for local companies and offering conference and meeting facilities.

Domestic travel has also changed. In the past, people relied much more on trains, coaches and buses for long journeys. Today the private car is used for most trips in the UK. Public transport services have been cut, while companies offering car hire services have grown up across the country.

DISCUSSION POINT

Is this a familiar scene? It may help to explain why millions of people each summer leave the UK's sandy beaches for the Mediterranean. Could the travel and tourism industry offer products and services to encourage people to stay in Britain, despite the weather? Can you think of any which are already available?

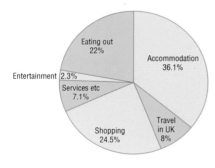

Figure 10 How incoming visitors spend money on leisure and tourism

Outgoing products and services

The UK's outgoing travel and tourism industry has grown rapidly in recent years, at the expense of the domestic industry. Until the 1960s, travel abroad from the UK was mostly be sea, which was time-consuming and expensive. The jet aircraft revolutionised opportunities for travel. New products and services quickly developed. The most important of these products was the package holiday. Tour operators put together a 'package' to a particular destination, including travel, transfer to accommodation, accommodation, and often catering and entertainment. Travel agents then sell these products to the public, who benefit from cheap rates and ease of planning.

Today the outgoing travel and tourism industry helps UK residents take millions of trips overseas each year. Almost half of these trips are bought as packaged products, with holidays to Spain, France, North America, Italy and Greece proving most popular. Almost three-quarters of people travelling overseas now use air transport.

	1980	1985	1990	1991	1992	1993
Spain	1938	2716	2817	2657	3084	3793
France	718	1100	1873	1878	2422	1982
Greece	628	1066	1346	1374	1583	1691
North America	219	40	470	501	586	646
Italy	605	522	443	444	509	449

Table 2   Numbers of people taking package trips to the main destinations, 1980–1993 (figures given in thousands)

Incoming products and services

Incoming travel and tourism brings people into the country to spend their money on transport, accommodation, food and drink, and visitor attractions.

Incoming tour operators organise products to attract visitors to the UK. These often centre on the country's cultural heritage. One popular tour is known as 'the milk run', a trip covering London, Oxford, Bath, Cardiff, Chester, the Lake District, York and Cambridge. Other popular products include trips to top sporting events and language study packages.

Once they have arrived, it is important that visitors can get the services they expect. These include transport, information, catering and entertainment. The British Tourism Authority, which has offices world-wide, collects information on what visitors to the UK are looking for and helps to make sure that the right products and services are available.

Travel products and services

Organisations providing travel products and services don't just cater for people going on holiday. The managing director of a chain of travel agencies explains:

 We provide travel products and services for people who want to travel for three reasons. The first is leisure travel – from an annual holiday to a simple day trip. The second is business travel. This differs from leisure travel because the customer doesn't choose where to go and the trip is usually booked by a company, often at short notice. The trip could be short or long, at home or abroad. It could be to a conference, trade fair or business meeting. Whatever the case, the company still needs the services of a travel agent. The third reason people travel is to visit friends or relatives, again either in the UK or overseas. **"**

Leisure travel

Everything from travelling to Australia on holiday, to a coach trip to Chessington World of Adventures.

When travelling overseas, most people buy leisure travel products and services – such as aeroplane and ferry tickets – from travel agents, rather than dealing directly with airlines or operators. Travel agents also offer products and services for some domestic leisure travel, but mostly as part of an organised tour or package.

Most people travelling within the UK buy tickets direct from the transport operators such as the regional railway networks and National Express. Although more and more people now use their cars for leisure travel, coach and rail travel are still popular with older people and students.

DISCUSSION POINT

The railway networks promote leisure travel by train in leaflets like this, which promise a cheap, convenient service to visitor attractions in the area, and often offer reduced entry.

What are the advantages of travelling by train instead of by car?

Why do you think so many people still choose to travel by car?

Business travel

An increasingly important part of the UK's travel industry. Many travel agencies now have staff who specialise in business travel and specialist business travel companies have been set up.

A young person who has just started work in the business travel section of a local travel agency explains his job:

> *Making travel arrangements for business travellers is often more complicated than for holidaymakers. Timing is vital, as they are usually rushing to attend meetings, conferences and exhibitions. Most of my work is over the phone, and I spend a lot of time faxing hotels, arranging car hire and making sure tickets are delivered or left for collection at the airport. A lot of business travel is arranged at the last minute, and I'm learning how to find my way around a computer database which has details of last-minute availability on flights all over the world. The important things are to offer clients an efficient service, and to make sure that the tickets they need are in the right place at the right time.*

Visiting friends and relatives

One of the most common reasons for travel. It could mean travelling fifty miles to spend the weekend at your sister's house in another city or going to visit friends in America.

Although people don't usually need accommodation when they visit friends and relatives, they are still an important part of the industry because they spend money on transport, catering and entertainment during their stay. Most people go by car to visit friends and relatives within the UK. If they go by public transport, they usually buy their tickets direct from the railway or coach operator. To visit friends overseas, people usually by their travel tickets from a travel agent.

Tourism products and services

Everything from a luxury cruise in the Caribbean to the bus timetables available in your local tourist information office.

Holidays and tours

Holidays and tours are sold as products by tour operators and travel agents. They fall into several categories.

Holidays and tours

- package holidays – which include travel, transfer to accommodation, accommodation, and sometimes food and entertainment
- specialist holidays – for sports enthusiasts, keen cooks, environmentalists etc.
- short breaks
- tours which involve visiting several different cities or areas
- full-board, half-board and self-catering holidays
- . . . and many more

ACTIVITY

People sometimes want to go on holiday with others who share their interests. There has been a huge rise in the popularity of specialist holidays recently to cater for this demand. Find out from a few of your friends the type of holidays they enjoy, their favourite hobbies and pastimes and how they like to travel. Then, based on your findings, design the ideal specialist holiday product for yourself and your friends. Think about travel, accommodation and catering, as well as the activities at your destination.

Activities at destination

Once travellers have arrived at their destination in the UK, there will probably be many products and services on offer for their entertainment – museums, theatres and historic houses, sports activities, walking and shopping. In the UK, activities like these are usually promoted by local tourist information offices. Travel agents also advise people what's on offer at a particular destination.

Vineyards	Pakenham Water Mill	
es were planted in 1972 and hg wine followed only later. Visitors may enjoy a tour iful 15th century od Manor House, museum, vineyard.	**Mill Lane Grimston End Pakenham Tel 01359 270570 or 01787 247179** **Open 1 April until 1 October Wed, Sat, Sun & Bank Hol Mon 2-5.30pm Open Good Friday** Admission **Adults £1.35**	A working watermill, souvenir shop, picnic area, river walk. Toilet for disabled. 

Accommodation

Tourists in the UK can choose from a wide range – hotels, guest houses, motels, self-catering cottages, caravans and camping sites.

The competition between accommodation providers is fierce and many tailor their products and services carefully in order to attract customers. The owner-manager of a large seaside hotel describes how important it is to offer what people want:

66 *In the past, most British families spent their long summer holiday by the seaside and we were packed out all summer. Now we're even fighting for trade during the summer holidays in August. We used to offer straightforward bed, breakfast and evening meal, but it's all much more sophisticated today. We've built a gym, sauna and swimming pool, and run special health and fitness weekends. We've linked up with a local golf course and organise golfing holidays. We also run themed breaks – 'murder mystery' weekends, writing workshops, and food and drink weekends. For businesses, we've developed good conference facilities, offering all the usual business support services.* 99

Catering

Many people buy food and drink as part of their holiday package, on a bed and breakfast, half board, or full board basis. Others prefer to sample the range of cuisine on offer in local restaurants.

Visitors to the UK can eat food from almost any part of the world, as well as the traditional British fare on offer in pubs and fish and chip shops:

66 *Tourists come to England and they like the idea of eating traditional roast beef and Yorkshire pudding by a log fire. That's what we serve up here, along with spotted dick, apple crumble and custard. Seeing me standing here wearing my chef's hat carving the joint helps to create the illusion that nothing's changed since Henry VIII was throwing bones over his shoulder. But me? I'd rather pop down the Chinese take-away!* 99

43

Transport

Good transport services are vital for the success of a country's tourism industry. The UK has good links with other countries through its air and seaports. Heathrow and Gatwick provide particularly important services for overseas travelling, handling over 70 per cent of the UK's air passenger traffic between them.

	1989	1994
Heathrow	39587	51366
Gatwick	21149	21045
Stansted	1319	3256
Luton	2828	1804
London, City	216	478

Table 3   Number of passengers using London's airports, 1989 and 1994 (figures given in thousands)

Within the UK, most people choose to travel by road. There are car hire companies in most towns and tourists from overseas can usually hire cars through their travel agent. National Express runs coach services between major cities. Smaller companies organise day trips and longer tours by coach.

Relatively few people now use rail services for leisure tourism, but they are still popular with many business travellers. It's difficult to work in a car (particularly if you're driving). Trains provide a comfortable seat, a table, catering services and reasonable communication via mobile phones.

Agency and information services

Tourists need information at every stage of their journey, so that they know where to go, where to stay, where to eat, what to do. They can get information from many different sources.

Figure 11 Information available for tourists

Information might be provided verbally over the phone or face to face, or be printed as a leaflet, brochure, timetable or advertisement.

Guiding services

Tour guides are employed to entertain and inform visitors, and to make sure
that they get the most out of an activity – whether it's a trip on an open-top
bus, or a week's tour of Scottish castles. Tour guides are usually hired by tour
and coach operators to explain the history and culture of a particular area to
tourists. Sometimes guides are also employed as tour managers to accompany
visitors on a tour of different parts of the UK. In this case, they are responsible
for checking all runs smoothly and helping the party book in and out of
accommodation.

Currency exchange

All tourists need money to buy products and services. Currency exchange
services enable people to change money easily. In the UK, they are
available at:

■ travel agencies

■ banks

■ specialist currency exchange outlets, found in cities and larger towns, at
airports and major railway stations.

The public, private and voluntary sectors

Like the leisure and recreation industry, the travel and tourism industry involves:

- public-sector facilities, funded and controlled by government
- private-sector facilities, funded and run by businesses
- voluntary-sector facilities, staffed mainly by volunteer workers and not aiming to make a profit.

Public sector

The public sector is playing an increasingly influential role in travel and tourism in the UK.

National or local?

Both. On a national level, public-funded agencies are responsible for overseeing tourism across the UK. The Government acknowledged the importance of tourism in 1969, when it passed the Development of Tourism Act which established:

- the British Tourist Authority (BTA)
- English Tourist Board (ETB)
- Wales Tourist Board (WTB)
- Scottish Tourist Board (STB).

The BTA was set up to encourage tourists to travel to the UK, and has offices world-wide which provide information and advice to would-be visitors. The ETB, WTB and STB aim to develop and promote tourism from within their own countries. They carry out marketing, provide information and support the development of facilities for tourists.

On a local level, the English Tourist Board is divided into regional tourist boards, which in turn oversee local tourist information offices. There is a local information office in most towns, providing free information services on travel, accommodation, catering, entertainment and so on.

Local authorities recognise the possible positive effects of tourism and are more involved than ever before in marketing their areas as tourist destinations. Many councils now have tourism departments, which provide guides and posters to market the area to visitors, run exhibitions for the public, organise conferences and provide tourist information centres.

Who does the work?

National and local public-sector organisations pay staff to promote tourism and provide services. The number of staff employed depends on the level of government funding. Local council members, who work on a voluntary basis, may also be involved in promoting tourism in their area.

How is the sector funded?

The national tourist boards are funded by central government through the Department of National Heritage. In 1993-94 they were given £32 million and raised a further £17 million themselves. They do not aim to make a profit. Tourist information offices at regional and local levels receive some grants from central government. They also rely on income from the hotels, tourist attractions and other facilities which they promote. In most cases they provide information services – and sometimes reservation services for hotels, theatres etc. – free of charge but they can gain revenue by selling maps, guides and advertising space.

Private sector

Most travel and tourism products and services – from travel and accommodation to sporting activities and theme parks – are provided by private-sector organisations. This means that they are funded and run by business organisations which aim to make a profit.

National or local?

Either. On a national level, many of the largest companies in the UK are involved in travel and tourism – for example, British Airways, Forte (hotels), McDonald's and the Tussauds Group whose attractions include Madame Tussauds and Alton Towers. On a local level, small hotels, guest houses and restaurants are also part of the private sector – run for profit. They may cater for people from across the UK and from other countries, but they are based in just one local area.

Who does the work?

People working in the private sector are paid for their time and expertise as chefs, receptionists, bar staff and so on. Many people working in travel and tourism are self-employed, running their own hotels, restaurants and tour guide services. In this case, the profits from the business need to cover their own living expenses.

How is the sector funded?

From the private capital of the organisations and individuals who set them up. Once a travel and tourism business is established, it has to make a profit by selling its products and services to tourists. Some of this profit is then ploughed back into the business to pay staff and maintain and upgrade facilities. Some of it pays investors back for their investment.

Voluntary sector

Most voluntary facilities are established to meet the needs of their own community. Overall, the voluntary sector plays little part in travel and tourism.

The National Trust is probably the most important voluntary-sector organisation involved in tourism, protecting historic buildings and gardens which attract millions of visitors each year. Recent years have also seen a growth in conservation holidays, with people paying to become volunteers working on a conservation project.

National or local?

Voluntary-sector organisations involved in tourism are run on a national level but provide products and services at a local level. The National Trust maintains heritage across the UK, but its individual sites can have an enormous impact on local tourism. For example, Clumber Park is owned by the National Trust but it attracts tourists to a particular area of the UK, in north Nottinghamshire. Similarly, conservation holidays are run by national organisations, but bring tourists to a particular part of the country.

Who does the work?

The large national organisations rely on a combination of volunteers and paid staff. Volunteers work as voluntary wardens, stewards and lecturers to keep costs low. Paid staff are employed to oversee the running of the organisation on a day-to-day basis.

How is the sector funded?

Organisations like the National Trust and the RSPB are charities which depend on voluntary funding. Most of their income comes from membership fees, gifts, legacies, selling merchandise and public appeals. Overall, their funding relies on people's generosity, and the hard work of volunteers.

A young conservationist explains the importance of people supporting voluntary organisations through activities such as conservation holidays:

66 *More and more people are now prepared to pay to become volunteers working on conservation projects. The money they pay covers the cost of equipment and people needed to run a project, and their time and effort ensures the conservation goal is achieved. The National Trust runs working holidays called Acorn Projects and Oak Camps, which depend on volunteers. The British Trust for Conservation Volunteers also runs this type of holiday. Activities include coppicing woodland, laying hedges and cleaning disused canals. The RSPB offers holidays for volunteer wardens in their reserves, observing birdlife and doing conservation work.* 99

ACTIVITY

Produce a chart comparing public-, private- and voluntary-sector travel and tourism facilities and services. Your chart should show:

■ whether the facilities and services are national or local

■ who is responsible for carrying out the work – paid staff, volunteers, or a combination of both

■ how each sector is funded (by grants, membership fees and so on), and whether it aims to make a profit

■ at least one example of a travel and tourism facility for each of the three sectors.

The impact of travel and tourism in the UK

The travel and tourism industry brings millions of people, billions of pounds, jobs, buildings and traffic to the UK. Inevitably, it has a major economic, social and environmental impact on the country – both positive, and negative.

Economic impact

The travel and tourism industry is big business. According to the World Travel and Tourism Council (WTTC), 'travel and tourism is the world's largest industry and a major contributor to economic development'.

Positive

Within the UK, travel and tourism has an enormous impact on the economy.

About 50,000 businesses in the UK are directly involved in travel and tourism, providing:
- travel and holiday packages – tour operators and travel agents
- accommodation – hotels, caravan parks, cottages etc.
- visitor attractions – theme parks, heritage attractions, wildlife parks etc.

Another 150,000 businesses are indirectly involved in travel and tourism, providing catering, transport, sporting activities, arts and education facilities.

On a local basis, tourists bring huge economic benefits to a region, area or attraction. Visitors spend money on accommodation, food, gifts and souvenirs, entertainment and leisure activities. Trade increases, businesses expand, and more people are employed.

Negative

In popular tourist areas, too much tourism can have a negative impact on local people's day-to-day life.

Positive impact

- Tourism represents three per cent of the total national output.
- It contributes over £22 billion to the British economy each year (£400 per person per year).
- The treasury gains £2.3 billion in VAT from tourism each year.
- 1.5 million people are employed in the industry.
- Tourism supports a range of other industries, including arts, entertainment, catering and leisure.
- It encourages investment in the environment and heritage.

(Source: 'Big Business for Britain' Tourism Society Report 1993)

Negative impact

- Although new jobs are created, they are usually seasonal.
- Local people sometimes have to pay extra taxes for services and facilities for tourists – for example, tourist information offices, leaflets and brochures.
- The price of land increases, and local people can't afford to buy property in their own area.

HOLMFIRTH, LAST OF THE SUMMER WINE COUNTRY

Holmfirth, the picturesque Yorkshire village where the long-running TV series 'Last of the Summer Wine' is filmed, has suffered negative effects from its fame.

Some local shops have gone out of business and been replaced by tea rooms and souvenir shops for tourists. Local people have to travel to other towns to buy things they have previously obtained in the village and the extra travel can be expensive.

Social impact

Positive

Along with its positive economic effects, tourism can have a positive social impact on a community. Money brought into an area by tourism can be used to provide parks, gardens, playing fields and community facilities such as village halls. Facilities built for tourists – such as leisure centres, swimming pools, golf courses and theatres – can also be used by local people in their leisure time. These facilities could not be built or maintained without the extra wealth provided by tourists.

Mr and Mrs Phillips run a pub in a small village in Devon:

66 *When tourists stay in our area, they bring extra trade which keeps local businesses, like ours, viable. Without the extra money they bring, we couldn't go on trading and our community wouldn't be as healthy and active.* 99

Sam Groves is a pensioner:

66 *In rural communities like mine, public transport wouldn't exist without the boost in numbers that tourism provides. It would cost me a fortune to have to take a taxi to see my daughter who lives ten miles away, and I'd find it difficult to get to see my doctor.* 99

School-leaver Jackie Dickson, aged 16:

66 *Tourism provides summer jobs which help young people like me to stay in the village. I'd have to try to find work in the town 20 miles away without it, and so would my friends. In the end, there would be only old people left here.* 99

DISCUSSION POINT

At some time in your lives, most of you will have been a tourist in someone else's village, city or region.

■ Have you ever felt that tourists like you were having a positive, or negative, social impact on the place you were visiting?

■ Do tourists have a noticeable effect on anywhere near where you live?

Negative

But there are negative social effects too, like overcrowding and loss of privacy. Narrow village streets swarm with tourists, making it hard for local people to go about their day-to-day lives. Residents who live in particularly picturesque spots may open their curtains to find a tourist peering in the window. Even in a city like London, the number of tourists strolling along pavements can make it difficult to get from A to B. And tourism can lead to an increase in crime, such as theft and fraud, committed by locals on the tourists.

In the long-term, tourism can change the whole life of a community. Local shops, often the centre of village life, disappear. Traditional jobs are replaced by employment in hotels and tea rooms. Even local customs can change to cater for the new tourist trade.

Environmental impact

Positive

Most people are aware of some of the negative effects which tourism has on the environment. But it's not all bad news. The money which tourism brings to an area can be used to maintain, improve and restore the environment. Tourists are less likely to visit an area which has an unattractive environment. So growing tourism can encourage local authorities to reclaim waste ground, restore buildings and rebuild derelict areas.

Negative

The negative impact of tourism is much more obvious; particularly in the countryside. The National Parks cope with over 100 million visitors a year, all of whom affect the environment in a small way. In the words of a National Park Officer:

66 *We don't always welcome increased tourism. Walkers and cyclists wear away the soil. Traffic causes congestion and overcrowding, and creates air and noise pollution. People drop litter and cause damage to farm properties. Wildlife habitats are also placed under enormous pressure.* **99**

The National Parks are particularly aware of the negative impact tourism can have on the environment. Although they recognise that tourism is important to the local economy, they also see the tremendous pressure it puts on the local environment. Their aim isn't to try to stop visitors – it's to help reduce their negative impact on the environment.

Unlike National Parks, built attractions are usually set up especially for tourists. Even so, the surrounding area may suffer because access roads cannot cope with the added volume of traffic. The result is huge, frustrating traffic jams, which create pollution and affect both tourists and local people. Unless they are carefully designed, new buildings to house attractions can also spoil the existing landscape or built environment.

LAKE WINDERMERE

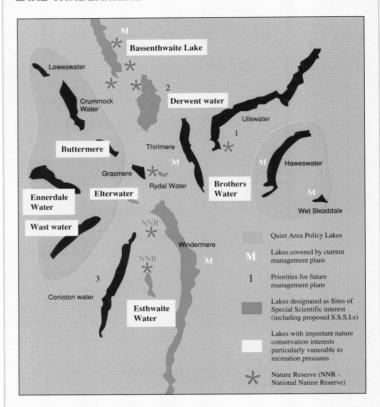

Lake Windermere is the largest lake in England and the busiest in the Lake District National Park. It provides a fresh water supply to the towns of Lancashire and Greater Manchester and is an important habitat for freshwater plants and animals. It is also one of the country's most popular sites for watersports.

Recreation activities that take place on Windermere range from rowing, swimming and fishing, to motor boating, water skiing and pleasure cruises. These create jobs and bring a lot of wealth to the area. But they also:

- cause pollution through litter, waste, oil spillages from boats, and noise from engines
- attract large numbers of people who trample on wetland plants and other vegetation
- disturb and destroy the breeding site for birds such as the goldeneye and mute swan.

To try to conserve the lake and surrounding land, the Windermere Steering Committee has created conservation zones, where no boats are allowed or there is a speed limit. Full-time staff also patrol the lake to check on litter, camp-fires and damage, and to make sure rules are followed.

ACTIVITY

Is it really possible for Lake Windermere to be a recreation and a conservation area at the same time? Produce two posters:

- one on behalf of a local conservation group, highlighting the negative environmental effects of tourism on the lake
- one on behalf of a local boating company, highlighting the positive economic effects of tourism on the area.

Show people the posters, and ask them whether they think the negative environmental impact of tourism outweighs its economic benefits.

The characteristics and impact of travel and tourism in a locality

The travel and tourism industry has transformed some areas of the UK. This section looks at the characteristics and the impact of tourism on one city – York.

Travel agencies are located in the main shopping areas of the city, offering travel and tourism services to both tourists and local people. There are two **tourist information offices** in York, one at the train station and one in the city centre. Both provide maps and leaflets, sell souvenirs, offer an accommodation service, and can book tours. There is also a special visitor's centre for York Minster.

York has an enormous number of **visitor attractions** – about 60 churches, museums and historic buildings are crammed inside the city walls. The most popular attractions include York Minster (northern Europe's largest Gothic cathedral), Jorvik Viking Museum, National Railway Museum, and the city art gallery. York also has a theatre and cinema, good sporting facilities, and a racecourse. It also holds special events, such as the York Mystery Plays and the annual St Nicholas Christmas Fayre. You can't walk for more than about 50 metres in central York without coming across a pub, tea shop or restaurant. **Catering provision** covers everything from traditional roast beef and Yorkshire pudding, to vegetarian, Indian and Mexican.

York offers the range of **accommodation provision** you would expect in a busy tourist city. Luxury five-star hotels cater for businesspeople and those on a generous budget. For those with less money, there's an enormous choice of cheap bed and breakfasts, as well as two youth hostels.

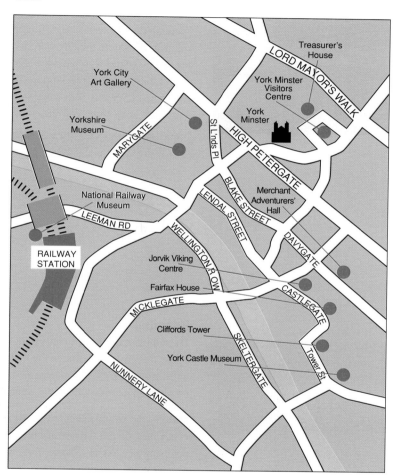

Until the Industrial Revolution, York was the second most important city in England. King George VI said that York's history 'is the history of England'. It is this history which has made York an essential stop on the UK's tourist trail. Its heritage means that there is plenty for visitors to see and do. It has good rail and road links and it offers the range of accommodation and catering facilities tourists expect in a modern city.

Facilities

To meet the needs of tourists, York provides a wide range of travel and tourism facilities.

Tour operators

A large number of tour operators are on hand to help visitors make the most of their time in York. Because the city itself is small, coach tours focus on attractions outside York such as Haworth and Castle Howard. Inside the city, open-top double-decker buses tour the major attractions. The Association of Voluntary Guides to the City of York organises two-hour walking tours of the city, led by guides who provide history and anecdotes along the way. At night, ghost walks visit the city's supposedly haunted buildings and alleys, called 'snickleways'. Visitors who don't want to go by foot can choose from river-boat tours, horse-drawn carriage trips, and even tours in cycle rickshaws.

ACTIVITY

Open-top bus tours are one of the most popular ways for tourists to see cities such as London, Bath, Oxford, Cambridge and Brighton.

A tour operator wants to set up an open-top bus tour in your nearest large town.

■ Plan a route for the tour on a map.

■ Mark points of local or historical interest and facilities which may be useful for tourists.

DISCUSSION POINT

How does an area's location affect which principals are based there?

Principal

The railway has played an important part in York's life for over 150 years. Today the city is the home of the National Railway Museum. Direct main-line trains arrive at York Station from all over the country and the regional railway provides an information service within the station.

Visitors who would rather travel by road can choose from several car hire companies, or visit the regional bus station. The National Express coach company also has an office in York, which is the destination for long-haul coaches from throughout the UK.

Products and services

The products and services on offer in York reflect its thriving tourist trade. Travel products and services – such as train tickets and tours – are widely available to help people travel to and from York, and to make the most of their time while in the city. Tourists can also get currency exchange services in travel agencies.

The large number of visitor attractions provide a range of products and services for visitors' entertainment – guided tours, information brochures, films and sporting activities. Accommodation meets all requirements and budgets and, in the face of competition, hotels and guest houses offer special packages to attract particular types of visitors. Catering provision in the city reflects the tourist trade, with a large number of tea rooms and old-fashioned restaurants providing traditional food and service. Although there are some fast-food outlets and take-away outlets, most of the catering products and services provided are designed to appeal to tourists drawn to York by its history.

Economic impact

Travel and tourism has brought enormous economic benefits to the city of York.

Positive impact

jobs – a large percentage of local people are employed in the tourism industry, working at visitor attractions, providing accommodation and catering services, and acting as tour guides

income – tourists travel to York from other parts of the UK and the world, spending money on accommodation, food and drink, visitor attractions, gifts and souvenirs

local trade – the millions of tourists who visit York each year spend money in all kinds of local shops, as well as in facilities designed for tourists

local wealth – travel and tourism is now the financial mainstay of York. Local businesses catering for tourists flourish, and the wealth created by travel and tourism is invested in facilities which are used by both tourists and the local community. The recently-built Barbican Centre just outside the city walls is a good example; it is a major concert and sporting venue visited by tourists, but also provides amenities for people who live in the area.

Along with all these benefits, travel and tourism has created some economic problems for York.

DISCUSSION POINT

What have been the positive
and negative effects of travel
and tourism in your locality, or in
a nearby tourist centre?

Negative impact

destabilising effect on the local economy – the city is very dependent on travel and tourism, and in times of recession it suffers from attracting fewer tourists, who spend less money.

seasonal jobs – although people visit York throughout the year, the largest number of visitors arrive in July and August; many local people are employed in seasonal jobs to cover this busy tourist period by offering catering and accommodation services, etc.

loss of local amenities – many shops providing products and services for the local community have been forced to close down, and have been replaced by gift shops and tea rooms for tourists, which dominate the city centre.

On the whole, local industries and livelihoods in York have not suffered at the expense of travel and tourism. Major employers, such as chocolate factories and the railway, are located away from the city centre, and are largely unaffected by tourism.

Key questions

1 What are the seven main components of the travel and tourism industry?
2 What are the four categories of organisations that offer travel services?
3 What are the differences between the two types of tours that are important to the UK?
4 Can you name the UK's three national tourist boards? What kind of information do they offer?
5 What are the four main types of transport in the UK?
6 Can you name the five main categories of travel and tourism products and services?
7 What are the three major types of impact that the travel and tourism industry has on the UK?
8 Why are there both positive and negative outcomes from these types of impact?
9 How can the characteristics and impact of tourism affect a locality?

Assignment

Set up a display on travel and tourism in your area. If the local library has an exhibition space, arrange for the display to be on view there. Or you could arrange for people to see it in your school or college reception area.

The display should show the main components of travel and tourism in the area and give examples of the products and services offered by each component, including:

■ domestic products and services
■ outgoing products and services
■ incoming products and services
■ travel products and services
■ tourism products and services.

One of the panels on the display should explain the difference between public-, private- and voluntary-sector facilities, and give examples of at least one facility in your area which is in each sector.

You might also like to record a commentary on cassette explaining the economic, social and environmental impact of travel and tourism in your area and highlighting both positive and negative points.

You will probably be able to collect useful information at your local tourist information centre, from the local authority's tourism department, by talking to people in the area, and by looking at local history books. Make your display as attractive as possible by including pictures from leaflets and brochures, photographs, charts and maps.

ELEMENT **1.3**

Preparing for employment

One of the main reasons why people do a GNVQ in Leisure and Tourism is because they are interested in getting a job in the industry. This element will help you think about what types of job might suit you. You will find out about the qualifications, skills and experience employers are looking for and investigate how you can get them. Although there are plenty of opportunities in leisure and tourism, you have to know how to present yourself well to employers – in your CV and job applications, and when you go for interview. You'll have the chance to see what employers expect and to practise these presentation skills.

66 *Anybody wanting to work for us would have to have the relevant qualifications and references and do a water test. People write in and send us their CVs and these go on file in case we're ever short of people. Because we have a good rate of pay and it's a nice place to work, our teaching staff tend to stay on.* 99

development manager, swimming pool

66 *There are no specific qualifications needed, although some companies would want you to have 4 GCSEs. But you would need to prove yourself competent at being able to make bookings, calculate prices and so on. Personality plays a big factor in your success so that even if you don't have the GCSEs you might still get the job.* 99

travel consultant in a travel agency

66 *The girl I employ rang and pestered me and offered to come and work for nothing! She doesn't work for nothing any more – I helped pay for her exams in addition to a small wage and now she is self-employed, though based here. As well as the physical work maintaining the horses, much knowledge is required for day-to-day care. She has a certificate in horse care in addition to the BHS exams she has done since coming here. The Jobcentre does advertise horse-related work and Horse and Hound – which is the most newspaper-like of the horse publications – has lots of adverts every week.* 99

owner of a riding school

66 *The council recruits people for work in our department through the personnel department, who advertise locally or in a national paper like the Guardian. People doing this work need an understanding of children's needs and to have experience of working with them. There are also two administrative posts in our department and for one of these you would need budgeting and financial skills as well as computer literacy. A lot of students help on our schemes in the summer, as well as people doing teacher training or sports training.* 99

community play officer in a city council

Finding out information about jobs in leisure and tourism

The leisure and tourism industry in the UK is very broad and there are many opportunities for employment either directly, or indirectly, in the industry.

Some jobs

- arts and entertainment – cinema attendant, theatre booking clerk, night-club manager
- sports and physical activities – sports coach, leisure centre receptionist, ground staff
- outdoor activities – National Park ranger, countryside manager
- heritage and visitor attractions – historic property manager, museum warden, theme park staff
- play – play scheme staff, crèche manager
- catering – kitchen assistant, chef, waiter/waitress, restaurant manager
- accommodation – hotel receptionist, porter, hotel manager, housekeeper
- travel services and tours – travel agency staff, tour operator staff
- information services – tourist information officer, tour guide
- transport – air cabin crew, coach driver, car hire manager

DISCUSSION POINT

Think of at least three more jobs in leisure and tourism for each component.

- With so many possible jobs, how do you find out more about what is actually available?
- How can you tell whether they are the right types of job for you?

The main sources of information are:
- careers advisers
- employment agencies
- Jobcentres
- advertisements
- reports of developments in the industry
- reports of changing local circumstances – for example, adding a new runway to an airport will create many more job opportunities
- other informed sources.

Careers advisers

Careers advisers are employed by the careers service to give people information and advice on all aspects of jobs – what jobs are like, what is available, training courses, opportunities for the future, and so on.

Talking to a careers adviser could be your first step in identifying leisure and tourism jobs which are likely to suit you. Your adviser will:
- interview you to find out your interests, experience and expected grades
- advise you on whether different careers are likely to be suitable for you, bearing in mind your qualifications and experience
- give you information about particular careers
- help you to work out an action plan for career development.

For people between the ages of 16 and 18, the careers service as well as the Jobcentre may provide information about employment. Your careers advisers

ACTIVITY

To make sure the interview with your careers adviser is as helpful as possible, prepare well in advance:

- put together information about your qualifications, work experience, interests, strengths, weaknesses and ambitions
- write a list of the questions you want to ask the adviser, especially if you already have ideas about the type of jobs you're interested in.

will have up-to-date information on job opportunities in the area and will be in touch with local businesses who employ staff. They will pass on job vacancies, arrange for you to go on training schemes, and act as a link between school and employment.

Employment agencies

Employment agencies are private businesses which make a living by filling job vacancies for employers. Their income comes from the companies who ask them to fill a vacancy – if you're looking for work, they don't charge you.

They usually advertise jobs for people in specific areas of work; for example, secretaries, catering staff, or nurses.

Jobcentres

Jobcentres are run by the government Department for Education and Employment.

Most of the vacancies advertised at Jobcentres are in the local area and are for people with some work experience. Staff in Jobcentres are trained to provide careers advice, give information and arrange interviews.

Advertisements

One of the best ways for organisations to make sure their job vacancy reaches a large number of possible applicants is to put an advertisement in a newspaper or magazine, or on the radio.

Radio

Local radio stations often advertise jobs in the area during normal advertising slots, or as part of a special feature on the area. Jobs in the leisure and tourism industry may be advertised before, during or after a programme on holidays or local leisure and recreation.

If you're listening out for jobs advertised on the radio, be ready with a pen and paper to note down the details so you know how to apply.

National newspapers

Most quality national newspapers – like *The Times*, the *Telegraph*, the *Independent* and the *Guardian* – have daily job pages. Although many of the jobs advertised are for people with experience, you may find some vacancies for school-leavers or useful information on training and higher education.

ACTIVITY

National newspapers usually group job advertisements by type of job. For example, they might advertise vacancies in computing on Monday, public sector jobs on Tuesday, jobs in the media on Wednesday, and so on.

Visit your local library and check the quality newspapers every day for a week. Make a chart showing what type of job advertisements appear each day, so that you know when it would be useful to look in a particular paper.

Local newspapers

If you are looking for your first job, local papers might be a better starting point than the national press.

THE SWANSDOWN HOTEL

Part-Time Staff
required for lunchtime waiting.
Experience preferred
but training is given.
Applicants must be over 18.

Please contact J Foster
on 01284 231 231

SICKLESMERE SPORTS
& LEISURE CENTRE

Position available for
LIFEGUARD

Appropriate qualifications for
children's and main pool essential

Applicants to contact: Kate Wilkins 01787 598348

Hunters Retreat

*The following positions are available
in our Traditional Country Hotel*

BREAKFAST CHEF
FULL-TIME RESTAURANT STAFF
PART-TIME BAR STAFF
KITCHEN PORTER

COMPETITIVE WAGES
SPLIT SHIFTS
EXPERIENCE NOT ESSENTIAL

Contact R Malik, Manager, by telephone
01287 359081

DISCUSSION POINT

Which local newspapers can you think of which might help you find a job?

Almost all local papers advertise some jobs – those that are delivered free through your door, those you have to buy, daily papers and weekly papers. Like national papers, daily locals tend to advertise particular types of job on a specific day of the week, so make sure you know where to look each day. Remember that you don't have to buy newspapers – you can look at them in your library.

ACTIVITY

■ Which part of the leisure and tourism industry would you like to work in?

– Catering?

– Sports and recreation?

■ Find out the titles of relevant trade press or specialist magazines.

■ Get hold of copies and see whether the jobs advertised in them might be suitable for you.

ACTIVITY

Start a scrapbook of cuttings from magazines and newspapers about developments in the leisure and tourism industry. As well as providing useful background on job opportunities, you might find it helpful to look through your scrapbook before going to job interviews.

Trade press and specialist magazines

Trade press and specialist magazines are printed especially for different parts of the leisure and tourism industry. For example, the trade press for the hotel and catering industry includes *Catering and Hotelkeeper* (weekly), and *Hospitality* (monthly).

All trade press and specialist magazines have advertisements for jobs in the industry. Make sure you look at the publications which are relevant to the type of job you're looking for.

Reports of developments in the industry

The leisure and tourism industry is growing and changing all the time. General reports on developments in the industry can give you useful ideas on new job opportunities. For example, you might read a feature in a specialist magazine about the success of theme parks in the UK and realise that working in a theme park would offer good long-term career prospects. Or you might watch a TV programme on new tour operators catering for independent travellers and decide that this would be a good opening for you.

You will be able to get some of this information from specialist magazines and the trade press. Keep your eyes and ears open. Leisure and tourism are topics of general interest and you will be able to find useful reports in all sorts of newspapers, magazines and TV programmes. Having a good general knowledge of the leisure and tourism industry will help you decide whether jobs really are for you, and will impress interviewers.

Reports of local changing circumstances

Jobs for 35 at new town hotel

Bury's newest hotel — Butterfly Hotels at Moreton Hall, just off the A45 — is scheduled to open in May and staff recruitment is about to begin.

Initially creating 30 to 35 jobs, the hotel is the second for the group, and follows in the footsteps of a similar successful venture at King's Lynn.

The new Bury hotel will have 50 well appointed bedrooms with facilities that include en-suite bathrooms, tea and coffee making equipment, telephone and television.

A French Provencal style restaurant and bar will be open daily.

Conferences

Ideally sited close to the fast routes to Ipswich and the East Coast as well as London and the Midlands, the hotel will provide first class

OPENING PLANNED FOR MAY

conference and business facilities for small and medium sized groups.

Five meeting rooms have been incorporated into the complex, ranging in size from those able to hold groups of

eight to 10 people to the largest room equipped to seat 50 plus in cinema-style comfort.

Vacancies

Recruiting staff for the new hotel is about to begin, the jobs on offer comprising mainly catering vacancies.

In addition to cooks, assistant cooks, cleaners, night porters and restaurant assistants, the management is looking for four receptionists whose flexible job description will include some help at the bar.

● Part of the Butterfly Hotels' new 50-bedroomed hotel taking shape at Moreton Hall, Bury, close to the A45.

Bury Jobcentre has been called in to help find the necessary staff and it is hopeful of the posts being filled quickly, many possibly by students emerging from the recently completed Manpower Services Commission sponsored course run at West Suffolk College by the Hotels and Catering Industry's Training Board.

Reports on developments in the leisure and tourism industry locally can provide useful information on job opportunities. Local newspapers might have reports on new developments in the community, such as leisure centres, visitor attractions and hotels. If you find out early that a new facility is opening you may get a headstart in applying for jobs.

As you travel around the local area, keep an eye out for buildings being renovated and find out what they're going to be. Often, signs on the building say who has bought the property and how they are going to use it. Word of mouth can also tell you about developments which might provide job opportunities. Ask people you know who work in local facilities whether any jobs are coming up in the near future.

Other informed sources

You can also look elsewhere for useful information about job opportunities. Some publishers produce books every year about careers.

Careers computer programs, which may be available at your school or college, hold large amounts of information about jobs.

> **Kudos** – an interactive program which offers advice on suitable jobs. You enter your qualifications and personal preferences (do you want to work as part of a team? do you want to work inside? and so on), and the computer lists a range of jobs which might suit you.
>
> **MicroDoors** – which has detailed information on jobs. You enter the title of a job you're interested in, and it will tell you about duties, working hours, and the qualifications and training you need, and will suggest linked jobs.

A careers adviser says:

66 *Talk to people who work in leisure and tourism. Ask friends and relatives to tell you about their jobs. Talk to staff at your school or college who will have a lot of general information about employment in the area. If you go on work experience, make sure you chat to people you meet about their jobs, to find out what it's really like to work in leisure and tourism on a day-to-day basis. Make the most of any links your school or college has with local companies by asking personnel departments for help and advice on jobs and training.* **99**

ACTIVITY

Over a period of a month, collect information about jobs in leisure and tourism. Keep a diary of your 'job search', making notes on:

■ the different sources of information you use
■ the type of information they supply.

Making sure jobs are suitable

Getting to know about employment in the leisure and tourism industry will give you ideas on the types of jobs you'd like to do. But you need to find out whether these jobs are likely to suit you.

What is it important to consider when deciding whether a job is suitable for you?

Circumstances

Things in your life like where you live, whether you have children and
whether you can drive. All of these circumstances can influence your ability to
do a job. If a job you're interested in is in a neighbouring town but there's no
public transport link and you haven't got a car, then the job won't be suitable
for you. If you have a child to look after, shift work would be hard because
you'd have to organise childcare.

Interests

Think about your hobbies and interests as well. If you're keen on sports, a job
in sporting environments such as leisure centres and sports clubs would
probably suit you. If you're interested in film and drama, you'd probably enjoy
working in a cinema or theatre.

Interest isn't enough to get you the job. You have to have the right skills,
experience and qualifications. In practice, few people are lucky enough to find
a job which exactly meets their interests. But thinking about what you enjoy
doing can help you decide what type of job would suit you. For example, if
you spend every spare minute walking in the hills, you're likely to find a job
behind a desk frustrating.

Qualifications

Most job advertisements say which qualifications applicants should have. They
give a good indication of whether a job is at the right level for you. For
example, if a job advertisement asks for a degree in tourism, you won't be
suitable – yet. If an ad says that no qualifications are needed, and you already
have GCSEs and expect to achieve a good GNVQ, you may feel that you
should aim higher.

WINGAWAY
E X E C U T I V E   T R A V E L

Require a
BUSINESS TRAVEL CONSULTANT

With minimum 3 years experience. Galileo trained.
Second language an advantage.
Apply to: Paula Smith
Tel: 01996 300222

Hawkwood Hall

requires an Assistant Hotel Manager
Minimum 5 years' experience in
traditional establishments

HCIMA Diploma an advantage

Apply in writing to
Mr C Butterworth
Hawkwood Hall
Ravens Copse
Nr Petersfield
Hants

FRENCHWAYS

require an experienced Resort Manager
for their operation in Nice.
Must speak fluent French, be trained
up to degree level in accountancy
and have a varied background
in Leisure and Tourism.

Apply in writing, with full CV, to:
FRENCHWAYS
Grove Road, Ferndown
Dorset

Present qualifications are those you have already achieved. They might
include academic qualifications such as GCSEs and vocational qualifications
like GNVQs or NVQs.

Anticipated qualifications are those which you are working towards at the
moment. Employers may take these into account when deciding whether you
would be suitable for a job.

Skills

Job advertisements also say which skills applicants should have. If you're looking for your first job, you may not be suitable for jobs which ask for specialist work skills.

If a job advertisement asks for general interpersonal skills – such as how well you work as part of a team, and how well you communicate with people – it may be suitable for you. Most employers are happy for you to learn specialist skills on the job. The important thing is that you show good general skills, and are willing to learn.

Experience

The amount of experience which a job advertisement asks for can be a good indication of whether the job would suit you. If you're looking for your first job and an advertisement asks for two years' administrative experience, it may not be suitable. But if it asks for experience of dealing with the general public, and you have a Saturday job in a shop, you may still be suitable for the job.

Work experience is very important when deciding whether jobs are suitable for you. Gaining experience in the workplace helps you know what you're good at and what you'd like to do. Even work in other industries will give you useful experience for jobs in leisure and tourism.

ACTIVITY

Produce a personal profile of yourself, summarising:

■ your qualifications – present and anticipated

■ your skills

■ your experience.

Keep your profile up to date. You can use it to help you explain to employers why you think you are suitable for a particular job.

Available opportunities

Whatever area of leisure and tourism you decide to work in, it's only useful to think about jobs for which there are opportunities available. An employment adviser explains:

66 *If you don't want to move, you have to look for job openings near where you live. However much you want to do a particular job, if there aren't vacancies the job isn't suitable. For example, if you live in London, it isn't realistic to decide you want to work as a National Park ranger. If the tourist trade is struggling locally and hotels are closing down, you may find it difficult to find jobs in the accommodation industry. So look out for the type of jobs advertised in your area and decide what would be suitable for you based on the opportunities available.* 99

John has worked as a hotel messenger on a work placement and is keen to find a job as a hotel porter. He sees this advertisement in the local paper and makes notes to help decide whether the job would suit him or not.

Gained some experience on IT placement. Organised taxis, carried guests' luggage.

There are good bus links to the city centre – transport no problem

HOTEL PORTER

Required to work in city centre hotel.
Must be able to deal courteously with guests,
provide usual portering services, and work well
with the rest of the hotel's team.
Some night shifts required.
No formal qualifications essential,
as training will be provided.
However, GCSEs in English and
Maths would be preferred.

Enjoy teamwork. On placement worked closely with porters and kitchen staff

Night shifts no problem. Night buses run. Am independent, & don't have to worry about causing family problems.

Keen to learn

Have GCSE English, not Maths. But preferred, not required…

ACTIVITY

Which of these jobs do you think would be most suitable for you? Make notes as John did, explaining how well the job relates to your circumstances, interests, qualifications, skills and experience.

Cupid Tours

FOR THE SINGLE TRAVELLER

REQUIRE A
SENIOR TRAVEL CONSULTANT

FOR BUSY INDEPENDENT AGENCY.
THE RIGHT PERSON WILL HAVE
AT LEAST 2 YEARS IATA & ABTA
EXPERIENCE, PREFERABLY
INCLUDING GALILEO.

APPLY IN WRITING
WITH FULL C.V. TO:
B.STONE PO BOX 995012
BOGNOR REGIS

THE WHISTLESTOP INN

Require a trainee
for all aspects of hotel service
Experience not essential
Suitable for school leaver
Contact: Mr H. Brown
Telephone: 01351 918452

Qualifications, skills and experience required for jobs

Qualifications, skills and experience are the three things employers usually ask for when trying to fill a job vacancy. If you don't have the qualifications, skills and experience required for a job, you probably won't even get an interview.

Vocational qualifications

Vocational qualifications are related to occupations and are designed to increase students' understanding of the world of work. They can be studied full time, part time, or on day release. GNVQs are vocational qualifications, so are NVQs.

Vocational qualifications have become much more widely available in recent years – the GNVQ you are studying is just one of the new courses now offered. A leisure and tourism teacher describes the value of the GNVQ:

66 *An Intermediate Leisure and Tourism GNVQ gives you skills, knowledge and experience which apply to a wide range of jobs in the leisure and tourism industry. During your course you will find out about how the leisure and tourism industry in the UK works. You'll get practical experience of marketing and promoting products, providing customer service, and organising an event. You'll also develop skills in using maths, communication and computers in the leisure and tourism context.* 99

More and more employers now know about GNVQs. You may even see job advertisements which ask for the Intermediate GNVQ in Leisure and Tourism. Some employers may ask you to achieve a merit or distinction grade, to show that you have developed good skills in planning, handling information, evaluating your work and producing high-quality outcomes.

Other vocational qualifications

- Advanced GNVQ – the level above the GNVQ you are working towards; you would need to continue studying, probably for another two years, to gain an Advanced GNVQ
- diplomas and certificates in specific areas of the industry, such as horticulture, cookery and transport management – these are often studied on a day release basis
- NVQs – designed for people already in work, to help them develop the skills they need to do a particular job

NVQs in leisure and tourism

NVQs are available in a wide range of areas related to the leisure and tourism industry – for example:

- sports and recreation
- spectator control
- museums, galleries and heritage
- travel services.

There are also NVQs for specific skills and expertise areas which can be used in almost any industry – for example:

- marketing
- administration
- accountancy
- management.

Many people study for vocational qualifications at the same time as working, in order to carry on learning and improve their career prospects. Here, a hotel chef describes her qualifications.

❝ *I left school when I was 16 with five GCSEs, including English and maths. I'd always enjoyed cooking and decided when I was quite young that I wanted to be a chef, so I got a job as a commis chef – that's a sort of trainee – in a hotel. My employer provided some in-service training, and then gave me day release to study towards a City and Guilds 706 certificate in Cookery for the Catering Industry. I really enjoyed the course so I decided to work towards the Caterbase NVQ and develop my practical skills in preparing, cooking and presenting food. Now I'm head chef, in charge of a large kitchen of 25 staff. One of my responsibilities is organising, and occasionally providing training, and I've started working towards an NVQ in Training and Development. I've found vocational qualifications extremely useful throughout my career.* **❞**

Academic qualifications

Academic qualifications are not so closely related to jobs. They are usually studied full time at school or college and involve learning the theory of a subject. The traditional qualification system in the UK is made up of the following academic qualifications:

- GCSEs – usually studied up to the age of 16
- AS and A qualifications – usually studied by 16- to 18-year-olds
- degrees – studied at university.

Academic subjects – like geography, history and chemistry – don't relate directly to work. But the knowledge they cover can be useful or essential when applied to a job. For example, an engineer has to understand the principles of physics before constructing a bridge.

Essential and helpful qualifications

Essential qualifications are those which employers insist you must have before you are capable of doing a job. For example, an employer may feel that in order to work as a hotel receptionist you must have GCSE English so you can communicate well in writing, and GCSE maths so you can calculate bills correctly.

Helpful qualifications are those which employers prefer you to have but which aren't essential for you to do the job. For example, an employer may feel that in order to work as a waiter, GCSE maths would be helpful for checking bills, but not essential.

If a job advertisement specifies that a particular qualification is essential, don't bother applying for the job unless you have the qualification. You will be wasting your own, and the employer's, time.

Qualifications in mountaineering are essential for rock-climbing instructors

If a job advertisement specifies that a particular qualification would be helpful, even if you don't have the qualification you should still apply for the job. Try to show that you have developed useful knowledge and skills in other ways. For example, if a job advertisement says GCSE maths would be helpful, but you don't have it, emphasise the number skills you are developing in your GNVQ.

Specific skills and experience

Being skilled at a job means that you have the knowledge and experience needed to perform tasks competently, professionally, and without supervision. This can only be achieved through training, practice and experience.

For this reason, people's first jobs usually require no, or few, job-specific skills. As they become more experienced they learn these skills and can take on more responsible jobs.

Specific skills in leisure and tourism vary enormously from job to job. The skills needed to be a coach driver are very different from those needed to work in a travel agency. Even within a job, the skills needed change with experience. While an assistant chef is weighing ingredients and preparing vegetables, a head chef will be making up recipes and overseeing cooking.

Jobs you apply for will probably only ask for a few basic skills specific to leisure and tourism. They might include things like organising events, organising travel for groups, or coaching awards.

Non-specific skills and experience

Some skills and experience are common to a number of jobs, not just leisure and tourism. These skills are sometimes called 'non-specific' or 'transferable' skills, because they can be transferred from job to job.

The first three skills on the list are covered by the core skills units in Communication, Information Technology and Application of Number. You will probably find that you have also developed the other skills on the list during work experience, school or college courses, hobbies and interests.

When you apply for leisure and tourism jobs, you may be asked for some of these non-specific skills and experience. Make sure you think carefully about how you have gained the skills through your experiences to date.

ACTIVITY

Read through this advertisement. Identify the leisure and tourism specific skills, and the non-specific skills, which are essential or helpful for the job.

CATERING ASSISTANT

**required to work in motorway fast-food restaurant.
We need someone adaptable, energetic and outgoing
to work in this demanding environment.
You'll need experience in dealing with the public
and working under pressure as part of a team.
Numeracy is important, as are good communication skills.
Experience of serving food to the public would be helpful,
and basic food preparation skills will be needed.**

How can you acquire qualifications, skills and experience?

There are plenty of opportunities to get the qualifications, skills and experience you need for jobs. More vocational, academic and training courses are available than ever before. You can study for them in a wider range of places – not just in schools and colleges, but also in the workplace. And you have more control over when you learn, and how long it takes.

Here are just some of the options which are open to people who want to gain qualifications, skills and experience.

Full-time courses

People who choose to take full-time courses spend most of their time each weekday working towards the qualification. Although they may get evening or weekend work to supplement their income, their time and energy is mainly devoted to gaining the qualification.

Courses usually studied on a full-time basis include:

- GNVQs
- academic qualifications such as A levels
- university degrees.

Most full-time courses follow the traditional academic year of three terms.

DISCUSSION POINT

What are the advantages of studying full time?

Part-time courses

Many people choose to study part time. They spend some of their time during weekdays, or else in the evenings, studying towards a qualification.

Employers who are keen for their employees to learn new skills may free them from work (with pay) to go to college, normally for one day a week. The students may also need to attend college one or two evenings in the week. This type of part-time studying is called day release.

Part-time courses are particularly convenient for busy people who wouldn't be able to study on a full-time basis. A young mother explains how part-time studying suited her circumstances:

66 *I used to work full-time at the sports centre. When my children were born I gave up work, and then went back part-time to work. I wanted to gain qualifications and progress in my career, and studying part-time fitted in with my routine. I took part-time courses in first aid and lifeguard skills, and am now a qualified swimming coach.* 99

Open-access learning

Open-access learning, or distance learning, is a way of gaining qualifications by learning at a distance from a college. Tutors send students assignments and students return their completed work by post (so these courses are sometimes called 'correspondence courses'). Postal contact can be supported by telephone conversations, tutorials and summer schools. Computers attached to the telephone line through modems are starting to be used in distance learning.

THE NATIONAL EXTENSION COLLEGE

'From little acorns, mighty oaks do grow': the NEC logo is an acorn, symbolising the fact that for many people distance learning courses are the start of something much bigger.

NEC has been developing and providing resources for distance and open learning courses for over 30 years. Many of these resources offer supported vocational training in areas like administration, business management, accountancy, marketing, IT and office skills. The College also offers a range of resources linked to academic and professional qualifications. As a provider of open learning, NEC's services include tutor support, administrative support and assessment guidance.

Open access learning is convenient for many people because it is completely flexible and can fit around a part-time or full-time job. In most cases, students can negotiate the speed at which they work. Studying at home, without the watchful eye of a tutor, requires time and self-discipline.

ACTIVITY

Find out about courses in leisure and tourism which you can study by open access learning. You could:

■ visit your careers office and talk to your careers adviser

■ talk to anyone you know who has completed an open access learning course – for example, a course at the National Extension College or an Open University degree.

Can you think of circumstances in which open access learning might be suitable for you?

Training programmes

Training programmes are provided by employers to help employees develop new skills and update existing skills, so they can continue to fulfil their role in the organisation. Organisations which have training plans for all employees can apply for the national 'Investor in People' award.

In organisations like these, managers talk to their staff regularly about their training needs and organise relevant training programmes:

■ training on the job – for example, a more experienced member of staff might explain how a computer system works

■ training outside the workplace – at a training centre, or in training rooms away from the main workplace; this training is often provided by specialist trainers.

INVESTOR IN PEOPLE

A pub manager describes her training programme:

66 *I was a librarian for many years, then I decided I needed more of a challenge. The idea of becoming a pub manager appealed to me. I had pub experience and wrote off to several breweries for information. I had to go on a variety of assessment courses, which tested my leadership and communication skills and my ability to act under pressure.*

I was lucky enough to be accepted and put on a licensee trainee manager programme. I spent six weeks learning the ropes in each of two pubs and three weeks on off-the-job training courses learning a wide variety of bar management skills. I got an NVQ qualification, a Food Hygiene Certificate, and a Craft Trainer award. I then spent some time as a relief manager, before I got my own pub. 99

Work experience

Work experience is an excellent way for students to learn the skills and gain the experience they need for jobs. A manager in a Compact scheme explains:

66 *As part of your GNVQ course, you will probably go on work placements organised by your school or college. They are particularly valuable because they give you a chance to work in leisure and tourism facilities, where you will develop skills which are specific to the industry as well as get some general work experience. When you start applying for jobs, you may find that your work experience will be very helpful in showing an employer that you are suitable for the job.* 99

Saturday jobs and evening work, although they may be in different industries, can still help you develop useful skills and experience. Dealing with the public, working as part of a team and communicating over the phone are important skills whether you are in a doctor's surgery or a leisure centre.

Work shadowing

This involves watching people at work – 'shadowing' them – to see what they do in their jobs. Work shadowing doesn't give you direct experience of a work placement. But it can help you:

■ understand the skills, qualities and experience needed to do a particular job
■ make up your mind whether a job is for you – spending a whole day watching a job can be an eye-opening experience.

ACTIVITY

Choose the three jobs which you are most interested in as a career.

Would it be possible to set up work shadowing for any of these jobs?

Talk to your teacher and careers adviser about opportunities.

On-the-job training

Training for many jobs is 'on the job'. You learn the specific skills you need as you do the job. People you work with act as trainers, showing you how to do different tasks.

An assistant in a fast food outlet describes his on-the-job training:

66 *I started working in the fast-food trade by chance – I just saw the job at the Jobcentre. I had no qualifications or experience, but was told that it didn't matter as training would be on the job. Everything – from cooking a burger to using the till – was taught to me as I went along. I've recently passed a test, so that I can teach the work to others and become a trainer myself.* 99

ACTIVITY

Look at these two job advertisements:

JUNIOR HOTEL RECEPTIONIST

Friendly and outgoing person needed for this city-centre post. Must have some office organisational skills, experience of dealing with the public, and good communication skills. We also require two good GCSE passes, including English. Training in using booking and finance systems will be given on the job.

SPORTS CENTRE ADMINISTRATION ASSISTANT

Well-organised, methodical person needed to help run the office. Some experience of office work desirable, along with typing and basic computer skills. Knowledge of the leisure industry helpful – job would suit a person with Intermediate GNVQ Leisure & Tourism. Opportunities for day release to study for Certificate in Recreation and Leisure.

■ List the qualifications, skills and experience needed for each.

■ If a 16-year-old without any qualifications or work experience was interested in doing one of these jobs in the future, how would you recommend she gained the qualifications, skills and experience she needs?

Ways of presenting personal information

When you find a job which would suit you, you need to apply for it. This means explaining to the employer:

- why you are suitable for the job
- why they should choose you rather than the other applicants.

Before you apply for a job, it's important that you have worked out what the employer is looking for. Look at the advertisement closely, listing all the qualifications, skills and experience required for the job. Make sure that you cover all of these points in your personal information.

UNIT

1

ELEMENT **1.3**

A recent Careers Advisory Service survey showed that employers turn down up to 75 per cent of people applying for jobs as soon as they read their applications. This doesn't necessarily mean that 75 per cent of people who apply aren't suitable for the job. But it does mean that they haven't presented their personal information well.

Letters of application

Some job advertisements ask you to write a letter of application for the job. Employers ask for letters to:

- check that you can communicate in writing
- make sure you are neat and careful.

So it's worth spending time planning, writing and laying out each letter of application you write. Check spelling carefully, and use a wordprocessing package if possible (some advertisements may ask you to apply in handwriting).

include the reference from the advertisement, if there is one

include your postcode and phone number

include a full name and job title

say where you heard about the job

include your age, school/college and qualifications

include work experience training

show you are keen

Print and sign your name

```
Your ref: NC/021/89/2                        41 Butchers Lane
                                             Bourne
                                             Lincolnshire
                                             PE72 1GT

Mrs L Price
Personnel Manager                            Tel: 01924  326437
County Buildings
Lincoln L1 3NG

28 September 1995

Dear Mrs Price

I wish to apply for the job of trainee leisure assistant which
was advertised in the Evening Standard on 18th September 1995.

I am 17 years old and left Shirley School in June 1992 with
GCSE grade D passes in English, Maths and Sports Studies. I am
currently working as an assistant at the local swimming pool,
where I have gained considerable experience of dealing with
the public and organising activities. I am currently studying
towards a Foundation Leisure and Tourism GNVQ on a day-release
basis.

I am extremely interested in the job advertised, and am
available any time for an interview. Bourne Swimming Pool
Manager, Mrs Jane Thomas, is happy to provide a reference if
necessary.

Yours sincerely

C Coper

Claire Coper
```

ACTIVITY

Find a job advertisement in your local paper which you could apply for. Write a letter of application for the job, remembering to:

- explain what you are applying for
- cover all the points mentioned in the advertisement.

Show your letter to your teacher and careers adviser, and ask them for feedback.

How could you improve it?

Application forms

Some employers ask job applicants to fill in an application form.
Application forms:

■ help to make sure employers get the information they need

■ help to reduce paperwork.

AVAILABILITY FOR WORK

As a 365 day a year operation we require staff to work
a variety of shifts, weekends and bank holidays. Please
indicate which of the following you would be able to work:

Weekends	☐ Yes	☐ No
Until 1.00am	☐ Yes	☐ No
Start at 7.00am	☐ Yes	☐ No
Christmas Day	☐ Yes	☐ No
New Year's Day	☐ Yes	☐ No
Bank Holidays	☐ Yes	☐ No

GENERAL

Do you have any commitments relating to the
performance of public duties that may affect your

MEDICA

Is there an
If yes, plea

A condition
required to
to undergo

TRANSF

Do you ho
Detail of a

Do you po
If no, how

Filling in an application form may seem easier than writing a letter of
application or filling in a CV. But it may not be. Application forms ask for the
same types of personal information contained in a letter of application or a CV
(see page 80), but you often have limited space and have to be selective about
what to include.

Tips for filling in an application form:

■ photocopy the form – you will only get one copy, so can't afford to
make mistakes;

■ practise writing answers on the photocopy before filling in the real thing

■ make sure you understand all the questions – if you're uncertain about
anything, ask a careers adviser or teacher

■ use black ink and make sure your handwriting is neat and clear

■ keep your answers concise and accurate

■ check that you have answered all the questions

■ check your spelling and punctuation

■ keep a copy of the completed form – if you get an interview, your
interviewer will probably ask questions based on your application.

ACTIVITY

Ask your teacher or careers
adviser for a copy of an
application form, and practise
filling it in.

Always send a brief covering letter with your application form, explaining that
you would like to apply for the job and are enclosing a completed form.

CV stands for *Curriculum Vitae*, a Latin phrase which means 'the story of your life'. This is exactly what a CV is – a summary of everything you have done and achieved in your life so far.

CVs

Many of the jobs you see advertised will ask applicants to send a copy of their CV. See page 79 for more details on CVs.

National Record of Achievement

Every school student in the UK has a National Record of Achievement (NRA) – a record of their achievements that helps them to make the most of their strengths.

Your NRA

- personal details – including a summary of your education and training history
- personal statement – your views on your progress and achievements
- qualifications and credits – details of your examination results, with certificates
- achievements and experiences – including progress in core skills, personal qualities, sports and social interests
- employment history – details of every full- and part-time job you have held
- individual action plan – a summary of your future goals and targets

If you are applying for jobs, the NRA can help you to work out your strengths and weakness, decide what you would like to do in the future, and show employers what you have achieved.

When you are applying for jobs, your NRA will provide useful information to help you write letters of application and CVs, and to fill in application forms. If you are asked to attend a job interview, take your NRA with you to give employers a clear summary of what you have achieved to date, and what you have to offer.

ACTIVITY

Look through your NRA, and make sure it is up to date. It should be a positive record of all you have achieved and activities you have taken part in, so try to make it as interesting as possible by including photographs and certificates. Your NRA must be signed by a teacher in order to be valid.

Interview

If you are invited to an interview for a job, it means you have overcome the first job-hunting hurdle. You have presented your personal information well on paper. Now it's your chance to do the same thing face-to-face.

Employers are looking for someone who:

- can cope with the work
- will enjoy the job and want to stay
- will work well with other staff
- is punctual and reliable
- will ask questions
- is very enthusiastic.

Your aim is to show that you meet all these criteria.

The interview is an opportunity to sell yourself and your achievements, and to persuade an employer that you are the right person for a job. Put yourself in the position of the employer.

Be cheerful – employers are looking for someone who will work well as part of a team and get on well with other staff.

Speak clearly and positively. This is your chance to show the employer you're right for the job.

Make sure you're well prepared. Decide what to wear. Check the time, place and how to get there.

STEPS TO A SUCCESSFUL INTERVIEW

On the day be prompt, smart and polite.

Make sure you're familiar with your CV or application form. The interviewer will probably refer to it.

Find out as much as you can about the job. The Personnel Department may be able to send you some useful information.

Prepare a list of questions to ask the interviewer. This makes you seem interested and enthusiastic.

Body language is the way our bodies send messages, often without us knowing it.

When preparing for a job interview, don't forget that your body language is just as important as the things you say.

Your body language can make all the difference to the impression you give an employer during an interview.

Actions speak louder than words

ACTIVITY

Choose a job advertisement in the local paper which you think you could apply for. Ask your teacher or careers adviser to arrange for you to have a practice interview. Remember all the points highlighted in this section, and think about body language.

At the end of the interview, talk about the roleplay and ask for feedback on techniques and presentation.

Think about the way your body is sending messages. You want to appear interested and alert, so:

- look at the person speaking – eye contact shows that you're listening
- lean forward in your chair – it gives the impression you're interested
- nod and smile while the interviewer is talking – it shows that you're listening
- don't cross your arms – it might give the impression that you've got something to hide.

Producing a CV

Getting your CV right is one of the most important steps towards getting the job you want. Your CV is an outline of your achievements. It aims to convince employers that they should give you an interview, and then give you a job.

CV quality

Content

- Does it summarise your achievements clearly and fully?
- Is the content well organised, with information in a logical order?
- Have you included all the essential information?
- Is all the content accurate? (Don't lie – you may be caught out.)
- Have you made sure your spelling and punctuation are correct?

Format

Your CV should be on A4 paper so that it is easy to file, and no more than two pages long.

Presentation

- Is your CV easy to read?
- Is it wordprocessed, so that it is clear, can be updated easily, and you can print out extra copies?

Always send your CV to an employer with a covering letter explaining which job you would like to apply for.

Check

Always ask someone to check your CV before you apply for a job – a fresh eye can often spot mistakes.

Information in CVs

- personal details – name, address, telephone number, age (or date of birth)
- subjects studied – details of schools and colleges you have attended and the subjects you are currently studying; even if you don't know the results yet, include details of qualifications you are working towards
- qualifications and awards – GCSEs, GNVQs, NVQs, City & Guilds, RSA and BTEC awards; list the subjects studied and results
- skills – make sure you include relevant skills in your CV. These might include languages, typing, using computer packages, driving, and so on
- experience – any employment you have had, including work placements, part-time work, and holiday work
- achievements – as well as qualifications and awards, things you achieve outside study can show that you have the qualities for a job; for example, if you are captain of a sports team, it shows you have leadership skills, or if you are on a college entertainment committee, it shows you have experience of working as part of a team
- personal interests and leisure activities – hobbies, sports, and activities such as Scouting or volunteer work which show what type of person you are; the achievements described above will probably fall into this category

The example on the next page shows how one student decided to present her personal information in a CV.

To judge whether your CV is suitable to send to employers, you need to assess its quality.

CURRICULUM VITAE

PERSONAL DETAILS

Name: Carol Williams
Address: 20 Laburnum Close, Kingswood, Hampshire S015 3JK
Telephone: (01233) 793472
Date of Birth: 21 December 1977

EDUCATION AND QUALIFICATIONS

1988–1990   St Saviour's Comprehensive School, Leicester
1990–1993   Madingley Comprehensive School, Southampton
GCSEs   English Language (C)   Mathematics (C)
                    Biology (D)   French (E)

WORK EXPERIENCE

1990–1992   Part-time work at Bradshaws Newspapers – delivery assistant.
                    Duties: organising papers for delivery; checking changes needed.

1993–1995   Full-time work at Budgens supermarket – checkout assistant.
                    I am responsible for checking shelves are well stocked, helping
                    customers, handling money, giving change, and cashing up at the
                    end of the day.

I have also worked regularly as a babysitter.

INTERESTS AND ACHIEVEMENTS

I have got grade 5 clarinet and play in the local wind band.
I enjoy swimming and train in a synchronised swimming team which takes part regularly in
competitions.

ADDITIONAL SKILLS

I have a certificate in First Aid.
I am currently learning to drive.

REFERENCES

Mr J Darling (Head Teacher)   Mrs G Simms (Personnel Manager)
Madingley Comprehensive School   Budgens
Ridge Lane   Robinson Road
Southampton SO23 4JL   Coney SO18 7HT

Key questions

1 What are the six main sources of information on jobs in leisure and tourism?
2 What five factors are important to consider when deciding if a job is suitable for you?
3 How do vocational and academic qualifications differ from one another?
4 Can you name four vocational qualification areas that are related to the leisure and tourism industry? And four that have a wider use?
5 How can you gain skills specific to the leisure and tourism industry?
6 Why are your non-specific skills and other experience also important for job hunting?
7 What are the seven ways you can acquire or increase your qualifications, skills and experience?
8 Why is it important to present personal information well?
9 What are the four main written documents that you can use to present your personal information?
10 What are the seven main areas of information you should include in your CV?
11 What are the steps to a successful interview?

Assignment

Get together the notes you have made by doing the activities in this element. Make sure that your notes:

■ identify two or three jobs that are likely to suit you
■ explain why you think they suit you
■ describe the qualifications, skills and experience needed for the jobs
■ say how you can get the qualifications, skills and experience
■ outline different ways of presenting information about yourself to employers.

Following the guidelines in the last section of the element, produce your own CV.

Show it to your careers adviser, teacher and friends, and ask them to evaluate:

■ quality of content
■ quality of format
■ quality of presentation.

Make any changes needed and keep a copy on disc for when you start applying for jobs.

UNIT **2**

Element 2.1

Investigating marketing and promotion

Element 2.2

Planning a promotional campaign

Element 2.3

Running and evaluating a promotional campaign

ELEMENT **2.1**

Investigating marketing and promotion

This element is about how leisure and tourism organisations get customers through their doors. Marketing helps organisations to provide the right products and services by finding out what customers want – and what they don't. You'll see what the basic principles of marketing are and how they apply in different situations. You'll also get a chance to look at some promotional materials. All this will help you with the other two elements in Unit 2. So it makes sense to do this one first.

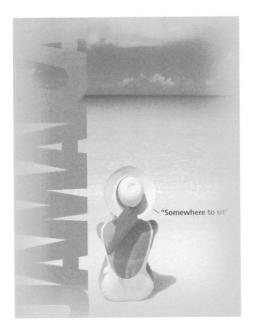

"Somewhere to sit"

66 We basically offer our services to everyone – whether it's an old person booking a coach holiday or a younger person wanting to book a honeymoon in the Maldives. It's very important to ask the right questions and to find out what people want – where they want to go, the price range and so on. **99**

travel consultant in a travel agency

66 If we are promoting ourselves we need to sell tickets. We've found that mailing lists are an excellent way of bringing people in to our concerts. We were invited to perform in a big hall recently and information was sent out to everyone on our mailing list. The concerts were sold out. So now we are building up our own database and we mail everyone on it every six months. This is definitely the most successful way of getting an audience. We have tried advertising but that isn't very successful. We've tried newspaper adverts and putting posters in music shops but it doesn't really work. The direct contact with customers is much more effective. **99**

manager of a band

66 Our income is from two sources – entry fees and sponsorship. We did quite a lot of market research before the first event so we had a good idea of how many entries we would have. Sponsorship is always a bit unsure. We started when companies could afford to sponsor, but for the past two or three years it's been harder to get. Our first sponsor was a typical family shoe shop. The race gave them a chance to advertise themselves to families and young people. Sponsors provide the prizes and cover the fixed overheads that we have to pay. **99**

organiser of a regatta

How marketing applies to leisure and tourism

Marketing helps to make a leisure and tourism product, service or facility a success.

Marketing means:

- finding out what customers need and want
- making sure the product or service meets these needs and wants
- deciding the right price for the product or service
- making sure it's available at the right place and time
- promoting the product and the organisation to customers through advertising, public relations (PR), special offers . . . and so on.

All leisure and tourism facilities – from small family-run restaurants to national attractions with their own marketing departments, such as Alton Towers – market themselves in some way. What do they aim to achieve?

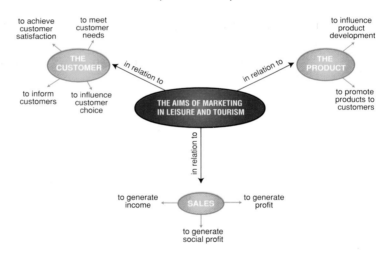

Figure 12 How marketing applies to leisure and tourism organisations

Meeting customer needs

If leisure and tourism organisations meet people's needs or wants they will attract and keep customers. For example:

- a woman with a baby might go to a leisure centre which has a mother and baby swimming class
- parents who want time to themselves on holiday might choose a tour operator which provides crèche facilities.

Marketing to meet needs and wants is done in two steps:

- find out what customers need and want, using market research (see page 101)
- use the information to develop products or services which meet these needs.

The managing director of a small tour operator which specialises in activity holidays overseas explains how important it is to meet customers' needs:

66 *This is a competitive industry. I have to be constantly in touch with what people want and need if I'm going to attract and keep customers. We carry out market research all the time into what our customers need from a holiday – we talk to them face to face and over the phone when they make enquiries, and send out questionnaires when they get back from a holiday. We then act on the information and try to develop the products people are looking for. It usually works. A couple of years ago our market research showed that older customers sometimes felt intimidated on walking holidays with younger people. In line with this we developed our 'Fit and Over Fifty' range, which is selling really well.* 99

Satisfying customers

Meeting customers' needs only doesn't always guarantee their satisfaction. People may want a particular product or service but only if they get it:

- at the right time
- presented in the right way
- in the right place
- at the right price.

As the tour operator explains:

66 *Keeping customers satisfied is just as important as meeting their needs. If our customers aren't happy with the way we sell them a holiday, they won't come back. What's more, they would probably tell their family and friends, and we'd lose even more customers. Never underestimate the power of word of mouth!* 99

Marketing helps leisure and tourism organisations to keep their customers satisfied by identifying:

- what people like and dislike
- what they expect
- how they think a facility could be improved.

DISCUSSION POINT

Think about times when you've used a leisure and tourism facility – for example, a sports centre, restaurant or cinema – and haven't been satisfied with the products and services offered.

- Were you unhappy because the product on offer didn't meet your needs?
- Or was the facility unsatisfactory in other ways?
- Have you ever been so dissatisfied with a leisure and tourism facility that you wouldn't go back?
- How could the facility improve to meet your needs and wants?

A family-run Italian restaurant carried out a survey of twenty customers to judge how satisfied they were with the products and services on offer in the restaurant. The table shows the results.

	excellent	satisfactory	could be improved
Variety on the menu	15	5	
Standard of service	10	7	3
Price of food and drink	12	6	2
Lighting	0	6	14
Music	0	10	10
Decoration (colour scheme etc.)	2	9	9

From this, the restaurant owners could see that customers were pleased with the food, drink and service offered by the restaurant but not with the atmosphere. After talking to customers over a period of a month, they decided to:

- redecorate the restaurant in new, quieter colours
- put candles on the tables and replace the overhead lighting with subtle wall lights
- play light classical music rather than the local radio station.

Generating income

Income is the money an organisation gets so that it can run its business. Most income in leisure and tourism facilities comes from customers who buy things. Some income may also come from loans, government grants and private investors who put in some of their own money.

All leisure and tourism facilities need to make money to cover the costs of employing staff, buying in materials and maintaining and updating equipment. Some facilities get funding from the government, some are private business organisations which raise their own funds, others are run on a voluntary basis.

Whatever their main source of funding, leisure and tourism facilities need to generate income by marketing their products and services to customers. Customers mean income for leisure and tourism facilities.

They pay entrance fees, buy food and drink, pay for court time and coaching, buy tickets for shows, pay to park their cars . . . and so on.

So one of the main aims of marketing in leisure and tourism is to attract customers and generate income from them. Advertising, articles in newspapers, special offers and sponsorship raise a facility's profile and promote its products to customers. Market research helps facilities to provide the products and services that customers need and want.

This combination of research and promotion helps to ensure that customers are attracted to a facility, spend their money, get the products and services they are looking for, and come back in the future – generating income for the facility.

ACTIVITY

Choose two leisure and tourism facilities in your area, one funded by the public sector and the other privately funded. Get hold of some of their advertising materials.

■ Can you see a difference between the two sets of materials?

■ Do you think that the differences are because one of the facilities aims to make a profit and the other aims to break even?

Generating profit

Profit is the amount of money left over in a business when all the expenses of running the business have been paid. Like all other organisations, leisure and tourism facilities have to make a profit in order to survive and invest in the future.

Profit comes from the money which customers spend. Effective marketing can generate more income, hence more profit. That's why organisations put time and money into marketing campaigns – to attract and keep customers:

■ a small bed and breakfast might advertise in local papers, produce a brochure to send to guests, print business cards, and try to get coverage in accommodation guides

■ a large facility, such as Chessington World of Adventures, might spend tens or even hundreds of thousands of pounds each year on marketing campaigns, including TV advertising.

Publicly funded facilities – like some sports centres – may not need to make a profit, but they have to break even in order to survive. Their advertising may be less glossy and expensive, but it still has to attract customers.

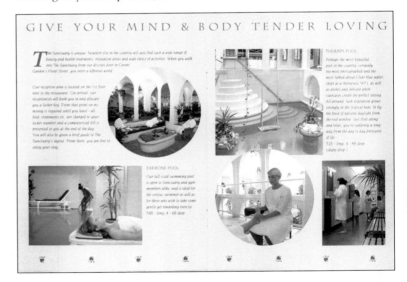

Social profit is the benefit brought to the community, or to a section of the community, by a business.

Generating social profit

Some leisure and tourism organisations exist mainly to help people in the community. Facilities in this category are usually either funded by the government or run on a voluntary basis. Like all other facilities, they market their products and services to make sure that as many people as possible know about, and benefit from, what they offer.

The manager of a town community centre talks about how she markets the facility:

66 *Our aim at the community centre is to provide activities for people from across the community to enjoy. Obviously, if people don't know what we've got on, they won't come. So we market our activities to make sure the community actually benefits from them. We advertise in the local paper – which gives us cheap rates, print a calendar which we deliver through people's doors and visit sheltered accommodation to let people know about the activities we run for over-60s. We also try to make sure that our calendar is displayed in doctors' surgeries, playgroups, the local hospital, and so on. We also carry out regular surveys in the community to find out what people would like from the centre. We've just started a new aerobics class for men over 50 – you'd be surprised what we find out from market research!* **99**

Informing customers

If people don't know about a facility, there won't be any customers. Most facilities produce brochures or leaflets with the basic factual information like:

- where the facility is located
- what products or services it offers
- opening hours
- entrance fees
- refreshment facilities, parking, disabled access, and so on.

This type of information is sometimes contained in newspaper advertisements as well.

Staff working at a facility can also help to inform customers, by making sure they have the knowledge to answer customers' questions.

Promoting products

Every day you can see and hear leisure and tourism products and services being promoted.

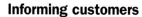

DISCUSSION POINT

A group is putting on a Christmas play, and wants to invite parties of elderly and disabled people from the local community to watch it.

- What information would you need to give them?
- Where would they see it?

Promoting leisure and tourism

- advertising campaigns on national television promoting a travel agency's latest special offers
- small ads in local papers advertising sports coaching
- radio interviews with the manager of a local leisure centre
- posters promoting concerts, plays, sporting events
- letters encouraging us to subscribe to cable television
- magazine articles about holiday destinations
- football teams sponsored by leisure and tourism organisations . . .

Promotional campaigns help to raise their profile as an organisation and encourage customers to buy their particular products and services.

Influencing product development

Getting the product right is the most important outcome of marketing. Customers won't buy a product they don't need or want, even if it is competitively priced and promoted well.

Organisations use the information they collect through marketing research – customer surveys, questionnaires, conversations with people, figures collected by other facilities – to influence the products they develop.

A town-centre cinema with three screens was badly affected by the opening of a large, out-of-town multiplex cinema. Here the cinema's manager describes how using marketing techniques helped them to redevelop the cinema's products:

66 *When the multiplex opened just four miles away, we were devastated. They've got nine screens, restaurants and burger bars, brand new furnishings, and seat thousands of people. We've got three screens, old seating and a kiosk selling popcorn and chocolates. But when we carried out a survey among local people, we found that the only reason they had deserted us was because of the choice of films at the multiplex – they actually preferred the more friendly, traditional atmosphere at our cinema. We decided to build on this. We brought back old-fashioned popcorn and ice-cream sellers, redecorated in 1930s style and launched a series of speciality nights showing classic films. Alongside this we ran an advertising campaign in the local papers, got coverage on local radio and television, and dressed up in costume to hand out leaflets in town. The result has been an enormous success – our audience figures are almost back up to their old level.* 99

Influencing consumer choice

Marketing tries to influence what people choose to buy. Organisations focus their marketing campaigns on the products and services they particularly want to sell to customers. The marketing manager of a leisure centre explains how she uses marketing to influence consumer choice:

❝ *At any one time we have several products which we particularly want to promote. It may be because we make a good profit on a product – for example, a year's family membership ticket. Or it may be because we feel it's a particularly good product which will win us customers. We offer potential members reduced rates to some classes to try to convince them to join. Sometimes, a product doesn't go well and we need to promote it to customers. Recently, we noticed that the number of people coming to us for swimming lessons was falling. We ran a marketing campaign promoting learning to swim, including articles in the local press about the importance of safety in water, ads for lessons, and special offers on courses. Now our pool's full of learner swimmers.* **❞**

The marketing mix and promotional activities

The **marketing mix** is made up of four interlinking parts, known as the 'four Ps':

■ price

■ place

■ product

■ promotion.

Like good cooking, successful marketing mixes the ingredients of the marketing mix together in the right proportions.

It doesn't mean there is always a fixed recipe. At different times, and in different facilities, the marketing mix needed will be different. For example:

■ a new facility may need to concentrate on promotion so that potential customers know that it has opened

■ a well-established facility trying to attract a new type of customer might decide to concentrate on improving its products to make sure it offers what people want.

Price

If customers feel that a product is fairly priced, they are more likely to buy it than if they think it's over-priced.

How do leisure and tourism organisations decide the price of products?

HOW MUCH DOES IT ACTUALLY COST?
In order to make a profit, the organisation has to charge more for the product than it costs to produce.

WHAT ARE THE AIMS OF THE ORGANISATION?
Does the organisation aim to make a profit? or can it offer reduced prices for the benefit of the community?

WHAT PRICE SHALL WE CHARGE?

HOW MUCH DO COMPETITORS CHARGE?
If a competitor is charging half as much for a similar product, the organisation's product won't sell.

WHAT IS THE DEMAND FOR THE PRODUCT?
The number of people wanting to use facilities and buy products varies throughout the year. Organisations need to change the price of their products in line with this.

Leisure and tourism organisations use a range of pricing methods in different situations.

Peak and off-peak pricing

Prices vary depending on the time of day or year, in line with the number of people wanting to use facilities. For example, sports centres usually charge lower fees for using facilities during the day, when most people are at work and demand is less than in the evening.

Low and high season pricing

Travel agents divide their holidays into low season, when relatively few people want to travel, and high season, when most tourists take their holidays. A holiday in the UK in February (in the low season) may cost a lot less than the same holiday in August (in the high season).

Group and special discounts

Discounts are reductions for parties of people or particular sections of the community. Group discounts attract large numbers of people to facilities and help to boost income overall. Special discounts or 'concessions' are often offered to pensioners, students and people with disabilities, so that they can afford to use facilities which might be too expensive otherwise. Facilities funded by the public sector often offer concessions.

CADBURY WORLD

The Cadbury World marketing team recognises the importance of groups to their facility – about 45% of all visitor traffic – and offers group discounts of up to 20%. The pricing policy in the shop reflects the expectations of visitors that chocolate at the factory would be cheaper. So Cadbury's adjusted the prices to meet this expectation.

Special offers

Low prices offered on a temporary basis to attract people to use a facility or to encourage them to buy a particular product. For example, a new restaurant might offer two meals for the price of one so that customers are tempted to try it and – if they like it – come back again.

Place

Place means two things in marketing:

■ where a facility is – its location

■ how it gets products and services to customers – the distribution channels.

Location

If a facility gets the location right, like this travel agent, it takes a major step towards establishing a successful business:

66 *We looked at several locations for our new shop – parades just out of town, units in the large undercover shopping centre. In the end, we decided that an empty shop in the middle of the high street was the place for us. People walk past us as they do their shopping and drop in to pick up brochures. We put posters about cheap flights and holidays in our windows so people notice what's available as they pass. It's easy for people to park – there's a multi-storey car park just along the street – and there's a bus stop right outside the shop.* 99

Many leisure and tourism facilities need to be located:

■ in a place with good transport links

■ close to where a large number of.people (potential customers) live or work.

For businesses like travel agencies, theatres, cinemas, restaurants and sports centres, this often means being in, or just outside, towns and cities. People are willing to travel further to reach visitor attractions and accommodation where they spend more time. But they still want an easy journey, and sites with good transport connections are at an advantage.

Distribution channels

Products often pass through two or three distribution channels before they reach customers. For example, products sold in National Trust shops come from various sources – some from the Trust itself, others from different suppliers. Like most other consumer goods, they pass through the hands of wholesalers and retailers before they reach the customer.

Ingredients and raw materials are bought from the wholesaler

Meals are prepared using the raw materials

Customers buy the final product

ACTIVITY

There is a similar distribution channel for holidays. A tour operator buys rooms, meals and flights (the raw materials of a holiday). When an operator's package holiday is sold to customers through a travel agency it pays a commission to the agency. Produce a visual flow chart, using photographs and illustrations, to show how this distribution channel works.

Product

The third part of the marketing mix is to make sure that products give customers what they need or want.

Some leisure and tourism **products** are things you can see and touch, like sports equipment. Many others are activities or experiences – such as a holiday, a visit to a theme park or a film – or services, like tennis coaching or guided tours round country houses.

Leisure and tourism organisations develop new products and redevelop existing products all the time based on customer feedback. For example:

■ mountain bikes were developed to meet people's need for a bicycle for riding on rough ground as opposed to shopping, racing or touring

■ theme parks introduce new rides every year

■ restaurants develop new menus

■ hotels offer new holiday packages.

This constant process of developing and redeveloping products is an important part of meeting customer needs and maintaining quality.

Another way of marketing products is branding them to give them a clear identity and to raise customers' expectations of what to expect. Many leisure and tourism outlets have strong brand identities: McDonald's, Adidas and many more. Building on these brands can help to ensure the success of products.

Promotion

Once you have the right product, at the right price and in the right place, you need to promote it – let your customer know that it's there and waiting to be bought.

Advertising

An expensive way to promote products and services – but it's effective. Advertisements appear:

■ on television and radio

■ in newspapers and magazines

■ at the cinema

■ on billboards and public transport.

Big leisure and tourism organisations can afford to run major advertising campaigns on TV and billboards. Small ones are usually restricted to putting ads in local newspapers.

The marketing manager of a national hotel chain explains how advertising is used for promotion:

❝ It's very expensive – we spend hundreds of thousands of pounds a year advertising our hotels. In return we're guaranteed space on the page, time on the radio or a slot on television. TV advertising is probably the most effective route, but showing even a short commercial at peak times is incredibly expensive. So we back up TV commercials with ads in national newspapers and magazines. It's important to put your ads in the right place for your target audience – our hotels are upmarket and cater for business people, so we advertise in quality papers like The Times, *glossy magazines like* Tatler, *and specialist business publications. Most of our advertising is national, but out of season we place some ads in local papers near our hotels offering special deals on honeymoon breaks, weddings, conferences and so on. ❞*

DISCUSSION POINT

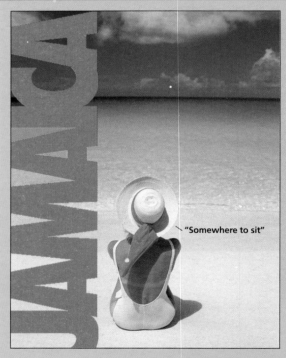

"Somewhere to sit"

■ Can you tell whether these leisure and tourism organisations are advertising their products to a national audience, or locally?

■ How clear are the messages?

■ How much impact do they have?

■ How could they be improved?

Sales promotion

Sales promotions aim to stimulate instant demand for a product. They are widely used in the most competitive bits of the leisure and tourism industry – package holidays or cross-channel journeys, for example. Customers are encouraged to buy particular products with incentives like:

- free gifts
- prize draws
- discount vouchers in magazines and newspapers, offering money off
- 'sale' offers on products.

Sales promotions are temporary. They aim to raise interest in a product quickly but only last for a short time. They are useful for leisure and tourism organisations because they are flexible and easy to put into practice.

Public relations

Public relations – PR – is one of the most cost-effective ways for leisure and tourism organisations to get themselves better known. The more people know and respect an organisation, the more potential customers it has. So good PR aims to:

- raise an organisation's profile
- give people a positive impression of its aims, efficiency and friendliness.

Organisations don't always pay directly for PR, like they do for advertising. Instead, they can invest their time in making sure that they make a good impression on the public and developing a strong corporate image. Friendly, informed staff and helpful telephone operators are terrific PR.

PR means making the most of the media – newspapers, radio and TV. Some leisure and tourism organisations have members of staff who concentrate on forming good relations with the media and getting good PR coverage for the company. Others hire firms of PR consultants to do it for them. A public relations consultant for a tour operator which organises exclusive faraway holidays explains:

66 *Companies hire us because we get them a good press – literally. For this company in the last three months we have written a newspaper article on the growing popularity of holidays in exotic locations, arranged an interview with the company's managing director on a holiday programme on national radio, featured one of its holidays on a TV holiday programme and listed them as one of the contacts in a magazine feature about travelling to paradise islands. They're getting very well known.* **99**

Travel

Travelogue

ALLSPORT/PASCAL RONDEAU

Mapped out
Cycling maps and touring packs are provided in Christmas breaks arranged by the Cotswold Cycling Company. Spend three days exploring country lanes and work off a few pounds between visits to the panto and tucking into Christmas pud. Prices start at £450 for three days (details 01242 250642).

Breaks with tradition
Liven up those days between Christmas and New Year with a Festive Filler break from Holiday Club Pontin's. Three-day breaks from December 27 cost £123 full-board for adults and £62 for children, or you could stuff your own turkey at a self-catering week at Camber Sands, Sussex, for £314 for a family of four (details 01772 621621).

Ringing in the new
The Lake District's handbell ringers and carol singers will be working overtime this winter. The South Lakeland Choir will be singing before the annual knockout domino championship at the Wild Boar Hotel (01539445225), where a three-night stay costs £229. Handbell ringers arrive at Rothay Manor (01539433605) on Christmas Eve for a sherry party as part of a four-night, £570 break which includes a cruise on Lake Windermere. And at the Beech Hill Hotel (0800 592294) beside Lake Windermere, carollers will join guests on Christmas Eve for hot chocolate and mince pies.

Bags of cheap fares
British Airways Holidays is planning discount Christmas shopping trips to European cities with a night in Paris for £95, a night in Amsterdam costing £119 and a quick jaunt to Rome for £175. To qualify, you must return with shopping bags laden before December 11 (details: 01293 723100).

ACTIVITY

Following a serious accident at a large leisure centre, the marketing manager is asked to generate some good PR to counteract any bad feeling in the community.

List ten different PR activities the organisation could try and rank them in order of importance.

DISCUSSION POINT

■ Why do you think personal selling is important to leisure and tourism organisations?

■ Can you think of times when you have decided not to use a facility again because staff weren't good at selling?

This kind of PR is effective because it appears as part of a newspaper or TV report. People are often suspicious of advertising and ignore it, but they tend to respect media reports more.

Personal selling

Personal selling happens when there is face-to-face contact between customers and staff. Staff with good personal selling skills make the most of these opportunities and many leisure and tourism organisations rely heavily on employees' selling skills:

■ travel agency counter staff sell holidays to customers

■ waiters and waitresses provide a polite, efficient service so customers go away happy – and come back again

■ reception staff at sports centres help customers make the most of their facilities.

Direct marketing

Direct marketing is when organisations identify their target customers and go to them directly, for example, by sending information in personally addressed letters through the post.

Mr W Jones
12 Munro Street
Southampton

Dear Mr Jones

Please find enclosed a taster of our latest issue of Mountain Runner. As you will see, we have kept up the superb quality of editorial content and photography for which we are known.

From subscription information here at Mountain Runner we know that our magazine appeals to ABC professionals:
81% of our readers are male.
77% are in the 22–48 age group
38% claim to read no other mountain activity magazine.

Mountain Runner is expanding the outdoor marketplace by covering a wide variety of activities with well written articles, practical advice and good photography. No wonder our readers are so loyal!

We hope to hear from you soon, with your subscription order for this "can't be missed" publication.

Yours sincerely,

J B Davenport

Jeremy B Davenport

Mrs R Hodgkin
62 Southgate Street
Northwood
Isle Of Wight

Dear Mrs Hodgkin,

Here we go again! Another new season of skiing is upon us and the holidays are drawing closer for which we are pleased to enclose our new 95/96 brochure.

As you were a valued visitor to our chalets in France last year we would like to offer you a **10% discount** on holiday prices this year, if you book before September !st 1995. **Don't delay** as some chalets are already fully booked on some dates!

As you know, all our resorts are recognised for their healthy snow records and local charm. As usual, this year we will be providing our Christmas Extravaganza Holiday Week, complete with a Christmas Eve torchlit descent by Santa and his helpers (all welcome to join in), and a deluxe Christmas season menu.

As ever, our emphasis is on personal service before and during your holiday, whenever you decide to go and we look forward to welcoming you back with us again this year.

Kind regards,

Martin Penn

Martin Penn

Leisure and tourism organisations are increasingly using direct marketing – also known as 'direct mail' – to promote themselves. They might want to send information about current offers or new developments, or a brochure or leaflet giving details of events.

The marketing manager for a four-star country house hotel explains how they use direct marketing:

❝ *We use direct mail a lot – mailing your message gives you the assurance that it will actually land on people's doormats! We mail two main groups of people. Firstly, we put together a mailing list from our records of people who've been guests at our hotel in the past. We usually send them a letter every six months, which is cheap to produce, outlining special offers and events coming up. Once a year we also send them our new brochure. Then a couple of times a year we buy mailing lists of prospective customers, and send them our brochure with a special introductory offer to try to tempt them. We get a good response to our mailings.* **❞**

ACTIVITY

Collect three or four direct marketing letters and compare them. Draw up a table of the advantages and disadvantages of this way of sales promotion.

Sponsorship

This means providing money to support an event, activity or cause – and getting publicity in return. More and more leisure and tourism organisations are now using this form of promotion:

- locally, leisure centres, visitor attractions and restaurants provide support for activities in their community
- nationally, leisure and tourism organisations are sponsoring everything from football teams to children's hospitals.

Thistle and Mount Charlotte Hotels has three hotels in Leeds:

Leeds United is sponsored by Thistle Hotels

❝ *The decision to sponsor Leeds United football team illustrates the group's commitment to the club and also to the city of Leeds where Thistle and Mount Charlotte Hotels has established substantial growth since relocating its head office to Leeds in 1976. Although the original sponsorship deal was for just one year, both parties were happy to sign up for a further two years, taking the partnership until the end of the 1995–1996 season.* **❞**

DISCUSSION POINT

A national chain of pizza restaurants which is particularly popular with children and young people has an annual budget for sponsorship. They have calculated that they could afford to sponsor one of these:

- a national cricket tournament
- a first division football team
- the new wing of a children's hospice.

Talk about the pros and cons of each option.

- How should the pizza chain spend its sponsorship budget?

Sponsorship can bring these benefits to the sponsoring organisation:

- it gets its name seen and heard
- if it sponsors a well-known event, team or cause, it gains prestige from being associated with something important
- if it sponsors a worthy cause, it gains the public's respect and gratitude.

ACTIVITY

Visit a travel agency and collect brochures produced by three tour operators offering similar types of holidays for families – for example, three lakes and mountains brochures, or three skiing brochures.

■ Does one stand out from the rest?

■ If you were producing a brochure for a similar type of holiday, would you try to make yours stand out? How?

■ Or do you think it would be better for your brochure to look like the others?

Producing brochures

Brochures are publications used to promote products and services to the public. You see a lot of them produced by leisure and tourism organisations, because:

■ people often travel to facilities in other areas, where they can't find out about them in passing – for example, we rely on the pictures and descriptions in travel brochures to tell us about holiday destinations

■ the leisure and tourism industry is very competitive, and an organisation's brochure can make it stand out from the crowd – for example, a visitor attraction with a good brochure or leaflet can stand out from other brochures in a tourist information centre

■ they are a good way to communicate with customers and potential customers by direct mail.

Marketing research information

Organisations do marketing research to find out what customers – and people who are not yet customers – need and want. When they're selling something, they want to know people's opinions about it and their preferences. Then they can use this information to make decisions like:

■ what new products shall we develop?

■ how much should we charge for them?

■ how can we improve our existing products?

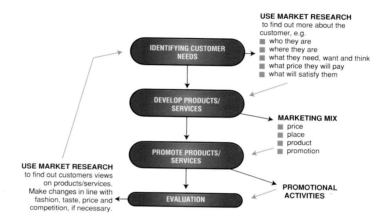

USE MARKET RESEARCH
to find out more about the customer, e.g.
■ who they are
■ where they are
■ what they need, want and think
■ what price they will pay
■ what will satisfy them

IDENTIFYING CUSTOMER NEEDS

DEVELOP PRODUCTS/ SERVICES

MARKETING MIX
■ price
■ place
■ product
■ promotion

PROMOTE PRODUCTS/ SERVICES

USE MARKET RESEARCH
to find out customers views on products/services. Make changes in line with fashion, taste, price and competition, if necessary.

EVALUATION

PROMOTIONAL ACTIVITIES

Primary marketing research

Primary research gives direct feedback on what customers want, need and think. It's done in various ways. Three common ways are:

■ surveys

■ observation

■ focus groups.

Interview surveys

A trained interviewer asks someone questions face to face and writes down their responses on a questionnaire. It's a good way to collect detailed, reliable information, but is expensive and takes a long time to carry out.

Written surveys

A questionnaire is given to customers and potential customers for them to fill in themselves. It's cheaper than interview surveys, but often provides less detailed information, and people's responses in questionnaires can be confusing.

Postal surveys

Questionnaires are posted to customers or potential customers for them to fill in themselves. Postal surveys are often used by tour operators, who post questionnaires to tourists after their holidays. One problem is that not

> **Primary research** means collecting information directly from people through surveys and observation. It's sometimes also known as 'field research' because it's done out there in the field, with actual people.

DISCUSSION POINT

Which primary marketing research methods would you recommend for:

- a sports centre which wants to know why more people use a competitor's facilities?

- a theme park which wants to know in what order visitors tend to go on different rides?

- a tour operator which wants to develop a new range of holidays for the over-50s?

- a museum which wants feedback from school groups after they have visited the facility?

everyone who gets a postal questionnaire bothers to fill it in and send it back – so there is a low rate of return. Sometimes there's a free draw to encourage a higher rate of return.

Telephone surveys

Calling customers or potential customers and interviewing them about their views and preferences over the phone. It can provide useful information, but people can be suspicious that interviewers are trying to sell them something and don't always like being called on the telephone.

Observation

Another way of collecting information directly from people is to watch what they do. Observation can also be a useful way for leisure and tourism organisations to find things out. Nowadays, it doesn't have to involve a person sitting watching what people do and recording the details. Instead, new technology can do much of the work – for example:

- closed-circuit TV cameras monitor people moving about a site
- electronic turnstiles count the number of people using a facility.

Focus groups

A good way of finding out detailed information on the opinions and views of a particular group of people. Focus groups bring together a small number of people from a similar background – for example, young people, or the elderly – who are the target audience for a particular product. A facilitator guides the group discussion, and records the group's views. Leisure and tourism organisations often use focus groups when they are setting up a new facility or product, or want to make major changes to existing products.

Secondary marketing research

Secondary research means analysing information from records held within the organisation, or compiled by other organisations. It's also known as **desk research** because it can be done without going into the field.

Secondary research does not involve collecting information directly from customers. Instead, leisure and tourism organisations can use:

- existing records of their customers – for example, attendance figures, customer complaints and membership lists
- information collected by other organisations – for example, survey specialists such as Gallup, Mintel, the Policy Studies Institute and the English Tourist Board. These organisations carry out general surveys of customer opinion and preferences and can be an excellent source of information for leisure and tourism organisations – for example, on buying patterns or visitor numbers.

Information about customers

■ whether they are male or female

■ how old they are

■ how often they visit

■ where they live

■ how they travel to the facility

■ what their jobs are

■ how much they earn

■ how much they are willing to pay for a product or service

THE NATIONAL MOTOR MUSEUM, BEAULIEU

The National Motor Museum at Beaulieu in Hampshire is the country's most famous collection of cars, commercial vehicles and motorcycles. They tell the story of motoring from 1895 to the present day.

The Museum has a computerised ticketing information system which automatically collects information about the people who visit. For example, recent figures collected in this way shows that:

■ 62% are adults

■ 29% are children

■ 9% are senior citizens

■ 70% are holiday makers

■ 30% are day trippers.

Information about customers

Leisure and tourism organisations use both primary and secondary marketing research to collect information about their customers.

They use this information to build up a customer profile – a picture of their customers. It helps them tailor their products and services to meet these customers' needs.

Information about customers' opinions and views

Most organisations carry out interview surveys to find out their customers' opinions and views on:

- what they like about a facility
- what they dislike
- how they think it might be improved.

If they're setting up a new facility, or considering a major change to existing products and services, leisure and tourism organisations may also use focus groups to collect more detailed information.

Information about customers' buying habits

Everyone has buying habits – what they spend their money on, how much they spend, whether they buy regularly or just occasionally. Knowing a bit about these habits can help leisure and tourism organisations provide the right products and services at the right prices. Computerised till and visitor records have made it much easier to collect this type of information.

The manager of a city-centre hotel with 80 bedrooms explains how she uses information about customers' buying habits:

66 We cater mainly for business people, so there's a constant flow of guests throughout the year staying for different lengths of time and buying different products and services. Our computer on reception keeps records of how long guests stay and whether they buy additional services such as room service and laundry. It's linked with another computer in the restaurant, which keeps records of the meals guests buy.

Every six months we analyse the information collected to see how our guests are spending their money. Last time we carried out the research we found that more guests were staying for over three days, more were choosing to eat an evening meal in our restaurant, and there was a growing demand for fax services. But fewer guests were using our laundry service, which had recently gone up in price.

As a result of our findings, we decided to put together a special 'business package' for guests staying for more than three days. We also extended the hours we serve evening meals in the restaurant, and slightly increased the cost of faxing. People obviously felt that our laundry service had become too expensive, so we brought it back down in price. 99

FORTE
BUSINESS GUARANTEE

Staying away on business?

Then there's something you should know

ACTIVITY

Choose two similar leisure and tourism facilities – for example, two sports centres, two cinemas, or two fast-food restaurants. Visit each, and make notes on:

- the range of products and services on offer
- how much they cost
- who they aim to attract with their products and services.

Write a short report summarising your findings. Based on your research, which facility would you choose to use? Explain how you think the facility you wouldn't use should change to take account of the competition.

Information about competitors

Parts of the leisure and tourism industry are highly competitive. Organisations need to keep up to date at all times with what their competitors are doing. It means keeping a constant watch on:

- new facilities, products and services being launched
- new technology being developed
- pricing – this is particularly important, because it can change so quickly and many customers will choose to buy from a competitor whose products and services are cheaper. Keen pricing in the travel industry is so competitive it can result in price wars between travel agents.

Collecting information about competitors in advance can be difficult, because organisations tend to keep developments secret for as long as possible.

Target markets and market segments

A market is a group of people likely to buy or use a particular product or service. Every individual is in many different markets – for education, food, holidays, insurance schemes, and so on.

All organisations need to know who their customers and potential customers are – their **target market** – so that they can provide the right products and services. Often, organisations break their target markets down again, into smaller pieces called **market segments**.

Target markets

Organisations often divide their overall target market into two types of customer:

- people who currently buy or use a product or service – for example, regular cinema-goers, people who use a park; they are called actual buyers
- people who might buy or use a product or service, but don't at the moment; they are called potential buyers.

All leisure and tourism facilities have more potential than actual buyers. For example, the target market for an indoor tennis centre might be all the people who enjoy playing tennis in the area and can afford to pay to use courts and equipment. Within this target market there will be more people who don't currently use the centre than people who play there regularly.

> ### DISCUSSION POINT
>
> What do you think would be the target market for these leisure and tourism organisations:
>
> - a motorway service station?
> - a country house hotel, 20 miles from the nearest major town?
> - a National Park?
> - a city-centre travel agency?

Market segments

Market segments are groups of individuals in a target market who have similar characteristics, needs and preferences. Dividing a market into segments can:

- help an organisation to check that it is satisfying all of its customers
- provide a focus for marketing campaigns, with different promotional activities concentrating on different market segments.

For example, a tour operator developing holiday products might divide its target market into segments like this.

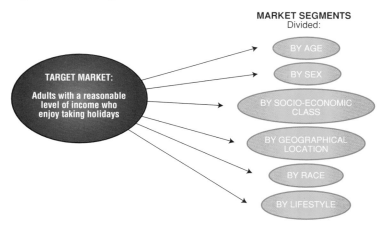

MARKET SEGMENTS
Divided:

TARGET MARKET:
Adults with a reasonable level of income who enjoy taking holidays

BY AGE
BY SEX
BY SOCIO-ECONOMIC CLASS
BY GEOGRAPHICAL LOCATION
BY RACE
BY LIFESTYLE

Markets can be divided (or 'segmented') in different ways, for example:

- by age
- by sex
- by race
- by socio-economic class
- by geographical location
- by lifestyle.

Divided by age

One of the most common ways for leisure and tourism organisations to divide their target markets into segments. Depending on where people are in their lives, they tend to have different leisure and tourism needs, likes and dislikes.

Retired single person (solitary survivor 2)
Low income.
Little to spend on leisure.

Single/widowed person in work (solitary survivor 1)
Restricted income.
Home and garden are centre of leisure.

Older couples, chief breadwinner retired (empty nest 2)
Restricted income.
Leisure centred on home (TV, radio, gardening).

Older couples, children left home (empty nest 1)
Higher disposable income.
Enjoy eating out, short breaks, overseas travel.

Couple with older children (full nest 3)
Low disposable income.
Leisure centred on the home (TV, radio).

Young couple with children (full nest 2)
Falling disposable income.
Spend less money on leisure.

Young couple with baby (full nest 1)
Enjoy family activities; parks, visitor attractions.
More likely to take self-catering holidays.

Young couple
Higher disposable income.
Enjoy cinema, eating out, more exotic holidays.

Young single person
Reasonable disposable income.
Enjoys pubs, bars, clubs, music.
Likely to take short-haul package holidays.

Disposable income is the money left over once you have paid for necessities like food, rent and clothing.

Targeting a market segment by age can provide an excellent focus for leisure and tourism organisations.

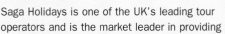

SAGA HOLIDAYS

Saga Holidays is one of the UK's leading tour operators and is the market leader in providing holidays for people over 50. The company was established in 1952 when its founder, the owner of a hotel in Folkestone, was looking for a way to attract guests during the low season. He thought of retired people and put together an all-inclusive holiday package for them. From these humble beginnings, Saga has grown into a large international organisation. It offers a wide range of holidays to cater for people with different interests and levels of disposable income.

Divided by sex

Some facilities find it useful to target market segments divided by sex (men and women). This is because:

■ men and women don't always enjoy the same leisure activities – for example, more men than women play football but more women than men do aerobics

■ traditionally, men and women have different tastes in style and decoration, and need different facilities – for example, hotel rooms designed for women will be decorated in light colours, contain a hairdryer and tissues, and so on

■ sometimes people prefer to be in single-sex groups – for example, women often prefer to exercise without men and all-female gyms are opening to meet this preference.

When leisure and tourism organisations are developing or promoting a product, they need to consider whether they are targeting it at men in particular, women in particular, or both sexes. This will affect the product they develop, the facilities they offer, and the way they carry out promotion.

The proprietor of a large hotel explains how its marketing strategy is influenced by its potential customers' sex:

66 *As we're just outside the city centre, we get lots of business people staying with us. Twenty years ago they were almost all men and our rooms and services reflected this – the bar was aimed at male drinkers, and our rooms were equipped with trouser presses and not much else. Over the last ten years more and more of our guests have been women and we've changed in line with this. We've redecorated rooms in a much softer style, with lighter colours and furnishings. All our rooms are now equipped with hairdryers, shampoo, cotton wool and tissues. We've made the bar and restaurant much lighter and brighter, so women feel comfortable to eat and drink on their own. We make sure we emphasise all these points – and the security of our rooms – in our brochures.* 99

The Ritz Hotel in London
supplies Japanese visitors
with pocket guides

Divided by race

Usually it would be considered discriminatory to target a particular market segment by race. But leisure and tourism organisations sometimes need to consider food, dress, language and religious customs when developing products and services to meet all their customers' needs. For example:

- in areas with a racially-mixed community, restaurants are often set up to meet the dietary preferences of particular ethnic groups
- hotels which have a lot of visitors from overseas may need to offer special food and facilities to meet their needs and expectations, translate signs into different languages and employ staff with language skills.

DISCUSSION POINT

Think of the food, dress and religious customs of two groups of people who live in the UK. What are some of the different ways in which leisure and tourism organisations might target their products and services to cater for these groups?

Divided by socio-economic class

Socio-economic class is a way of categorising people depending on the job they do and their income. It is based on the theory that people of a similar background have some similar likes and dislikes, share some common interests and spend some of their money on similar things.

Leisure and tourism organisations usually have a clear idea of the socio-economic classes they are marketing their products to. Often they break down information on their customers in this way.

The most common way to divide people into social class is by the occupation of the head of the household, as the table shows.

Social grade	Social class	Typical occupations
A	Upper middle	Higher managerial, administrative and professional (e.g. judges, surgeons)
B	Middle	Intermediate managerial and administrative (e.g. lawyers, teachers, doctors)
C1	Lower middle	Supervisory, clerical, junior management (e.g. bank clerk, estate agent)
C2	Skilled working	Skilled manual workers (e.g. joiner, welder)
D	Working	Semi-skilled and unskilled manual workers (e.g. driver, postman, porter)
E	Those at lowest level of subsistence	Pensioners, casual workers, students, the unemployed

If a visitor attraction decides that its target market segment is made up of people in the C1, C2 and D classes, it will tailor its product and prices to meet what it thinks these people want.

Divided by geographical location

Every leisure and tourism facility knows the geographical area or areas in which its target market lives. For example:

■ a family-run pub in a town may decide that its geographical market segment covers the town itself and villages within a radius of two miles

■ Cadbury World, a national visitor attraction based in Birmingham, focuses its marketing within a 50-mile radius of Birmingham, although it also recognises target market segments in Yorkshire, East Anglia and the south of England.

The marketing manager of a living museum describes how the target geographical market affects the way the museum is marketed:

66 *After carrying out customer surveys and looking at other attractions in the north of England, we decided that our main geographical market was within 20 miles travelling distance of the museum. We drew a circle on the map and planned how we could market the museum throughout this area. I placed advertisements in all the local papers, and made sure that our leaflets and brochures are on display in all the tourist information offices within the area. I also ran a series of commercials on local radio and television – luckily one station covers the whole area.* 99

Divided by lifestyle

Some organisations think of people according to their lifestyle – car dealers are one example. The chart shows a typical lifestyle classification, which divides people into five types according to what they need and like to do.

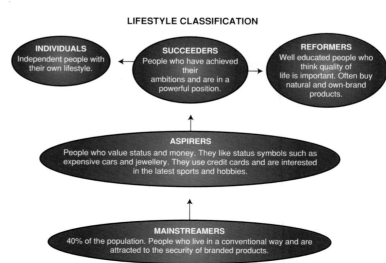

LIFESTYLE CLASSIFICATION

INDIVIDUALS
Independent people with their own lifestyle.

SUCCEEDERS
People who have achieved their ambitions and are in a powerful position.

REFORMERS
Well educated people who think quality of life is important. Often buy natural and own-brand products.

ASPIRERS
People who value status and money. They like status symbols such as expensive cars and jewellery. They use credit cards and are interested in the latest sports and hobbies.

MAINSTREAMERS
40% of the population. People who live in a conventional way and are attracted to the security of branded products.

Based on segments like these:

■ an exclusive hotel might decide that it particularly wants to target 'aspirers', who are likely to spend a lot of money on extravagant breaks

■ a tour operator which specialises in adventurous holidays for independent travellers might decide to target 'individualists'.

66 *Trailfinders was founded in 1970 as an agency and information centre for the independent traveller. Having identified and serviced a gap in the market for non-package travel, Trailfinders continues to respond to the changing requirements of independent travellers.* **99**

DISCUSSION POINT

For each of the different lifestyle groups shown on the chart, identify:

■ a sport you think they would enjoy

■ a type of holiday you think they would enjoy

■ a visitor attraction you think they would visit.

The marketing mix and target markets

There is a close relationship between target markets and the marketing mix. Dividing a target market into different segments can help organisations make good decisions about pricing, product development, promotional activities and place.

Pricing and target markets

An organisation which has identified its market segments can look at the amount of disposable income this group of people has and find out their buying habits. Then the products and services can be priced according to people's pockets. If the price for a product is already set, the organisation can target the market segment which it thinks will be happy with the price.

Target market division	Relationship to pricing
By age	As the lifecycle chart on page 107 shows, most people have different amounts of disposable income at different stages of their lives. Young couples without children can on average afford to pay more for a product than couples with families.
By socio-economic class	Dividing people by the occupation of the head of the household (see page 109), someone in grade B would probably have more disposable income than someone in grade E. Middle-class people can on average afford to pay more for a product than working-class people.
By geographical location	Some areas of the country are wealthier than others. Looking at the location of its target market segment can help an organisation decide how much people will be willing to pay.
By lifestyle	People's lifestyle priorities, as shown on the chart on page 110, affect the amount they are willing to pay for a product. So aspirers, who enjoy the status of buying something expensive, will pay more than mainstreamers, who tend to play safe.

The owner of an exclusive health farm describes the relationship between the facility's target market and pricing:

66 *Staying at our health resort is extremely expensive. Our product is very special, and this is reflected in its high price. From the outset, we marketed our resort to sections of the population we knew could afford to pay for this exclusivity. Our promotional campaigns focus on people who fall into the middle and upper middle class socio-economic bracket – younger people without families, and older people whose children have grown up and left home. We definitely appeal to the aspirers of life. We recently introduced low season packages for retired people, which we offer at a slightly lower price as they have less money to spare.* 99

Place and target markets

A leisure and tourism organisation which has already established the location of a facility can target particular market segments in its locality. If the target market segment for a facility is decided before its location, looking at their needs and preferences can help decide where to locate.

Target market division	Relationship to place
By age	Different age groups have different levels of mobility, both in terms of physical fitness and methods of transport. For elderly people, who often rely on public transport and can't walk too far, it is particularly important that a facility is near to a bus stop or railway station. Younger people may be more concerned with being able to reach a facility quickly by car.
By sex	Women have particular security needs which organisations aiming to sell their products to women need to bear in mind when deciding on a location. For example, it would be inappropriate for a women's gym to be down a badly lit alleyway.
By geographical location	It is important that a facility is located within easy reach of a large population centre. Organisations need to consider geographical markets when choosing the location for a facility.

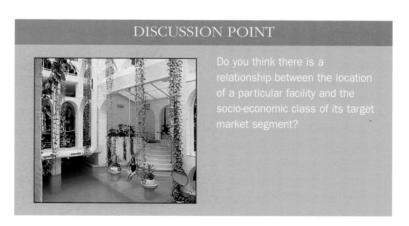

DISCUSSION POINT

Do you think there is a relationship between the location of a particular facility and the socio-economic class of its target market segment?

Promotion and target markets

Promotion should always be carefully targeted at a particular audience. The marketing director of a chain of national travel agencies explains how the target market for a particular product affects the promotional methods used:

66 *It's really important for us to think about the target audience for every piece of promotion we buy. What appeals to the target market? What do they read? Where do they go? How important is price? For example, we've recently run big promotional campaigns on two types of holidays – skiing packages, and bargain winter breaks for the over-60s.*

The skiing packages are mostly aimed at young, single people travelling in groups, with plenty of money to spend on having a good time. We ran an advertising campaign for these in the quality national newspapers, sporting magazines and style magazines such as GQ and The Face. We also put advertising posters on the London Underground and ran a short commercial on late night TV.

We took a different approach to promoting the over-60s breaks. Money was more of a concern for this target market, so we offered a 5% reduction if they booked within a month. We advertised in tabloid papers, on local radio, and daytime television. We also managed to get coverage for the packages on one of the TV holiday programmes. **99**

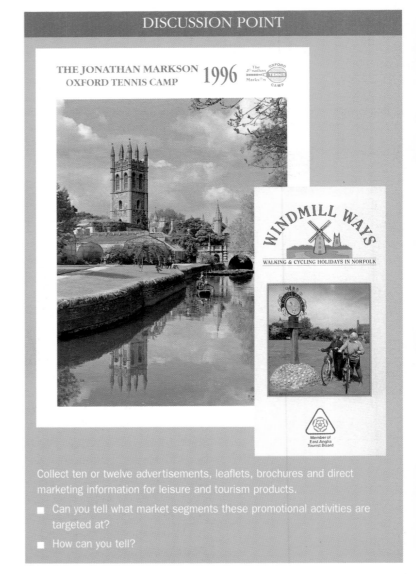

DISCUSSION POINT

Collect ten or twelve advertisements, leaflets, brochures and direct marketing information for leisure and tourism products.

■ Can you tell what market segments these promotional activities are targeted at?

■ How can you tell?

Product and target markets

Successful products meet the needs and preferences of their target markets.
So it's good to think carefully about the target market before developing
the product:

- identify the target market first
- find out the needs and preferences of customers in this target market
- develop a product which meets these needs and preferences as closely
  as possible.

Age, sex, race, socio-economic class, geographical location and lifestyle can all
make a major difference to the type of products people need and want.

DISCUSSION POINT

A new leisure centre with a wide range of sporting and refreshment
facilities is opening near to where these people live. They each belong to
one of the target market segments for the centre.

- What products should the centre offer in order to appeal to each
  individual or family?

115

BANGERS

Imagine our fictitious company, Bangers, is one of the leading fast-food companies in the UK. Today's fast-food sector is one of the most competitive in leisure and tourism, and the public has an enormous choice of:

- what to buy
- where to buy it
- at what price.

Bangers realised that to meet this challenge it needed a high-profile marketing campaign. It began by carrying out marketing research to identify its customers' needs. This centred on five questions covering the marketing mix and target markets.

Question	Area covered
Do more people eat out?	PRODUCT
What type of restaurant do people want? Eat in? Drive through? Take away?	PLACE
Who visits the restaurant? Families? Young people? Children?	MARKET SEGMENT
What do people want to eat? Do different types of people like different things?	MARKET SEGMENT AND PRODUCT
Who eats at Bangers? What do they want to eat?	MARKET SEGMENT AND PRICE

The findings of the research were:

- eating out is expanding – 75% of adults buy fast food, 94% of people under 34 buy fast food
- most people choose to buy takeaways
- the types of restaurant people like depends on when they want to eat, but all must be easily accessible
- families visit restaurants most, but young adults and teenagers are also important customers
- people want a good quality, good value meal.

From the research, Bangers identified young families, young adults and teenagers as its target market segments. It then used the marketing mix to make changes to meet their needs.

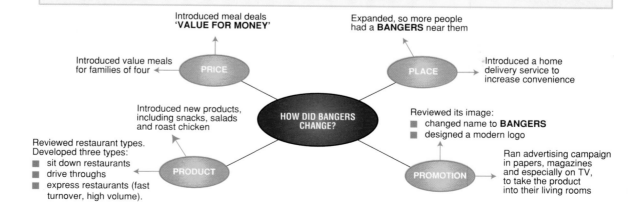

Key questions

1 What are the eight main ways in which marketing can benefit leisure and tourism organisations?
2 What are the four parts of the marketing mix?
3 What benefits can sponsorship bring to an organisation?
4 Why are brochures used a lot by the leisure and tourism industry?
5 Why do organisations do market research?
6 What's the difference between primary and secondary market research?
7 How do leisure and tourism organisations use market research to help them make decisions?
8 What is the difference between target markets and market segments?
9 Can you give six examples of market segments?
10 Why does dividing target markets into different segments help organisations make decisions about pricing, product development and promotional activities?

Assignment

Choose one leisure and recreation organisation, and one travel and tourism organisation. Find out:

■ what each organisation aims to achieve through marketing
■ how they use the marketing mix
■ the types of marketing research they use, and the information they aim to find out through research
■ the target markets and market segments of each organisation.

Write a report on marketing in both organisations for a weekly magazine, covering all of these points. You should:

■ describe how the two organisations carry out their marketing
■ show the differences and similarities between them
■ explain how the four Ps of the marketing mix relate to the target markets for each organisation's products and services
■ illustrate your report with examples of the organisations' promotional materials
■ if possible, use quotes from people who are involved in marketing the organisations.

ELEMENT **2.2**

Planning a promotional campaign

In this element you will look at how a promotional campaign is planned, so that you can plan one of your own. You'll see how people go through the various stages of planning and how they decide on the objectives of their campaign. But things don't always go according to plan . . . What sort of factors could affect the success of the campaign? And how detailed does the plan have to be?

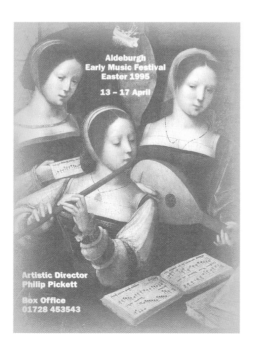

66 We aim to provide what people actually want, so we do as much consultation as possible. We listen to the children we work with and get the parents to fill in a feedback form which we evaluate at the end of the summer. We also interview people who attend 'Playfest' – where we spend a week going to different venues and providing a day of activities. All this helps us plan our promotional campaign for the next year. 99

organiser of a summer festival for children

66 We are a fairly new facility and this is a strong marketing point. We are newer and cleaner than the other local pool. In our promotional campaigns we target people wanting a family swim. We have a lot of parking space so we also appeal to the disabled and parents bringing school children. We target special groups who want to use the pool separately from everyone else, such as muslim women. We don't tend to run big campaigns because these are not particularly cost effective and can be disappointing in what they achieve. 99

development manager, swimming pool

66 We mainly run promotional campaigns in up-market guides. They emphasise those things which are different about what we have to offer – we are non-smoking and vegetarian and tend to go for people who want this sort of atmosphere. We also promote ourselves in guides abroad because foreign visitors are particularly interested in unusual settings and buildings. 99

owner of a guest house in Bradford on Avon

66 It's essential to plan the promotion so that we get to customers when they are ready to book. For a May festival we aim for the end of January. Our research showed that the longer the selling period for tickets the greater the box office income. Once when we slipped with the publicity by a week and a half our income slipped too. There are definitely two distinct periods for promotional campaigns. You need to get the early birds and then those that like to make late decisions. So you need maximum exposure at these two times. But we find there's no point sending anything out before Christmas. All we do before Christmas is send out some pre-publicity – just a taster inviting people to fill in a form to send off for full details. 99

festival manager

Stages in promotional campaigns

Stages in a promotional campaign

- RESEARCH
- PLANNING
- PREPARATION
- IMPLEMENTATION
- EVALUATION

A **promotional campaign** is an organised course of action which aims to raise the profile and appeal of a product, service or organisation.

In leisure and tourism industries, promotional campaigns can range from simple local initiatives to complex national projects costing millions of pounds. For example:

- a snooker club advertises in local papers and delivers leaflets to people living in the surrounding streets
- a national travel agency launching its summer breaks arranges commercials on national TV and radio, organises features and advertisements in national papers and magazines and offers special discounts on holiday prices.

Whether they cost £1 million or £100, promotional campaigns should always include five basic stages.

Research

Researching a promotional campaign means finding out what you want to promote, and who you want to promote it to.

Leisure and tourism organisations regularly carry out marketing research to find out information about their customers and potential customers. They can use the information to:

- help them recognise problems and changing situations which they need to respond to through a promotional campaign
- identify the target market segment for a promotional campaign
- identify the best way to communicate to this target market segment.

Without research, promotional campaigns would be guess work, as this theatre manager explains:

66 We always have a promotional campaign on the go, whether it's a short-term push on a particular show, or a long-term project to promote the theatre as a whole. Either way, we need to know about our customers to make sure it's effective. A few months ago, our records showed that attendance was low during the week, so we handed out questionnaires and talked to members of our Friends of the Theatre group. The results showed that people associated theatre-going with the weekend and didn't think they had time to come to performances after work. We decided to run a campaign with the aim of increasing attendance on week nights by 10%. We put ads in local papers and offered reductions on tickets. We targeted office workers in particular, and faxed information about midweek performances – with details of special offers – to offices in the area. 99

Planning a promotional campaign means deciding what you want to achieve and making plans to achieve it.

Planning

Careful planning can make all the difference to the success of a promotional campaign.

Planning a campaign

- look at research findings
- identify the objectives of the campaign
- identify any additional marketing research needed
- decide the target market for the campaign
- divide the target market into segments to give the campaign a clear focus
- agree what methods of promotion to use
- decide which media to use for advertising
- set time schedules for the plan, with clear goals to achieve by certain dates
- identify anything which could affect the campaign, such as a competitor's campaign. This is called action planning.

HOW FIT ARE YOU?

Fitness Assessment Service at Riverside Leisure Centre

Riverside Leisure Centre

RIVERSIDE LEISURE CENTRE

Marketing research showed the Riverside Leisure Centre that few people used its fitness assessment service. The centre decided to run a promotional campaign with two aims:

- raise awareness of fitness assessment
- recruit 50 new customers over two months.

To find out who would be interested in fitness assessment, the centre organised interview surveys with customers. These showed that young people under 30 should be the target market for the campaign, with a particular focus on women. Keeping in mind their target market segments, the centre decided to advertise in the health pages of the local paper, at the cinema, and on a local radio station which appealed to young people. Realising that many young people were short of money, they also decided to offer a 10% reduction to people who applied within two months.

ACTIVITY

Using the information in the case study as a starting point, write a memo to staff at the Riverside Leisure Centre outlining the promotional campaign for the fitness assessment centre. Include a list of factors which could affect the campaign.

Preparation

Once an organisation has a promotional plan, it can be tempting to leap straight into action. Leisure and tourism organisations are often under pressure to produce instant results and it's easy to rush things.

But promotional campaigns are often complex and need careful preparation to ensure that all runs smoothly. It might mean:

- producing advertisements for TV, radio, magazines or newspapers
- writing and printing leaflets, brochures, posters, notices and hand-outs – and taking photographs for them
- organising PR events to tell journalists more about a new product or facility
- preparing letters and a mailing list for a direct mailshot.

Big leisure and tourism organisations sometimes employ advertising agencies to run campaigns for them. A major promotional campaign may take several months to reach the TV screens and newspaper pages. Even small organisations arranging to print a new brochure or organise a local direct mailing need to spend time making sure every detail is perfect before putting their promotional campaign into action. Promotion is the public face of an organisation, and it has to make sure that it sends the public the right messages.

Implementation

With all preparations made, the promotional plan can be implemented. It may mean several different promotional activities going on at the same time, as the organiser of a music festival describes:

66 *We launched the festival last week, after several months of planning and preparation. We decided that the main promotional push should be two months before the festival start – plenty of time for people to sign up, but not so long that they'll forget about it. So last week advertisements appeared in the local paper; we put posters up at different sites around town and took leaflets round to the local libraries. Really, it was a question of everyone involved working as a team, and making the best use of the budget and time we had.* 99

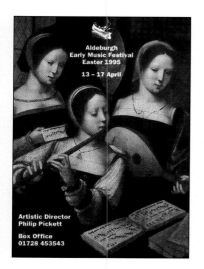

Aldeburgh
Early Music Festival
Easter 1995

13 – 17 April

Artistic Director
Philip Pickett

Box Office
01728 453543

Evaluation questions

- Did it inform people, as intended?
- Did it raise awareness?
- Did it make people buy the product or service?
- Did it improve the facility's image?
- Did it increase sales?
- Did it attract new customers?
- Did it help to keep existing customers?

Evaluation

Evaluating a promotional plan means assessing whether it achieved its aims and thinking about how it could have been improved.

At the end of a promotional campaign, people involved stand back and evaluate its success or failure. They ask questions about the campaign, based on the original aims identified at the planning stage.

Not all of these questions will be easy to answer. Organisations may carry out more marketing research to find out more; for example, they might interview customers and potential customers to discover their views, or analyse records of sales over a period during and immediately after the campaign.

Whether the results show that the campaign was a success or a failure, evaluation can provide useful guidelines on how to do it better in the future.

DISCUSSION POINT

- Why do you think evaluation is a useful process?
- What does it achieve?

The objectives of promotional campaigns

Objectives are the things you are trying to achieve by taking a particular course of action, such as having a promotional campaign.

Having clear objectives for a campaign establishes the marketing mix because it:

■ forces the organisation to pin down exactly what it is trying to achieve

■ ensures that everyone involved in the campaign is clear what its goals are

■ helps the organisation to decide the target market segments for the campaign

■ helps the organisation to decide what promotional activities to use

■ provides a set of measures against which the campaign can be evaluated after it has finished.

There are three key questions when identifying the objectives of a promotional campaign.

Key questions for campaigns

Can the objectives be achieved?

Be realistic. If objectives are set which can't be achieved using the staff, time and resources available, then the promotional campaign will automatically fail. Setting unrealistic objectives is demoralising and makes people feel they are taking on an impossible task. To avoid this, many promotional campaigns focus on just one or two objectives.

Are the objectives specific enough?

Good objectives are clear and specific – for example, 'to increase sales by 10% in three months'. If they are too broad or vague – for example, 'to improve our performance' – people don't really know what they mean and it's much harder to measure success or failure at the end of the campaign.

Are the objectives set within a timescale?

Decide a specific, realistic timescale for the campaign. Set start and finish dates and 'milestones' by which certain things have to be done. Setting a date for evaluating the campaign can provide a deadline for achieving objectives.

DISCUSSION POINT

A hotel says that the objective of a promotional campaign is to 'increase the number of guests staying in the hotel'.

■ Do you think this is a good objective for a promotional campaign?

■ How would you change it?

The objectives of leisure and tourism campaigns usually fall into one of seven categories:

■ to inform

■ to raise awareness

■ to make people buy the product and so improve sales

■ to improve and enhance the image of the organisation

■ to improve and enhance the image of the product

■ to attract new customers

■ to help keep existing customers.

Inform

Leisure and tourism organisations use promotional campaigns to inform people about:

- the features of a product or service
- when a new facility is opening
- a new product or service when it's first introduced
- changes to an existing product or service.

So what type of information do they need to communicate?

All of this information is factual – things that customers need to know so that they can use a facility or buy products and services. It's best to use written materials for this, such as leaflets, brochures, letters and magazine advertisements. Customers can then keep the information to look at when they need to.

DISCUSSION POINT

Travel brochures are one of the best-known ways in which the tourism industry informs its customers.

- What information do travel brochures usually contain?
- Are there other ways in which organisations could pass on this information to customers?

prices

Accommodation	HOTEL JOLLY HARBOUR	FLIGHTS
Accom. Code	1846	To Antigua from Gatwick
Prices based on	2 B'ROOM/4FFPP	
Board Basis	SC	FOR FULL
No. of Nights	ADULT **14**	FLIGHT DETAIL SEE PAGE 6
1 May-27 May	**509**	
28 May-22 Jun	**519**	
23 Jun-6 Jul	**539**	
7 Jul-20 Jul	**569**	
21 Jul-10 Aug	**609**	
11 Aug-31 Aug	**579**	
1 Sep-14 Sep	**579**	
15 Sep-28 Sep	**539**	
29 Sep-19 Oct	**539**	
20 Oct-31 Oct	**539**	

Supplements per person per night

H/B £22.70.

2 BEDROOM
3 Adults   3.80
2 Adults   11.40

Prices are in £s are per
FULL FARE PAY-ING PASSENGER (FFPP)
and are guaranteed (see page 4).
They include airpo taxes and Air

Raise awareness

Promotional campaigns help to raise customers' awareness of products and services, or the whole organisation. A tour operator specialising in holidays to Australia describes how the organisation went about raising people's awareness of holidaying 'down under':

❝ *People think that Australia is expensive to visit and much too far for a fortnight's holiday. In fact, prices of flights have dropped in recent years, it's cheap to stay in certain places and the journey isn't as bad as they imagine. We needed to raise people's awareness of Australia as a holiday destination. We ran advertisements in national newspapers and magazines, telling people that Australia's accessible and cheap. At the same time, we offered holiday packages to journalists from national papers and invited them to report on what they found. As a result, there have been three major reports on visiting Australia. We think our campaign has made people more aware that they could go to Australia and has got our name known across the country.* ❞

Make people buy

Direct selling is a key objective when running promotional campaigns. Campaigns are usually about trying to make customers buy products and so improve overall sales and profits. All other objectives relate to this one.

Advertising is probably most widely used in leisure and tourism campaigns to boost sales. Advertisements which aim to sell don't contain important information which customers need to keep and use. Instead, they should:

■ grab the attention
■ make an instant impact
■ be memorable enough to prompt the customer to buy a product or visit a facility.

So they need to be professionally produced and attractive. Large leisure and tourism organisations often pay advertising agencies a lot of money to run major selling campaigns.

Far from the maddening crowd...

Get away from the crowded beaches and discos. Settle back in your hammock and watch the sun go done. The tranquil beaches and quiet luxury of your own beach cabin await you. For further details of the perfect holiday, contact your travel agent.

ANTIGUA

TWO WEEKS IN THE SUN

from only £699

Visit Sunny Antigua
see your travel agent for details

- Which one of these advertisements would make you most likely to buy the holiday? Why?

- What do you think makes a good selling advertisement?

For quick results, organisations may arrange sales promotions such as reduced prices, special offers and two for the price of one deals. These increase sales of particular products in the short term. Direct mailing of letters or leaflets can be a good way to tell a target market segment about sales promotions. In leisure and tourism organisations where personal selling is important, such as travel agencies, staff training in sales techniques can also improve sales.

Improve image

Sometimes organisations try to improve the public image of its products, or of the organisation as a whole. This may be because:

- a product has changed and is better than it was before
- the organisation's image is old-fashioned and needs to be updated
- the organisation is aiming at a new target market and needs to update its image to win new customers
- a mistake or accident has damaged the image of a product and/or the organisation.

Fatal accidents in outdoor activity centres recently damaged the image of activity centres across the UK. Here the manager of one centre describes how they went about improving its image:

66 *At the time there was obviously a lot of mistrust about safety and several groups cancelled their bookings. We realised we needed to do something quickly and decided that the best thing to do was to let people see for themselves. We put advertisements in the local paper and sports centres, emphasising the quality of our staff and facilities and inviting the public to a free half-day's activities. We asked the press to come along and report on the sessions and made sure our staff knew how to sell the centre to visitors. We also introduced special offers for group bookings to try to encourage schools and youth groups back. Bookings are now back up to the same level as before and our safety procedures are as tight as they can be.* 99

Attract new customers

Leisure and tourism organisations are always keen to attract new customers, especially when they are:

- opening up a new facility
- launching a new product or service
- trying to build a new image.

To attract new customers, organisations have to make sure that people know about their products and services. The most effective way to do this is through advertising and direct mailing, which guarantees that every household in a target area receives information.

Once people know about a product or service, they have to be persuaded to try it. Facilities often use sales promotions to attract new customers – for example, special offers on membership fees, or vouchers offering two meals for the price of one.

A new bar and restaurant aimed at under-25s is opening up in your area. Write and produce an advertisement to go in the local paper with the aim of attracting new customers. The example below might give you some ideas of how to go about it.

FROM NOVEMBER 6TH TO DECEMBER 31ST 1995

at rollers

KIDS GO FREE!*

To celebrate the start of the rollerskating season we have a very special offer – at Rollers during the months of November and December up to **two children can skate absolutely FREE** when accompanied by a full paying adult.

All you have to do is bring this completed leaflet with you when you visit Rollers and for every full paying adult **we will admit two kids ABSOLUTELY FREE.** Adult price £3.45.

The offer is valid every day including weekends and holidays from 6 November to 31 December 1995.

Terms and conditions
- Kids are children up to 15 years
- An adult is aged 18 years and over
- This offer does not include skate hire
- Up to 2 children per full paying adult – extra children pay normal child's rate
- 2 full paying adults can bring 4 children

- This offer cannot be used in conjunction with any offer voucher or promotion
- This offer is not valid for Friday disco sessions or all night skates.

01284 701216

Rollers, Station Hill, Bury St. Edmunds

ADMIT TWO CHILDREN FREE*

AT rollers   BF1

Adult's name

Address

                    Postcode

Child's name

Child's date of birth

Child's name

Child's date of birth

Address (if different)

                    Postcode

PLEASE BRING THIS COMPLETED COUPON

Keep existing customers

Organisations have to attract new customers, then keep them – and at the same time hold on to their existing customers. Customer loyalty is very important in leisure and tourism. Regular customers mean a regular income, and happy customers often come back with friends.

Here the manager of a small restaurant explains how he and his staff keep customer loyalty:

66 *We do all we can to make sure that customers who visit once want to come back again – preferably with their friends and family! We hope they'll come back because of the excellent food and service. But to encourage them we leave cards and books of matches printed with our name, address and phone number on the tables, so they remember us and have the number to hand when they want to book again. We make sure we get to know customers who visit regularly – people really appreciate it if we remember their names and where they like to sit. At Christmas, we give a free bottle of wine to our regulars. I'd say about 75% of our customers have been to the restaurant before.* 99

ACTIVITY

Collect a range of promotional materials produced by leisure and tourism organisations – leaflets, brochures, advertisements and direct mail material. Working in a small group with two or three others, produce a chart listing each piece of material you've collected and identifying its objectives. Is there a link between the objectives of promotional material and its layout and style?

What affects the success of a campaign?

Evaluation – finding out what worked and didn't work – is an important last stage in planning promotional campaigns. It helps the organisation to:

- decide the objectives of future campaigns – if a campaign's goals haven't been achieved, they may need to be tackled again
- decide which promotional activities to focus on in the future – for example, if advertising on local radio was unsuccessful, it might be better to advertise in local papers in the future.

So how do leisure and tourism organisations judge the success of their promotional campaigns?

UNIT

2

ELEMENT **2.2**

Criteria for success

To assess the success of a campaign, look back at the original objectives and ask whether they have been achieved.

Whatever the original objectives of the campaign, these things often affect their success.

Criteria for success

Getting the marketing mix right by:

- doing good marketing research
- targeting the market properly
- using the right media
- getting the timing right
- keeping the campaign within budget
- changing – or reinforcing – people's perceptions
- using staff with the right skills
- knowing the legal and professional constraints
- designing and presenting the information well.

Success? Have we ...

... attracted new customers?

A hotel which ran a promotional campaign with the objective of attracting new business guests might judge its success by monitoring customer records.

... improved our image?

A football club which ran a campaign to improve its image in the local community might judge its success by interviewing members of the public to find out whether their views have changed.

... improved sales and made people buy the product?

A travel agency which ran a campaign with the objective of increasing sales of skiing holidays might judge its success by monitoring sales figures.

Doing good marketing research

Knowing the market lays the foundations for promotional campaigns. Before they even start planning, organisations carry out marketing research to find out information about the needs, opinions and preferences of their target market. Then they use the information to make decisions about:

■ the objectives of their campaign

■ who it's aimed at – the target market segment

■ what promotional activities to carry out.

These are all important decisions. If the marketing research they are based on is wrong, not detailed enough, or irrelevant, the campaign may fail. If the research is accurate and detailed, it provides an excellent starting point.

Targeting the market

Leisure and tourism organisations have to target their promotional campaigns at the right market. According to the marketing manager who produced the campaign plan shown on these pages:

66 *It's essential to know from the outset who you are trying to influence through a campaign. Only once you have identified your audience can you decide what promotional activities to carry out, what media to use, and how to present your message.* 99

DISCUSSION POINT

Here is a list of products, who they are being promoted to, and how they are being promoted. The list has got confused. How would you match up the right products, people and promotional activities?

Product	Target market	Promotional method
Honeymoon cruises in the Caribbean	Children under 10	Advertisements in specialist business magazines, national papers
Half-term football coaching	Pregnant women	Advertisements in bridal magazines, women's glossy magazines
Ante-natal swimming classes	Businessmen	Posters in schools and sports centres
Bargain business breaks	Newly-weds	Leaflets in the local medical centres and hospitals

Using the right media

The **media** is any means of communicating with the public – for example, on television or radio, in newspapers or magazines, in cinemas, on outdoor sites such as billboards and public transport.

If an organisation chooses the wrong media, it can mean that the target audience doesn't get the message or the campaign goes way over budget. When deciding which media to use for a campaign, leisure and tourism organisations should consider:

- the target market for the campaign – who needs to see the advertisements?
- the budget for the campaign – advertising on television is beyond the budgets of small leisure and tourism organisations
- geographical location – where should the advertisements appear?
- timing – when should they appear?
- frequency – how often do people need to see them?

Getting the timing right

The timing of a campaign can make the difference between success and failure, as the marketing manager explains:

66 *If a leisure and tourism organisation wants to promote a one-off event – anything from a film or exhibition to a football match – it's vital not to advertise too early or too late. If you do it too early, people forget about it or lose interest before the event. If you do it too late, they don't have time to book tickets or they've already made other plans for the date.* 99

Many leisure and tourism products and services are linked to seasons. So they need to be promoted at particular times of the year – for example, hotels advertising summer weekend breaks in Britain will have little success if they promote them in November. Making sure television and radio advertising appears at an appropriate time of day can also be important. For example, it's best to advertise children's products during children's programmes on TV and travel products during the breaks in holiday programmes.

Over the page is a media schedule and budget for just one product. This gives a complete breakdown of newspaper advertising over a two-month period for a particular campaign. It shows the size of each insert and whether it will be monochrome or in colour, the cost per entry, the position on the page reserved for the advertisement, and when it will appear in each newspaper. This is typical of a national press campaign.

131

CLIENT		DATE:	7.11.95	THE MEDIA BUSINESS
PRODUCT		PLAN NO:	1	PRESS PLAN
CAMPAIGN		REVISION NO:	6	
PERIOD – OCT/NOV 95		STATUS:	PROPOSED/BOOKED	

PUBLICATION	CIRC ,000	SIZE	EST COST	POSITION	NO.	TOTAL COST	OCT 2	9	16	23	30	NOV 6
DAILY EXPRESS	1,274	20X3 MONO	£2,700	fr 1/2 news edge pre section	5	£13,500		MO			WE	FR
		25X4 MONO	£4,500	fr 1/2 news edge pre section	2	£9,000	TH		TU			
DAILY MAIL	1,758	20X3 MONO	£4.110	fr 1/2 r/h corner	3	£12,330				MO		MO
		25X4 MONO	£6,850	fr 1/2 r/h corner	1	£6,850			TU			
		25X4 MONO	£6,850	Money Mail	1	£6,850	WE					
GUARDIAN	403	25X4 MONO	£2,000	fr 1/2 main news edge	3	£6,000				TH		TU
(Colour A: B not available)		25x4 COLOUR	£3,700	outside back cover	0	£0						
		20x3 MONO	£1,200	fr 1/2 main news	2	£2,400		TH			FR	
INDEPENDENT	290	25X4 MONO	£1,425	fr half o/edge	3	£4,275	FR		MO			
		20X3 MONO	£855	page 2	1	£855				WE		
INDEPENDENT ON SUNDAY	316	25X4 MONO	£1,513	fr 1/2. o/s edge	1	£1,513			SU			
		20X3 MONO	£908	Inside story. solus o/s edge	1	£908		SU				
THE SUN	4,086	20X3 MONO	£6,300	p2 or ERH, not Sun Woman	1	£6,300			WE			
DAILY MIRROR	2,489	25X4 MONO	£7,800	1st or 2nd 25x4 or tv	0	£0						
		20x3 MONO	£4,680	front half	1	£4,680		WE				
DAILY RECORD	765	25X4 MONO	£3,000	front half	0	£0						
	765	25x4 MONO	£2,600	front half	2	£5,200	FR		WE			
	765	25X4 COLOUR	£3,400	front half	0	£0						
		20x3 MONO	£1.560	front half	5	£7,800				FR	TH	
TODAY		25X4 MONO	£1,600	front half RH O/edge	1	£1,600	TH/FR					
		20X3 MONO	£960	assets(finance) front page solus	1	£960		TU				
MAIL ON SUNDAY		20X3 MONO	£4,920	front half, solus on John Junor	1	£4,920			SU			
SUNDAY MAIL	853	25X4 MONO	£3,100	front half	0	£0						
		25x4 COLOUR	£4,000	front half	0	£0						
		20x3 MONO	£1,860	front half	4	£7,440		SU				SU
THE OBSERVER	464	25X4 MONO	£2,500	front half main news RH o/edge	0	£0						
S TIMES	1,239	25X4	£9,500	Main news RH edge	0	£0						
TIMES	632	25X4 MONO	£2,500	PAGE 2 OR 3	0	£0						
		25X4 MONO	£2,500	front 1/2	5	£12,500				TH	TU	
		25X4 COLOUR	£4,000	front 1/2	0	£0						
		20x3 MONO	£1,500	front 1/2	0	£0						

TOTAL ESTIMATED GROSS COST	£115,881	
TOTAL CLIENT COST	£98,499	All dates and positions subject to availability.
NUMBER OF INSERTIONS	44	Firm dates will be confirmed at point of negotiation.

Keeping within budget

Leisure and tourism organisations have to be efficient and in most cases need to make a profit. Promotional campaigns can be expensive and keeping within a set budget is very important:

66 *Every promotional campaign has a budget; whether it's £100 for printing leaflets for a bed and breakfast or £1 million for advertising a national chain of hotels. Whatever the budget is, stick to it. This means calculating the costs of the campaign carefully and taking into account every detail, including the expenses involved in things like paying outside experts such as advertising agencies and PR agents, producing material and distributing it, buying advertising space and offering sales promotions.* 99

Even if a campaign meets its other objectives, it could still be considered a failure if it goes badly over budget:

66 *One company recently ran a major promotional campaign involving national TV, radio, magazine and newspaper advertising. They had a budget at the outset but didn't realise they'd underestimated until too late. The commercials took ten days to film instead of five, and the costs became astronomical. The price of advertising space in national magazines went up, and they spent thousands more than expected. By the end, the campaign was almost £30,000 over budget. Even though sales increased, the company needed all the extra business just to cover the high costs of the campaign.* 99

Changing – or reinforcing – people's perceptions

Perceptions are the way people see and understand something.

Every time a leisure and tourism organisation runs a campaign, it aims to make an impression on the public – it aims to affect the public's perception of its products or services. For example:

■ a theme park might want to make people think it is an exciting place to visit

■ a country house hotel might want to create the impression of exclusivity and luxury.

Whether they succeed depends on people's perceptions of the product or service the campaign is promoting. An organisation can spend thousands of pounds on advertising, but if people ignore it or misinterpret the messages they are trying to put across, the campaign will fail. That's why it's useful to do some market research before launching major campaigns, to find out how a sample of people perceive it. If they get the wrong impression, the advertisements can change.

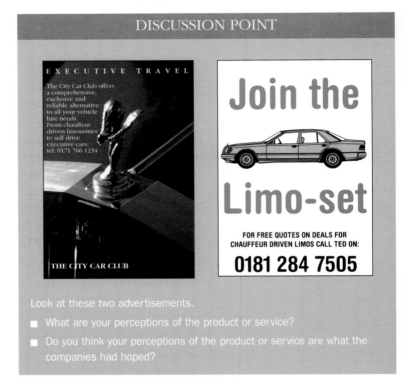

DISCUSSION POINT

Look at these two advertisements.

■ What are your perceptions of the product or service?

■ Do you think your perceptions of the product or service are what the companies had hoped?

Using staff with the right skills

If you don't have the right staff with the right skills to put a promotional campaign into practice, don't even start. Checking staff have the skills needed is an essential part of planning.

If staff don't have the skills needed for a campaign, the organisation can:

■ provide extra training – for example, a sports centre which wants to produce one-page leaflets about the different courses on offer might decide to send a member of staff on a course to learn desktop publishing

■ get the help of outside experts – for example, a chain of restaurants which wants to revamp its image and produce new advertising materials would probably employ an advertising agency to coordinate the project and employ the skills of designers, writers, photographers, and so on.

Knowing the legal and professional constraints

If organisations fail to follow the correct procedures or break the law, it could mean failure for the campaign and bad publicity for the organisation.

Legal constraints include:

- the Trades Descriptions Act 1968, which states that products should be described clearly and accurately, with correct photographs
- the Consumer Protection Act 1987, which states that it is an offence to mislead customers about the price of products.

Travel brochures are particularly affected by these laws because of the large amounts of information they contain. Each year trading standards departments – which are responsible for ensuring companies keep to the law when advertising – receive over 25,000 complaints about holidays. Many of these relate to accommodation and facilities not being described accurately in brochures, and surcharges or taxes not being stated.

Designing and presenting the information well

The quality of design and presentation is one of the most obvious factors affecting the success of a campaign. If promotional materials are well written, designed and presented, they are much more likely to succeed than if they don't communicate well and are unattractive.

Promotional materials need to catch people's attention, make them read on, and encourage them to buy a product or find out more. Many leisure and tourism organisations follow the AIDA guidelines (attention, interest, desire, action):

- attract attention – use colour, pictures, striking graphics
- get people interested – use language and images that the audience can relate to easily
- get them to want it – create a desire to buy the product or use the service
- trigger an action – by letting the customer know what to do and giving them information about where to find the product or service.

Preparing a detailed plan

Plans are there to:

- provide a structure to work to
- remind the team of their objectives and responsibilities
- monitor progress
- evaluate the final success or failure of the campaign.

Here is a checklist to use when putting together a plan for a promotional campaign.

Objectives

Aims of the campaign:

- inform
- raise awareness
- make people buy a product
- improve the image of a product
- improve the organisation's image
- increase sales
- attract new customers
- keep existing customers.

Are the objectives identified:

- realistic in terms of
  - staff
  - time
  - budget
- specific
- measurable or easy to evaluate
- set in a realistic timescale.

Marketing research

To find out more about:

- customers' needs
- customers' preferences
- customers' views and opinions
- competitors' products.

Information collected through:

- face-to-face surveys
- self-completion questionnaires
- observation
- focus groups
- the organisation's own records
- other organisations' research.

Target markets

Who are the:

- actual buyers of the product or service
- potential buyers of the product or service.

Market segments

Within the target markets are market segments identified by:

- age
- sex
- race
- socio-economic class
- geographical location
- lifestyle.

Promotional activities

Promotional campaign includes:

- advertising
- sales promotion
- public relations
- personal selling
- direct marketing
- sponsorship
- producing brochures.

Type of media

Advertisements appear:

- on national or local TV
- on national or local radio
- in national or local newspapers
- in magazines
- in cinemas
- on billboards or public transport.

Time schedules

For a one-off event:

■ how long before the event should promotional activities start?

■ when should promotional activities end?

■ at what time should advertisements appear on radio and television?

For a long-term promotional campaign:

■ when should promotional activities start?

■ when should promotional activities end?

■ at what time should advertisements appear on radio and television?

Factors which could affect the campaign

Could the success of the campaign be affected by:

■ the quality of marketing research?

■ the budget available?

■ people's perceptions of promotional materials?

■ staff skills – are any outside experts needed?

■ legal and professional constraints?

■ the design and presentation of information?

ACTIVITY

You may find this checklist useful when you prepare your own detailed plan for a promotional campaign. Make a version for your portfolio which you can refer to as you work, adding any information from other parts of the unit that you think might be helpful.

BRITAIN WELCOMES JAPAN

The Britain Welcomes Japan campaign was set up in 1991 with two aims:

- attract more Japanese visitors to Britain
- raise the profile of Britain as a quality destination to visit and buy from.

The campaign involved British tourism, retailing and manufacturing industries. It was coordinated from the British Tourist Authority's (BTA's) office in London, with close links to the BTA's Tokyo office.

Planning for the campaign began in 1990, a year before it was launched.

Objectives

Britain Welcomes Japan aims to:

- raise awareness in Britain of the importance of the Japanese market
- raise awareness in Britain of the needs and unique requirements of Japanese visitors
- improve the welcome offered to Japanese visitors by the tourism, retailing and other related industries
- make practical suggestions to the industry on improvements to products, product presentation and other facilities and services to meet the needs of Japanese visitors
- enhance a positive attitude to Britain among the Japanese by preparing them for a special welcome.

Marketing research

The campaign needed information on the needs and preferences of Japanese visitors to Britain. Marketing research showed that:

- visitors from Japan have more than doubled since 1985 and are expected to reach 1 million by the mid 1990s
- more and more Japanese travellers now visit just one country, rather than touring Europe
- Japanese visitors spend on average £539 per visit and the average length of stay is 6.9 days
- package tours are becoming less popular, as Japanese travellers become more confident and selective
- in the past, 90% of Japanese visitors stayed in London, but this is changing as they become more confident and experienced
- Japanese visitors expect polite and unobtrusive service, prompt attention to complaints and a welcome in their own language.

Target markets

The Britain Welcomes Japan campaign focused on potential customers rather than actual customers. Its target market is Japanese people who:

■ enjoy travelling

■ are interested in Britain

■ have enough disposable income to travel here on holiday.

Market segments

Within this target market, the campaign identified important market segments:

■ 'Office Ladies' – Japanese women with a high disposable income who are happy to take long holidays; knowledge of the world and English lessons enhance their status

■ business people – the Japanese don't want to be excluded from European markets

■ 'Silver Group' (older people)

■ English language students

■ honeymooners – 97% of all Japanese couples honeymoon overseas, and they return with a gift for each of their wedding guests (good news for retailers).

Promotional activities

The campaign planned a wide range of promotional activities, including:

■ a campaign logo, using the Japanese word for welcome

■ a press gathering at a London hotel

■ a campaign prospectus setting out the objectives of the campaign

■ two special publications – *Caring for the Japanese Visitor*, for providers of accommodation, literature, shopping, transport and guiding services and *Facilities Survey*, listing hotels, restaurants, retail outlets and tourist attractions which make a special effort for Japanese tourists

■ a campaign database

■ a newsletter

■ seminars.

Type of media

The campaign did not use advertising.

Time schedules

The campaign was launched in 1991 and aimed to ensure that by 1995 Japanese tourism was Britain's second largest market in value terms after the US.

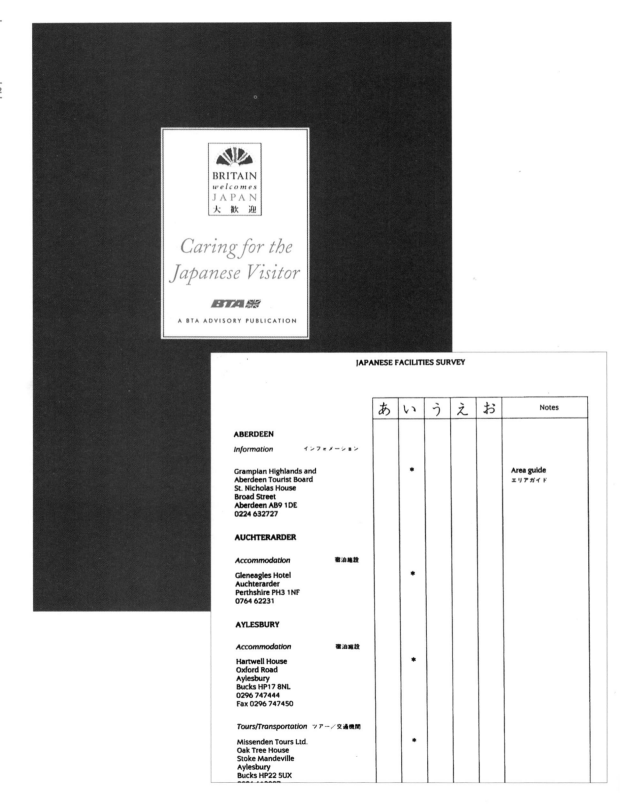

BRITAIN
welcomes
JAPAN
大 歓 迎

*Caring for the
Japanese Visitor*

BTA 🇬🇧

A BTA ADVISORY PUBLICATION

JAPANESE FACILITIES SURVEY

	あ	い	う	え	お	Notes
ABERDEEN						
Information インフォメーション						
Grampian Highlands and Aberdeen Tourist Board St. Nicholas House Broad Street Aberdeen AB9 1DE 0224 632727		*				**Area guide** エリアガイド
AUCHTERARDER						
Accommodation 宿泊施設						
Gleneagles Hotel Auchterarder Perthshire PH3 1NF 0764 62231		*				
AYLESBURY						
Accommodation 宿泊施設						
Hartwell House Oxford Road Aylesbury Bucks HP17 8NL 0296 747444 Fax 0296 747450		*				
Tours/Transportation ツアー／交通機関						
Missenden Tours Ltd. Oak Tree House Stoke Mandeville Aylesbury Bucks HP22 5UX		*				

Key questions

1　What are the five key stages of a promotional campaign?
2　What are the three key questions that help identify the objectives of a promotional campaign?
3　The objectives for leisure and tourism campaigns usually fall into one of seven categories. Can you list them?
4　Why is evaluation after a campaign helpful to organisations?
5　Can you name three outcomes that show a campaign has been successful?
6　Why is it important to have a detailed plan for a promotional campaign?

Assignment

Write a four-page handbook for new staff at a leisure or tourism facility, explaining how the marketing department runs promotional campaigns. The handbook should:

■　explain the different stages in promotional campaigns
■　describe the objectives of promotional campaigns
■　explain factors which can affect the success of promotional campaigns.

The handbook should give a clear overview of promotional campaigns. Use it to prepare a detailed plan for your own campaign. Choose something that you can manage with the resources you have – for example, promoting a new coaching or sports course, a coach tour, or a local one-day event. Make sure your plan:

■　sets objectives
■　identifies marketing research you need to carry out
■　identifies target markets
■　identifies market segments
■　identifies promotional activities
■　identifies the type of media you will use
■　sets time schedules
■　identifies factors which could affect the campaign.

ELEMENT **2.3**

Running and evaluating a promotional campaign

This element shows you what actually happens when a promotional campaign is up and running. You'll look at different sorts of promotional material and see what people do to make the best use of resources, including each other. And when it's all over, how do you judge the success of a promotional campaign? What things could be done better next time?

66 *In order to run our summer programme a budget is drawn up and submitted to the managers. We have a meeting in the autumn at which we review how it went and think about how to change it next year.* 99

organiser of a summer festival for children

66 *We have marketing meetings frequently where we discuss promotion for the shows. If it becomes clear that we need to change the direction of our campaign, we do so as quickly as possible. For example, one production we put on sold quite badly at the matinees, even though the month before a different production did well. We realised that the first play appealed to a younger audience who came in the afternoons, whereas the second was a play for older people. The students interested in it were mostly in the sixth form and came in the evenings rather than during the day. So we changed the publicity to emphasise discounts on afternoon performances.* 99

press and publicity officer at an entertainments venue

Preparing promotional materials

Promotional materials are printed or recorded information used to tell people about a new product, service or facility.

Leisure and tourism organisations use a wide range of materials in promotional campaigns.

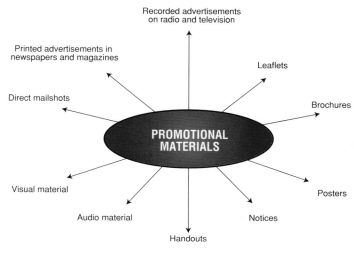

Figure 13 Promotional materials used in leisure and tourism

In their plans, they decide what promotional activities to carry out and what media to use for advertising. Based on these decisions, they start to prepare promotional materials. It can take a long time to get all the materials written, designed and printed or recorded before they are distributed to the public. Because promotional materials are often the main way that people form an impression of an organisation or product, it is important that they are right.

Advertisements

Advertisements for leisure and tourism products and services are prepared in different ways depending on the size of the organisation.

Large organisations pay advertising agencies to prepare their advertisements. Smaller ones can't afford to pay agencies and play a greater role in preparing their own advertising materials.

Advertising agencies

- a creative team – writes the words and slogans, designs printed advertisements, arranges photography and organises the filming and recording of TV and radio commercials
- buyers – buy advertising space in newspapers and magazines, or air time on TV and radio
- a print and production team – produce the finished advertisement

The leisure and tourism organisation identifies the campaign objectives and plays an important part in making sure the final product meets its needs. But the actual preparation of the materials is handed over to the agency.

Most small organisations use local newspapers. A sports centre produced this checklist to help administrative staff prepare advertisements.

Advertising checklist

1 Decide what the objectives of the advertisement are – what we want to say, who we want to say it to, and when we want to say it.

2 Look through the local papers and decide where you think it would be best to place the ad. Are there regular sporting feature pages to tie in with? Think about how, when and where the ad should appear so that it stands out from the crowd and isn't lost on the page.

3 Ring the advertising departments to find out the circulation of the paper and their rates for different size ads. Remember to ask whether we can use colour.

4 Choose which paper to advertise in. Find ads similar to the one we want to place and find out how much it will cost. Don't be afraid to bargain – we may be able to get a cheap rate if we agree to place a certain number of ads each month.

5 Decide on our key message – keep it clear, simple and persuasive. Write the ad in four sections:

   – a headline which grabs the reader's attention

   – the main text explaining what we offer

   – a request for action (e.g. 'come in and see!')

   – information about where we are and how to get in touch.

6 Decide whether to use illustrations. We have artwork for our logo and most papers are happy to print it. It helps to grab attention and present a professional image.

7 Take the text and any illustrations to a graphic design studio. Explain to them what we're looking for, and they'll put the ad together quite cheaply ready for you to give to the paper.

Most small leisure and tourism organisations don't have the budget or the expertise to prepare a television commercial. Radio commercials are a lot less expensive, and the advertising department at local radio stations will help organisations to put their ad together. Cinema advertising is also relatively cheap and most cinemas have standard commercials that organisations can tailor for their own use.

Leaflets

Leisure and tourism organisations distribute leaflets free to:

■ inform customers about the features of a product or service

■ give useful information such as prices, opening hours, telephone numbers and so on.

ACTIVITY

Prepare an advertisement for an event. Working in a team with two or three others in your group, look through your local papers, find out their circulation and decide which it would be best to advertise in. Decide:

■ where in the paper the advertisement should go

■ what it should look like.

Then write and design the ad.

A **leaflet** is a sheet of paper, often folded in half or thirds, which is printed with information about a product, service or facility.

As with advertisements, leaflets produced by large leisure and tourism organisations tend to be different to those printed by small organisations. Large organisations' leaflets:

■ are designed by a graphic designer
■ are usually printed in colour
■ often feature photographs and illustrations
■ are printed on good-quality paper.

Small organisations often produce their own leaflets using word processing or desktop publishing packages and take them to a local print and copying shop for reproduction, normally in just one or two colours. Even with a limited budget, organisations can make their leaflets stand out by using illustrations and printing on coloured paper.

Brochures

Brochures are extremely important promotional materials for leisure and tourism organisations. Like leaflets, they are used to inform customers, but they are longer and usually more expensive to produce.

Tourist facilities in particular rely on brochures to communicate information about what they offer – hotels send brochures to prospective customers, resorts have guides to the area which they give to holidaymakers. Best known of all is the travel brochure. Tour operators prepare colourful brochures about their holidays, which are then distributed as sales material by travel agencies.

ACTIVITY

Go to a travel agency, and look at a rack of brochures. Pick out the three which stand out most from the others on the shelf. Ask a few of your friends to do the same thing, and see if they choose the same brochures. Look carefully at the materials you choose, and decide what it is that makes them stand out from the crowd.

A tour operator in the competitive 'summer sun' market describes how they go about putting together brochures for a new season:

66 *We start getting our brochures together long before they reach the travel agencies. We give them a distinctive style to make them stand out – the front cover is particularly important because it's what the customer sees first on the shelf. Inside, we always have an introduction, a contents list and an index, as well as detailed descriptions of our holidays. And of course, hundreds of photographs. Accuracy is very important as the laws are strict. Our information and pictures have to be constantly updated – if customers can claim they were misled, we're in big trouble. And then there are all the practical considerations, like what weight paper to use and how many pages to have.* 99

Notices and posters

Huge posters on billboards, small notices in shop windows – they can be simple, local and cheap or national and expensive. Whatever their size, posters and notices must be bright, clear, bold and attention-grabbing. A designer in an advertising agency explains:

66 *Words should be kept to a minimum and messages should be simple. Get a good graphic designer to design them. Colour is important to make an impact. Even if you're a small organisation such as a guest house or restaurant, your posters and notices should be professionally produced and printed. It's vital that the things you show the public are well designed and give a professional impression.* 99

Information displayed in public places should be updated and replaced regularly. Leaving information on display about events which happened last month gives a bad impression.

Hand-outs

Simple printed materials distributed free, usually to inform potential customers of forthcoming events and special offers.

Small leisure and tourism organisations often use hand-outs as a way of giving information to people who live or work locally – for example, a bar which is launching a regular early evening 'happy hour' might ask a member of staff to stand outside a shopping centre nearby distributing hand-outs. Because the information is put straight into people's hands there's less need to get their attention by using colour and illustrations. Instead, hand-outs should put the message across as quickly and concisely as possible.

Unlike brochures, organisations can easily produce hand-outs themselves using wordprocessing or desktop-publishing packages, and reproduce them using a photocopier or local printer. Using coloured paper can be a good way to make people take more notice of messages.

Audio material

Audio materials are sometimes used by leisure and tourism organisations to give out information. Heritage sites, museums and galleries sometimes use audio cassettes as talking guidebooks.

Audio materials can also have a promotional use. They can be used to accompany visual displays about products and services or at exhibitions to give out information or to attract people to the organisation's stand.

They can also be used to provide promotional information for people who find printed materials difficult to use – people with visual impairment, for example.

Visual material

Now widely used by leisure and tourism organisations as promotional materials. Visitor attractions such as monuments and natural environments rely heavily on photography to attract people to their facilities – they put together photographs of buildings and countryside as calendars, books of postcards and visual guides. These have two purposes:

■ they are sold to customers to generate income

■ they promote the attraction to people who see the pictures.

Some organisations now use videos and CD-ROM, as well as printed materials, to promote their products and services:

■ Alton Towers has produced two videos focusing on different areas of the curriculum for students to use before visiting the theme park

■ travel companies have started making videos of holiday destinations which customers can watch in travel agencies

■ the National Gallery has produced a CD-ROM featuring its paintings.

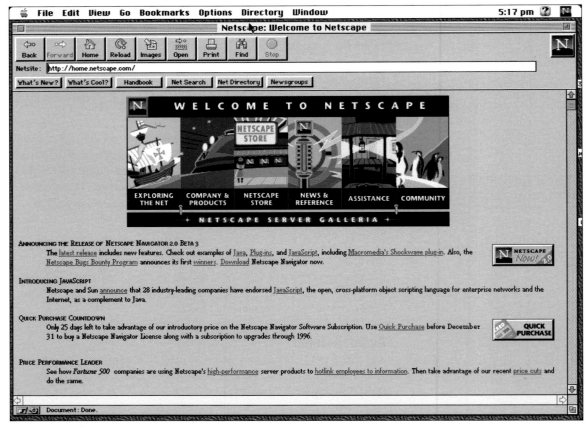

Some leisure and tourism organisations promote their products and services on the World Wide Web

DISCUSSION POINT

With developments such as CD-ROM and the Internet, how might leisure and tourism organisations use visual material for promotion in the future?

ACTIVITY

A good way to ensure people pay attention to direct mail materials is to encourage them to reply – by including an order form, a reply card, or a reply-paid envelope.

■ Write and design a direct mail letter for a local sports club which is keen to recruit new members.

■ What would you include in the mailshot to ensure a good response to the promotion?

Direct mailshots

Direct mailing is a way of distributing promotional material to a target market in a particular area. The danger is that unless the material is really effective, it will be thrown straight into the bin without a second look.

The owner of a home-delivery pizza company describes how they prepare material for direct mailshots:

66 *It's easily our best way to attract customers. Information about our products and services lands on people's doormats, they keep it in case they fancy a takeaway, and we get new customers. We've developed a good line in leaflets, which describe our pizzas and give information on prices and how to order. We get these designed and printed at a local print shop, and use colour and photographs to get people's attention. When people order pizzas we keep computer records of their names and addresses, and then mail out personalised letters offering special deals. We check the spelling of people's names carefully, and sign all the letters by hand to make them seem more personal.* 99

Participating effectively in a campaign

Promotional campaigns involve a team of people:

- playing an active part at each stage of the campaign
- working together towards achieving the campaign's objectives
- making the best use of resources available – money, time, other people, materials, equipment, information.

Success depends on the commitment, enthusiasm and efficiency of everyone who puts the promotion into practice.

Playing an active part at each stage

People take different roles in each stage of the campaign – it's no good everyone doing the same thing. But there's plenty of work to go round and people can choose the jobs that suit them best.

Stage of the project	Tasks and responsibilities
Research	<ul><li>carry out primary marketing research – surveys, observation, focus groups</li><li>collect secondary marketing research – looking at existing records</li><li>analyse the findings of marketing research to find out about customers' needs, opinions and preferences</li><li>recognise problems and situations which may need to be changed through a promotional campaign</li></ul>
Planning	<ul><li>look at research findings and identify the objectives of the campaign</li><li>identify any additional marketing research needed</li><li>identify the target market for the campaign</li><li>identify market segments</li><li>decide what promotional activities to use</li><li>decide which media to use for advertising</li><li>set time schedules for the plan</li><li>identify factors which could affect the campaign</li><li>produce a detailed plan for the campaign</li></ul>
Preparation	<ul><li>produce any advertisements needed – e.g. for papers, and magazines</li><li>buy space on the page</li><li>arrange the production of ads needed for TV, radio or cinema, and buy space on air</li><li>produce leaflets, brochures, posters, notices and hand-outs</li><li>organise PR events to tell journalists about the campaign</li><li>prepare letters and a mailing list for a direct mailshot</li><li>monitor costs when preparing materials</li></ul>
Implementation	<ul><li>distribute promotional materials such as hand-outs, notices and posters, leaflets and press releases</li><li>check that advertisements are printed or broadcast at the correct time</li><li>produce extra materials and arrange distribution, if needed</li></ul>
Evaluation	<ul><li>look back at the original objectives of the campaign. Were they achieved?</li><li>talk to customers, potential customers and staff about their views on the campaign</li><li>monitor sales to see whether the campaign had an effect</li><li>evaluate the performance of the team, and of individuals</li><li>make recommendations on how campaigns could be improved in the future</li></ul>

ACTIVITY

Keep an activity log for a promotional campaign you are involved in. Make notes on your responsibilities and actions at each of the stages listed above.

■ Did you take on tasks and responsibilities at every stage of the campaign?

■ Did you perform them effectively?

Members of a marketing team have their own skills and interests, and take on particular roles and responsibilities based on these. But it's important for everyone to be involved to some extent in each stage of the promotional campaign. For example:

■ if people are involved at the research stage, they will understand the underlying causes of the campaign

■ if they're involved at the evaluation stage, they will be able to use the knowledge they have developed during the project to help improve future campaigns.

Working together with others

Teamwork plays an important part in the success of a promotional campaign. If team members communicate well and work together they will stand a much better chance of achieving the objectives of the campaign.

The airline's marketing director explains how important it was that all her team worked together to achieve the campaign's objectives:

66 *Our latest promotional campaign was a major initiative, involving a considerable investment in terms of time, money and resources. The campaign lasted six months from research to implementation. During this time we held weekly team meetings. These gave us an opportunity to update each other on progress, agree targets for the next week, and organise any support needed. This was vital to ensure the team worked together well, as we're not all in the same office, and communication can be difficult.* 99

ACTIVITY

People have different skills and knowledge. They should have different roles in a marketing team to make the most of their strengths. Hold a planning meeting to decide who should take on particular responsibilities in your team. Draw a diagram showing the organisation of your team, adding arrows to show how different team members will need to communicate at different stages of the project.

Resources

■ budget

■ time

■ people

■ materials

■ equipment

■ information

Making the best use of resources

Leisure and tourism organisations are all in business and need to make the best use of resources at all times.

Budget

Money is the resource which has to be monitored most closely. All organisations – from the tiniest bed and breakfast to national travel companies – only have a certain amount of money for marketing.

From this overall budget, money is allocated to individual promotional campaigns. Promotional budgets are decided at the planning stage. It's then up to the team to make sure it uses the money in the best way possible.

DISCUSSION POINT

If you were on the staff of the
playgroup, how would you
suggest spending the budget of
£800? Think of alternative
promotional activities, and then
find out estimated costs for
them. How would you make the
best use of the money
available?

SUNSHINE PLAYGROUP

A well-established playgroup run as a
workers' cooperative had a budget of £800
for a campaign to promote its summer
activities. After considering a range of
promotional activities, the playgroup staff
decided to spend the money as follows:

■ getting posters designed	£180
■ getting advertisement designed	£100
■ getting 100 posters printed	£200
■ four weeks' advertising in local paper	£240
■ paying for posters to be distributed	£55
■ total cost of the campaign	£775

Time

Time is important in promotional campaigns for two main reasons:

■ the timing of promotional campaigns – if time is wasted, deadlines may
be missed

■ time is money – organisations pay staff for the time they spend carrying out
promotional activities.

Timescales for a promotional campaign are decided at the planning stage.
Every member of the marketing team should know their deadlines, and
keep to them.

DISCUSSION POINT

Think about your own use of time when working towards GNVQ
assignments.

■ How do you make sure you use time well?

■ Would any of the techniques you use also be useful when working on
leisure and tourism promotional campaigns?

People

In many ways, the most important resource. With the right support and skills
from staff to put projects into practice, organisations stand a good chance of
success. The owner of a small firm making souvenir badges explains:

66 *The trick is to make the most of the different skills, knowledge and
experience of your staff. People are suited to different roles and
responsibilities. You need to recognise this when you're deciding how to use
staff for a promotional campaign. If people are given tasks and responsibilities*

which match their skills, they feel they are able to make a valuable contribution to the team effort. We find that this in turn increases their enthusiasm and commitment, which is fed back into the campaign with positive results. **99**

It is also important that organisations recognise when their staff don't have the skills needed for a promotional campaign. Where this is the case, they either need to arrange staff training, or to employ someone with the right skills from outside.

ACTIVITY

Next time you take part in a team project, look carefully at the way the team works. List the different team members, and identify their particular skills, knowledge and experience.

■ What roles and responsibilities would match each person's skills?

■ Does the project demand any skills which you don't have between you?

■ Can you develop these skills through extra training?

■ Do you need to ask for someone else's help?

DISCUSSION POINT

Computers now make it easier than ever before to mail information to a large number of people efficiently and accurately. Can you think of any disadvantages to computer-generated mailings?

Materials

However much money and time an organisation invests in developing promotional materials for a campaign, it will be wasted unless the material is used well.

To be effective, materials must reach the people they were intended for. This means keeping careful control over the distribution process.

Distribution tips

■ Spend time checking mailing lists for direct mailshots, making sure names are spelt correctly, addresses are accurate, and so on.

■ Get your leaflets and brochures well displayed in shops, sports centres and other suitable places.

■ Check the sites of notices and posters, and make sure that any damaged or out-of-date materials are replaced.

■ Monitor advertisements to make sure they appear where and when they should.

Equipment

Equipment used during promotional campaigns includes photocopiers, telephones and desktop-publishing packages. Organisations may need to arrange extra training to ensure equipment is used efficiently and to its full potential.

DISCUSSION POINT

Think about the equipment you use regularly for GNVQ assignments.

■ Are you making the best use of it?

■ Is there any equipment you need extra training in using?

Information

Leisure and tourism organisations have enormous amounts of information which can be useful at all stages of promotional campaigns – things like marketing research findings, mailing lists and new customer details. Information about past campaigns can also play an important part in new promotions. Staff who have already been involved in campaigns have useful experience and knowledge. Promotional materials produced in the past, and by other organisations, can provide good guidelines when developing new materials.

BRITAIN WELCOMES JAPAN

The British Tourist Authority's Britain Welcomes Japan campaign aimed to increase the number of Japanese people visiting Britain.

The campaign was launched with a press gathering at a London hotel. As a result the initiative was reported in the *London Evening Standard* and *Hotel & Caterer* magazine. A campaign prospectus, related publications, and a campaign newsletter helped to maintain momentum. The BTA also set up a database of products and services in Britain specially prepared for Japanese visitors, and operators which make a special effort to welcome them. To support the campaign in the UK, the BTA's office in Tokyo produced a newsletter for distribution to the travel trade in Japan.

A series of seminars for the travel trade and retailers gave advice on marketing to the Japanese. Many already had facilities in place for Japanese visitors, including:

■ hotels with Japanese guest relations managers

■ Japanese translations of leaflets, guides and audio tours

■ a hotel which provides Japanese set menus, newspapers, dressing gowns and slippers

■ shops with Japanese speaking assistants.

Evaluating the campaign

Looking back at the original objectives for the campaign

Measuring whether they were achieved:
- by questioning staff, potential customers
- by monitoring sales

Preparing an evaluation report on:
- the success or failure of the campaign
- the success of promotional activities
- the contribution of team members

Making recommendations for improving future campaigns

When it's all over, at the end of the campaign, organisations carry out an evaluation to assess:

- whether the campaign achieved its objectives
- how successful different promotional activities were
- the contribution of different team members
- how the campaign could have been improved
- what lessons can be learned to inform and improve future campaigns.

They collect the information they need to measure whether objectives were achieved by:

- monitoring sales
- asking people questions.

Monitoring sales

Many leisure and tourism promotional campaigns aim to:

- increase sales
- make people buy products
- attract new customers
- keep existing customers.

All of these can be measured by monitoring sales, for example:

- counting the number of visitors using electronic counters
- monitoring the number of sales using computerised till rolls
- monitoring the levels of occupancy in accommodation.

If the objectives set at the start of the campaign were specific enough, organisations can measure accurately whether they were achieved. For example, if a sports centre aimed to increase use of its swimming pool by 10% over a month, it can measure whether it achieved this by comparing the number of people using the pool in the weeks immediately before and after the campaign.

Promotional activities which aim to increase sales or attract new customers are usually easier to evaluate than activities with less obvious objectives. Direct mailings and printed advertisements can include reply cards or coupons for customers to return. The success of personal selling can be measured by keeping records of the number of sales made by different members of staff.

DISCUSSION POINT

Think about the promotional campaign you are involved in.

- Does it have objectives which can be measured by monitoring sales?
- If it does, how are you going to carry out the monitoring?

Questioning

Not all the objectives of promotional campaigns can be evaluated easily with facts and figures. It's harder to measure whether a campaign:

- informed customers
- raised their awareness
- improved a product's, or an organisation's, image.

One way of evaluating whether these objectives have been achieved is to carry out surveys with existing customers, potential customers and staff. For example, a facility might:

- hand out questionnaires to customers visiting the facility
- carry out face-to-face interviews with people in the target market who don't currently use the facility
- organise a meeting with staff, to get their views on how customers have reacted to the campaign.

The information collected then needs to be compared with the results of marketing research carried out before the promotional campaign. Comparison is most effective if similar research methods are used before and after the campaign.

The success of promotional activities such as PR and posters, which are hard to measure by monitoring sales, can also be assessed when questioning customers and staff.

ACTIVITY

Prepare a short questionnaire to evaluate whether your promotional campaign achieved its objectives. Include questions which evaluate the success of different promotional activities.

Evaluating against objectives

As the table on the next page shows, different objectives for leisure and tourism promotional campaigns are evaluated in different ways.

Objective	Example of a specific goal	Evaluation method
To inform	Make sure visitors to a sports centre know about all the facilities on offer	Survey to find out level of knowledge of facilities before and after the campaign
To raise awareness	Raise awareness that a new bar/ restaurant is opening in town	Questioning potential customers to find out whether they have heard about the bar
To make people buy the product	Increase sales of a particular product by 25% during the month of the campaign	Monitoring sales using till rolls and stock counting
To improve image	Improve the image of a fast-food chain following a food poisoning scare	Questioning customers, potential customers and staff to find out their views of the restaurant. Monitoring sales
To improve sales	Increase hotel bookings by 10% in comparison to the previous year	Monitoring sales by looking at computerised records of bookings and occupancy
To attract new customers	Get 30 new members to join a health and fitness club each month	Monitoring the number of new members joining up
To maintain existing customers	To get 75% of customers to return to a family-run restaurant	Customer surveys to find out how many people have been to the restaurant before, and questioning staff

ACTIVITY

Produce a table like the one shown here for your own promotional campaign. Identify:

- the general objectives of the campaign
- your specific goals
- how you will evaluate whether you achieved them.

Own and others' contributions

Because the campaign will have been organised and run by a team of people, it is also useful to evaluate the contribution of individual team members. This involves looking at what was expected from each team member and then judging how completely and how effectively they performed.

DISCUSSION POINT

Why is evaluation a useful process? How can you make it effective?

Here are some ways to evaluate team members' contributions.

Evaluating self	Evaluating others
list what you did and check it against what was expected of you	observe and make notes
ask for feedback from other team members	fill in a questionnaire
list what you did then put a tick against those you thought went well and a cross against those you thought went less well	hold a one-to-one feedback and discussion session with the person concerned
	hold a group feedback and discussion session

Keeping a log or diary of what happened and who did what will help you when you come to evaluate the success of the event and your contribution to it.

When giving feedback to others, make sure your comments are constructive. Emphasise the good things they did and give suggestions on how things that went less well might be improved. Evaluation is a way of recognising achievement and helping things to go better next time, not a squabble over who's to blame for things that were less than perfect.

| Section 2.3.4 | # Recommendations for improving future campaigns |

The lessons learned from evaluation are used to improve promotional campaigns in the future. Sometimes the people involved in a campaign write evaluation reports summarising their findings and making recommendations for future campaigns.

COACH TOURS

This is part of an evaluation carried out by the manager of a small coach tour company. Marketing research had shown that bookings on day trips were down, and local people were unaware of the range of trips on offer. So the company ran a six month promotional campaign to:

- inform customers about the range of day trips on offer
- increase the number of bookings on day trips by 15% in comparison to the previous year's figures
- improve the image of the company.

As part of its campaign the company:

- produced new leaflets and hand-outs to promote the coach trips
- printed notices and posters which it displayed around town
- offered reductions for group bookings.

At the end of the six months, the company organised an evaluation to see whether the campaign had achieved its objectives. Face-to-face interviews carried out with potential customers in town showed that more people now knew that the company ran day trips, although their image of the company was unchanged. Sales figures revealed that bookings were up by 20% on the previous year.

When the evaluation was finished, the manager made these recommendations for future campaigns.

Objectives

We achieved two out of three of our objectives – to inform people about our trips, and to increase bookings. Our research showed we didn't improve people's image of the company – we were probably trying to achieve too much at once. In practice, our promotional materials focused on informing people about trips and trying to encourage them to book, not on impressing them with the company's image.

I have learned the importance of having focused objectives rather than trying to spread our resources too thinly. I recommend that we follow up the objective of improving the company's image in a future campaign.

Research

We used the same marketing research methods before and after the campaign – face-to-face interviews. They were a good way of finding out detailed information, but took a long time, so we couldn't carry out as many as we'd hoped. In future I'd like to experiment with other methods of collecting information from customers – giving questionnaires to people to fill in after trips would probably be a good way to get the same types of information.

Our computerised booking system worked well for monitoring sales, and could be used in the same way for campaigns in the future.

Planning

66 *Before launching the campaign we thought hard about what we were trying to achieve and how to go about it. But we probably got too enthusiastic, and jumped in without planning carefully enough how to coordinate everything. I think that's why there was an overlap in information on two different posters, and one set of leaflets wasn't printed in time for the trip.*

The main lesson we learned for the future was to set a detailed time schedule for the plan, with clear goals to achieve by certain dates. I think if we'd had a detailed timetable to work to, the campaign team would have been calmer. 99

Preparation

66 *We have never produced so many promotional materials before! I think we probably tried to prepare too many of them in-house. The notices and hand-outs we did on the desktop publishing system were fine, but we wasted a lot of time trying to design our own leaflets and posters. Next time we'll go straight to the copy shop in town and use their graphic designer. When we eventually did ask for her advice, she instantly sorted out all our problems.*

Again, because of lack of experience, we underestimated how long it took to print materials and cut it all too fine on several occasions. In future, we should allow much more time for printing. 99

Implementation

66 *Overall, the campaign ran smoothly. We distributed hand-outs, got our notices and posters displayed in prominent places and checked regularly that they were still in place. I recommend that we follow a similar course in the future.* 99

Evaluation

66 *Carrying out marketing research to find out if people's knowledge and views had changed was very time-consuming. Next time we should try using questionnaires that customers complete themselves. We held an evaluation meeting a couple of months after the campaign had finished to talk over the project and people's contributions. But by then staff had lost interest and forgotten a lot of points. Next time I'll definitely hold an evaluation meeting sooner – perhaps during, as well as after, the campaign.* 99

ACTIVITY

Using the headings used by the coach company manager, write your recommendations for future campaigns based on the evaluation of your own promotional campaign. Make sure your recommendations are:

- practical
- realistic.

Key questions

1 Can you name eight different kinds of promotional materials that could be used in a campaign?
2 In what three ways can team members be involved in a campaign to bring about its success?
3 Can you name the six essential resources for a promotional campaign?
4 At the end of a campaign what five things can be assessed through evaluation?
5 How does monitoring sales after a campaign add to this process?
6 Why is it helpful to ask people questions after a campaign?
7 Can you think of three or four ways to evaluate your own or other team members' contributions to a campaign?
8 Why can campaign reports be useful for planning improved future campaigns?

Assignment

Keep a log or diary of how you helped to run the promotional campaign you planned in Element 2.2. You could write it or record it on cassette. Note down or record:
■ what your role was during the campaign
■ how you worked together with other people in the team
■ what resources you used.

Your tutor or another assessor will be observing your contribution to the campaign. Use the completed log or diary to remind you and your assessor what you actually did.

Keep a copy of any promotional materials you helped produce. Add a note saying what you did – for example, write copy for a leaflet, design the artwork for a poster or organise the delivery of tickets to local outlets.

Use a wordprocessor to produce a summary of your team's evaluation of the campaign. Make a file with four columns. Look at the following headings and decide which are relevant to your campaign. Write the relevant ones in the first column:
■ how the campaign informed people
■ how it raised their awareness
■ how it made people buy the product
■ how it improved the image of the organisation
■ how it improved sales
■ how it attracted new customers
■ how it maintained existing customers.

In the second column, write an evaluation of your own contribution against each heading. In the third column, write an evaluation of how other people in the team contributed to the campaign. In the fourth column, note down what methods you used to evaluate your and other people's contributions.

Using your experience of running this campaign, prepare and give a presentation making recommendations on how you would improve future campaigns. Be prepared to say:
■ how you feel your objectives could be made clearer
■ what extra research you would do next time
■ how you would improve the planning process
■ what you would spend more time preparing in future
■ how you would run the campaign itself differently
■ what you would do to make the evaluation process more useful.

If you are giving the presentation with others in your team, you may decide to present one of these points each. But make sure you discuss all the points when you're preparing what to say.

UNIT 3

Element 3.1
The principles of customer service

Element 3.2
Information and customer service

Element 3.3
Sales techniques and customer service

Element 3.4
Providing and evaluating customer service

Customer service

ELEMENT **3.1**

The principles of customer service

What's it like to work in the 'front line' of a facility, providing a service to customers? This element shows you what customer service is and why it's so important in the leisure and tourism industry. You'll see the benefits of providing an excellent service to customers – benefits to them, to you and the organisation. You'll also see how front-line staff communicate with customers and the skills they use.

66 *We try to give a good impression in the shop by being helpful, smiling but not pushy. We have a policy of greeting people when they enter the centre, but then leaving them to browse. We prefer people to come to us rather than pester them. But we do have to keep an eye out for customers who look like they need help, so we can be ready to give advice if needed.* **99**

manager of a Tourist Information Centre

66 *We try to make a good first impression by greeting people when they come in and show that we're willing to help. We must look as though we have plenty of time for them, even though we might actually be very busy.* **99**

travel consultant in a travel agency

66 *We deliberately didn't look at what other people offered when we started. We had no experience of bed and breakfast but we very much wanted to do it the way we like to have it done for us. That way we knew that customers would be getting a good service!* **99**

owner of a guest house in Bradford on Avon

66 *My job involves running a car and van rental fleet. The work includes answering the telephone to making bookings with our customers when they come in, dealing with rental agreements and invoicing, delivering and collecting vehicles. I'm in contact with customers all the time. The skills you need in a job like this are a good telephone manner, being good with numbers, neat handwriting, a clean driving licence, and being polite and considerate with customers. What I like about the job is meeting lots of different people, and there is a lot of job satisfaction in having all the cars hired out and exceeding targets.* **99**

car rental manager in a car rental business

What is customer service?

All leisure and tourism organisations need customers:

- sports centres need to attract people wanting to play sport
- travel agencies need people to buy their holidays
- restaurants need customers to come and eat their food
- art galleries need people to look at their paintings . . .

. . . and so on. Leisure and tourism organisations exist to please customers. Without customers they go out of business.

> **Customer service** is the way in which leisure and tourism organisations treat their customers, giving them what they want and need and making the experience enjoyable.

Customer service includes:

- direct contact between staff and customers – for example, a waitress serves food in a restaurant, a travel agent sells a holiday
- indirect contact with customers – for example, a hotel cleaner makes sure a room is clean and tidy ready for customers to use
- making sure customers get the products and services they want and need.

When organisations recognise the importance of customers, they put each individual customer at the centre of all their activities. It's called 'customer service', which is about three things:

- caring for customers
- meeting their needs – for help, advice, information, products and services, security and safety
- making the customer satisfied.

Caring for customers

Customer care is what happens – or should happen – every time there is direct contact between a customer and staff. Everybody working in leisure and tourism needs to know how to care for customers. Good customer care can make all the difference between gaining and losing a customer. Here one woman describes how her experiences helped her to decide which travel agent to use to book her family holiday:

66 *When I wanted to book a holiday for the family, the first place I went to was the travel agency in the High Street. As soon as I walked in I had my doubts. The office was dirty, piles of brochures were lying around and the posters were advertising out-of-date holidays. There were two people behind the counter, but when I tried to attract their attention one walked off and the other picked up the phone. I walked out in disgust. I knew that round the corner there was a small local travel agency so I tried in there. It was a different experience. The office was clean, bright and cheery and I was greeted by a smiling member of staff. She listened to what I wanted, showed me brochures, looked up prices and made suggestions. When the phone rang, she asked another member of staff to deal with it. You can imagine who got my booking.* 99

Customer care is in the hands of an organisation's staff – from the maintenance staff who make sure facilities are clean and tidy, to sales staff who deal directly with customers. Successful organisations recruit and train staff who can provide good customer care. The personnel manager of a large chain of fast food restaurants explains what he looks for in the people they employ:

❝ *Our staff are our public face. So we make sure that they are our greatest asset. Anyone working for the company must be polite, cheerful and efficient, creating a positive picture which will draw people back. An outgoing personality and good communication skills are helpful, as these leave a long-lasting impression on customers. We provide all our restaurant staff with uniforms, so customers can identify them easily. Our customers want attention, courtesy and efficiency, and we make sure they get it.* ❞

DISCUSSION POINT

Some leisure and tourism organisations train their staff to greet customers with a standard welcome greeting, others leave it to the initiative of individuals. How would you feel if you went into a restaurant and were faced with the following greetings:

- 'Yeah. What d'you want?'
- 'Hello. My name's Vanessa and I'm your waitress for this evening. Can I get you something to drink?'
- 'We are greatly honoured to welcome you as one of our many, highly valued customers. May I say how wonderful it is to be of service to you this evening?'

What are the advantages and disadvantages of these approaches?

Meeting customer needs

Customers are drawn to a leisure and tourism organisation in the first place by the products and services it offers. But at different times, different customers may need:

- help
- advice
- information
- the feeling of being secure and safe.

Products

Organisations use marketing research to identify what products customers are looking for. Then they provide them. A tour operator explains the importance of offering the right products:

❝ *If you don't give people what they want, you're not providing good customer service. We know what our customers expect and we put together the products they're looking for. At one end of the market we sell standard self-catering holidays to Greece. We know there are five or six other brochures offering similar, or the same, accommodation as us. Customers looking for this type of holiday want value for money, so we price our products competitively to give them what they want. At the other end of the market, a couple booking a trip to a paradise island base their decision more on empty beaches and romantic sunsets than price. So we tailor products especially for them. It's all part of providing good customer service.* **"**

Help

Customers using leisure and tourism facilities often rely on an organisation's staff for practical help. For example:

■ helping a hotel guest find a parking space and carrying their luggage
■ explaining to someone in the gym how to use a piece of equipment safely
■ showing a cinema-goer to a seat in the dark.

Leisure and tourism organisations need to:
■ identify the different types of help their customers might need
■ make sure staff are trained, equipped and available to provide it.

Advice

Customers using facilities often ask staff for advice, to make sure they enjoy activities in safety and to the full. For example:

■ asking a travel agent about different types of holiday insurance
■ asking the waiter what's good on a menu
■ making sure from a member of staff whether a particular ride at a theme park is safe and suitable for young children.

Organisations need to make sure their staff:
■ know enough about the area they work in to give good advice
■ are trained how to give it clearly and politely
■ know that if they can't offer sound advice, they should ask someone with more experience – passing a question on to someone else may take longer but it's a whole lot better than giving bad advice.

Information

Customers often just need straightforward information. For example:

■ someone in the audience at a theatre asks the person selling programmes for directions to the toilets
■ a visitor to an art gallery asks an attendant for information about a picture
■ someone joining a sports centre asks the receptionist about opening hours.

To meet customers' information needs, staff need to know about the facility they work in and the products or services it provides. Sometimes this can be a basic level of knowledge about prices and features. Or it may mean knowing what information to pass on to customers in the form of leaflets, brochures or maps. Some members of staff may need much more detailed information in order to meet customers' needs. For example, the Science Museum in London employs 'explainers' to work in some of its galleries, who answer visitors' questions about exhibits.

ACTIVITY

Interview a member of staff who works in a leisure and tourism facility. Ask them:

- what type of help they give customers
- what type of advice they give
- what type of information they give.

If they're not sure of the difference between help, advice and information, explain it to them using examples. Using the information you have collected, write a short leaflet to help someone new to the job do these three things well.

DISCUSSION POINT

Have these people received good customer service:

- a swimmer whose purse goes missing when she leaves it on the ledge as she dries her hair?
- a restaurant customer who suffers food poisoning after not choosing what a waiter suggested from the menu?

Security and safety

People nowadays are very conscious of security and safety. Customers want to be sure that they and others around them will be safe when using a facility, and that their belongings will be secure. Making sure that this is the case is an important part of good customer service.

It means:
- giving information and advice to customers – how to use a piece of equipment properly, what to do with personal belongings
- making sure that staff follow health, safety and hygiene regulations
- checking that staff know how to use equipment safely.

Making the customer satisfied

The goal of customer service is to provide products and services that customers are happy with. So why is customer satisfaction so important?

According to the US Office of Consumer Affairs:
- 90% of dissatisfied customers take their custom elsewhere
- one unhappy customer will tell at least nine others
- 13% of unhappy customers will tell at least 20 others.

As this suggests, it doesn't take many dissatisfied customers a week before an organisation loses hundreds of potential customers. Satisfied customers have the opposite effect. They tell their family and friends, and business booms.

The difficulty for leisure and tourism organisations is that only a small percentage of dissatisfied customers actually complain. This can make it very hard to judge whether people are satisfied or not. Many organisations carry out primary marketing research – face-to-face surveys and written questionnaires – to measure:

- whether they are caring for customers well
- whether they are meeting customers' needs.

QUESTIONNAIRE

RESERVATIONS
How did you hear of The Kings Bridge Hotel?

....

How was your reservation made?

When your booking was made, was it handled
courteously and efficiently?
If not, please indicate why you were dissatisfied

Directly to the Hotel? ☐ ....

Through a travel agent? ☐ ....

Company booking? ☐ ....

Other - please specify.................................. ....

Please evaluate the following services:	Excellent	Good	Unsatisfactory	Comments
RECEPTION:				
Welcome from the desk staff	☐	☐	☐	....
Efficiency of desk staff	☐	☐	☐	....
Service from porters	☐	☐	☐	....
Message handling	☐	☐	☐	....
Telephone operation	☐	☐	☐	....
Bill preparation and check out	☐	☐	☐	....
BEDROOMS:				
Cleanliness	☐	☐	☐	....
Comfort	☐	☐	☐	....
Bedroom and bathroom supplies	☐	☐	☐	....
Laundry/dry cleaning service	☐	☐	☐	....
Heating/ventilation	☐	☐	☐	....

Are there any maintenance requirements in your room?...Room No:...............

BARS:				
Comfort and general atmosphere	☐	☐	☐	....
Friendliness and efficiency of the staff	☐	☐	☐	....
Selection of non-alcoholic and alcoholic beverages	☐	☐	☐	....

RESTAURANTS:
In which restaurant did you dine? ....

	Excellent	Good	Unsatisfactory	Comments
Welcome from the restaurant staff	☐	☐	☐	....
Comfort and general atmosphere	☐	☐	☐	....
Efficiency of service	☐	☐	☐	....
Choice of wines	☐	☐	☐	....
Your enjoyment of the meal served to you	☐	☐	☐	....

Then they change the customer service they provide in line with their findings.

ACTIVITY

A sports stadium wanted to find out whether customers coming to events were satisfied with the customer service they received. A questionnaire produced the following findings (summarised here):

- 82% thought the stadium was dirty

- 17% thought staff at the stadium were very helpful, 42% thought they were quite helpful, 41% thought they weren't helpful at all

- 31% thought the signs in the stadium should be improved

- 91% thought the stadium should stage a wider range of events

- 74% were concerned about customer safety in the case of fire.

Write a memo to the sports stadium's manager:

- listing the findings in order of importance

- explaining what steps you think should be taken in order to improve service and achieve customer satisfaction.

What does customer service achieve?

Effective customer service means:

- caring for customers well
- meeting their needs for help, advice, information, security and safety
- providing the right products and services.

Providing effective customer service benefits the customer, the organisation and the staff who work for it.

Customer satisfaction

Good customer service makes customers satisfied. Don't underestimate the importance of satisfying customers – and the dangers of leaving them dissatisfied.

> 66 *This is my favourite restaurant in town. If I reserve a table, there's never any confusion and I never have to wait. I like the staff because they're friendly and efficient – some of them remember my name and ask me how I am. The food's great and there's a wide choice for vegetarians, which suits me. I've brought most of my friends here at some point and lots of them have become regulars too.* 99

> 66 *I went there last week, and no way would I step inside the door again. There were dirty dishes on the table, ashtrays full of old cigarette ends and food on the floor. I waited ten minutes for someone to take my order and another ten minutes before it arrived. When it did arrive it was the wrong thing. I was so hungry by then that I started to eat, but it was really horrible. The next day I felt ill, and I'm sure it was because of this place. I've warned all my friends and family and after seeing me walking round looking green they won't go near it.* 99

Customer loyalty and repeat business

Organisations which provide good customer service are likely to have loyal customers. Customers who are loyal feel a sense of commitment to a particular facility, and will choose to return there in preference to others.

> **Repeat business** is when a customer comes back again and again with similar needs (or with different needs), and spends money each time.

It's always best if organisations can build up a solid base of loyal customers and repeat business so that they have a regular income to rely on. Customer service makes this possible.

Building up good one-to-one relationships with customers is important. Customers like to feel they are recognised and valued as individuals. They are much more likely to bring repeat business if they like and know the people they are dealing with.

ACTIVITY

Over the next week, make notes on two occasions when you are a satisfied customer, and two occasions when you are a dissatisfied customer.

- What caused you to be satisfied or dissatisfied?
- What have been the results of your experiences as a customer?

DISCUSSION POINT

Talk about leisure and tourism facilities where you are a loyal customer.

■ Do you go to the same sports club each week, or do you regularly go to the same cinema?

■ What part does customer service play in winning your loyalty?

Increased sales and profitability

Good customer service wins customer loyalty and repeat business. This increases an organisation's sales. In a private-sector facility aiming to make a profit, more sales mean more profit.

The manager of a busy pub describes how he sees the link between effective customer service and increased sales and profitability:

❝ A few months ago I decided to make sure our customer service was really up to scratch. I began by talking to our regular customers about what needed to change. They told me more guest beers and a wider range of food – they wanted more choice. I took on two new bar staff and sent them on a training course in customer care. They're both good with the customers, and the pub has a much friendlier atmosphere. I noticed that we saw our regulars more often, and that people who used to come in maybe once a month were now in several nights a week. When I checked sales figures last month, I was pleased to see that sales were up by over 20% from three months ago. ❞

Enhanced reputation

In the competitive leisure and tourism industry, organisations with a good reputation win out. If people have a positive impression of a facility and its products they are more likely to buy. It may mean that:

■ a restaurant is known in the district for its friendly staff and excellent chicken dishes
■ a well-known high street travel agent has a reputation for being well-established and dependable.

All leisure and tourism organisations try to create a good impression. The type of customer service they provide helps them to do this. For example, you wouldn't expect exactly the same type of service in a traditional hotel and a lively, fashionable bar. But you would want the staff in both to be efficient and friendly. Customers who have enjoyed the service and been satisfied with the products on offer spread the word to their family and friends, enhancing the facility's reputation in the community.

Job satisfaction

If you have ever had a job or work experience which brought you into direct contact with customers, what did you enjoy most about it?

Many people find their job is most satisfying when they are able to help a customer, and feel they are providing good customer service. When customers are happy, staff have fewer complaints to handle, tend to work together better, and the atmosphere in general is more positive. This was certainly the experience of one college-leaver who started working as an assistant receptionist in a large hotel:

66 *When I first started, I hated my job. I didn't know what I was supposed to be doing, couldn't answer guests' questions, and felt uncomfortable when they complained. A couple of times I snapped back at them because I felt so clueless. I even took two days off sick because I couldn't face going in. The personnel manager took me to one side and asked me what my problem was. I explained that I felt useless around guests so she gave me three days' extra training in customer care and service. Since then, my whole attitude to the job has changed. I enjoy going in the mornings. I get a real buzz out of helping guests and seeing that they are pleased with the work I do.* 99

Staff are happier when they provide good customer service. It increases their enthusiasm for the job and they feel more committed to the organisation. This in turn improves the customer service they provide.

Safe and secure environment

As part of customer service, all leisure and tourism organisations should be committed to ensuring a safe and secure environment for their customers.

People have a right to use facilities in safety, and to be secure while using them. Organisations can help to make sure this is the case by:

■ giving information and advice
■ checking that health and safety guidelines are followed at all times
■ training staff and customers to use equipment safely.

If customers feel safe, they are much more likely to return than if they feel threatened in any way. If an accident does happen, it can have serious long-term effects on a facility's repeat business, sales and reputation.

ACTIVITY

Talk to two or three people who have contact with customers in the course of their everyday work. Ask them what brings them most job satisfaction, and what they find most dissatisfying about work. Make notes on your findings, highlighting any links you find between job satisfaction and the quality of customer service.

DISCUSSION POINT

What types of security and safety do customers have the right to expect at:

■ a restaurant?

■ a hotel?

■ a theme park?

■ an outdoor activity centre?

In each case, how could security and safety be provided as part of customer service?

The importance of customer service

Customer service is important to:

■ customers
■ the organisation
■ employees.

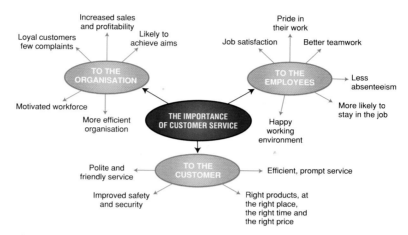

The organisation

Customer service can be seen as a cycle involving employees, customers and management. The aim is to achieve the organisation's goals.

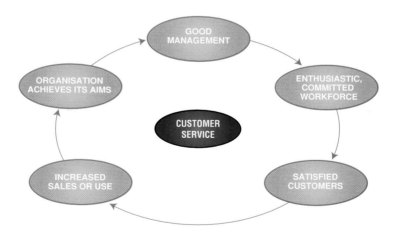

Figure 14 The cycle of customer service

Good management is needed to help employees provide good customer service. With the right training, resources and products staff can concentrate on meeting customers' needs and making them satisfied. Both of these bring financial benefits to the organisation.

An organisation which helps its staff provide good customer service is more likely to have a motivated and happy workforce and happy customers.

Employees who are happy in their jobs:

- take less time off sick, saving the organisation money on sick pay and relief cover
- stay in their jobs longer, saving money on recruitment
- work harder on a day-to-day basis.

Satisfied customers:

- spend more money and are more likely to return
- tell their friends and families about the facility, attracting new customers.

The result is a more efficient organisation, and increased sales or use. Whether the organisation is in the public or private sector, it is more likely to achieve its aims if it provides good customer service.

Customers

The customer is at the centre of customer service. In recent years, customers have come to expect more and more of the service they receive from leisure and tourism organisations. So why is good customer service so important to customers?

66 When I walked in it was packed. I thought it'd be a nightmare booking our flights. But the staff were friendly and efficient and there was a really good atmosphere in the shop. I actually quite enjoyed myself! 99

66 We've never been here before but the attendants have been really helpful. They told us how to get around the gallery, showed us where to get refreshments and gave us advice on what pictures not to miss. 99

66 The queue was massive, and I didn't think I'd get my food in time to get back to college for my next class. But the service was fast and I've still got plenty of time. 99

66 We came along to see whether there are any activities we can join in. We're pleased there are so many classes for the over-50s. They're cheap, and at the right times so we can get here by public transport. 99

66 Safety was the most important factor when we decided to bring the kids here. The staff have been excellent, they know exactly what they're doing, explain everything well, and we haven't worried at all. 99

ACTIVITY

You've just come back from a pizza restaurant with a friend, and you're extremely dissatisfied with the service you've received. Here's what happened:

- the restaurant was dirty
- staff didn't take your order for over 15 minutes
- the waiter didn't know what all the different items on the menu were and had to ask the chef, wasting more time
- when it finally arrived, the food was cold
- when you got up to go, the waiter asked you rudely where his tip was.

Write a letter of complaint to the restaurant manager, describing the poor customer service you have received. Point out to the manager why it's important that the restaurant improves the quality of its customer service – both for the sake of its customers, and the sake of the organisation.

Employees

Employees who feel they are providing a good customer service are likely to feel satisfied in their work. As a result, they are more likely to:

- be enthusiastic about, and committed to, their jobs
- make an extra effort for customers – they try to be friendly, efficient and polite at all times
- take pride in their work
- cooperate with other team members, in order to provide as good a customer service as possible
- take less time off sick
- stay in the job for longer
- enjoy it more.

Section 3.1.4

Types of communications

Providing good customer care is often about communicating well.

Employees who deal directly with customers need to enjoy working with people and be good at communicating with them – face-to-face, in writing and over the phone. Customers should come away from any type of communication feeling they have benefited from the contact and with a positive impression of the organisation. Following a few basic rules helps staff to achieve this:

- don't leave customers waiting
- always be polite
- always be honest.

These simple guidelines apply to all the different types of communications used by leisure and tourism organisations.

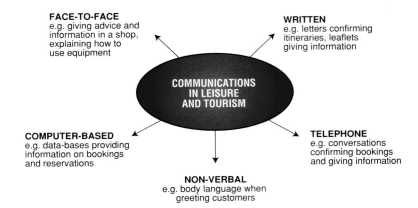

FACE-TO-FACE
e.g. giving advice and information in a shop, explaining how to use equipment

WRITTEN
e.g. letters confirming itineraries, leaflets giving information

COMMUNICATIONS IN LEISURE AND TOURISM

COMPUTER-BASED
e.g. data-bases providing information on bookings and reservations

TELEPHONE
e.g. conversations confirming bookings and giving information

NON-VERBAL
e.g. body language when greeting customers

Face-to-face

Face-to-face communication takes place whenever customers and staff meet. In leisure and tourism, this might be when:

- a customer goes into a travel agency to book a holiday
- a tourist goes into an information centre to find out about visitor attractions in the area
- a customer goes to a ticket office to get tickets for a performance
- a parent goes to the sports centre reception to book swimming lessons for the children.

A customer service manager explains to staff how they are expected to deal with customers face-to-face:

66 *Dealing with customers face-to-face is probably the most important thing you will do in this job. As soon as customers walk in they get an impression of you based on your appearance, so you have to look smart and approachable. Listen to what people say to you and reply clearly. Sound enthusiastic and interested in what they want. Remember that customers are human beings with feelings and emotions. They come to us with needs, and it's up to us to handle these in the best way possible. You're on the front line.* 99

In writing

Sometimes organisations put information down on paper for customers to keep and refer to in the future. In leisure and tourism, this might be when:

- a sports club sends a letter to notify members that membership fees are due
- a travel agency sends an invoice to a business customer asking them to pay the amount outstanding on their air flights
- a theatre sends tickets to a customer with a letter highlighting future performances.

All written communication sent to customers should:

- be easy to understand
- be clearly laid out on the page, following standard conventions
- include a contact name, address and phone number, so customers can ask for more information if they need to
- use language and grammar correctly
- use correct spelling.

Dear

Welcome to OUT WALKING, the country's No. 2 in walking – selling 21,380 every month.

I have enclosed for you a back issue, along with a great copy of the TRAIL'91 feature we published last February.

It was such a good success that we are now planning to continue with the same quality and style but this time with more exciting trails, all for 1992!

OUT WALKING caters for all walking be it long distance walking, backpacking and camping, with 83% taking a walking holiday every year, so by advertising your trails particularly alongside such strong editorial coverage, you will be in very good company.

The sheet enclosed shows various sizes of advertisements. However due to the popularity of our holiday spreads, we can now offer very special rates on eighth and quarter page colour advertisements along with any feature. TRAIL'92 is scheduled to feature in our MARCH issue which will be on sale from the 10th of February. Therefore I suggest that if you are interested in using an ad space you should start planning now.

We hope that you enjoy the enclosed issue of OUT WALKING and find it useful and we will telephone you in the next few days to discuss your requirements.

In the meantime should you need any further information please don't hesitate to phone us on (01721) 547385.

Yours sincerely

Jane Smith
Senior Telephone Sales Executive
OUT WALKING Magazines

On the telephone

People get on the telephone when they want to communicate or find out information quickly. In leisure and tourism, this might be when:

- tickets arrive at a travel agency, and a member of staff phones the customer to tell them they're ready to be picked up
- a customer rings a theatre to reserve tickets over the phone using a credit card
- a hotel rings a business to check what equipment is needed for a conference
- a customer rings a sports centre to find out what time it closes.

An airline put together this checklist for telephonists working on its enquiry line.

Telephone checklist

- always answer the telephone within three rings
- state the company's name, say who you are, and ask how you can help
- no one can see you smile over the phone – make sure your tone of voice and the words you use show that you are friendly and helpful
- make sure you have easy access to a computer monitor, so you can answer enquiries quickly and efficiently
- have a pen and paper to hand, so you can make notes on the customer's enquiry if necessary
- never leave a customer waiting without explaining why
- make sure the customer is happy and has all the information they need before ending the call
- finish the call appropriately, using the other person's name if possible

On computer

Computers are good when you're trying to find out or record information quickly and efficiently. In leisure and tourism, this might be when:

- a travel agency customer wants to find out about flight availability
- a hotel guest wants to see if another guest has checked in yet
- a customer wants to reserve theatre tickets over the phone.

Usually staff look at information on screen. Information can also be printed out to provide a written record, if necessary. For example, many travel agents give their customers computer-generated itineraries for trips. The manager of an agency explains:

66 *We use a computerised reservations system which contains a central bank of information about scheduled airline bookings, car hire, hotel accommodation, and leisure activities such as sports events and what's on at the theatre. Our staff use their computer terminals to make reservations for customers. These days, computers are an essential support service and source of information. But we find that customers still want advice and personal contact when choosing a holiday.* 99

Non-verbal communication

We all use body language to communicate our emotions and feelings. Our bodies send messages when we're not even aware of it. In leisure and tourism, this may be when:

- a customer walks into a travel agency and approaches a member of staff
- a porter greets a guest arriving at a hotel
- a cinema usher shows a customer to their seat
- a customer asks a receptionist for information on prices.

DISCUSSION POINT

Look at each of the images here. Decide what you think the member of staff is like.

■ Does she like her job?

■ Is she friendly and willing to help?

■ Does she respect customers?

■ How do you think she was feeling at the time?

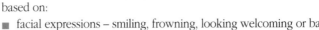

In all of these cases, both people form instant impressions of one another, based on:

■ facial expressions – smiling, frowning, looking welcoming or bad-tempered

■ eye contact – meeting someone's eye shows you're interested and ready to listen

■ posture – leaning forward shows you're interested, lounging back suggests you can't be bothered

■ position of the body – for example, crossing your arms puts distance between you and the person you're talking to.

Listening skills

Good communication doesn't just mean being able to talk well. It also means being able to listen well. Listening is particularly important for people working in customer care, so they can take in what customers want, answer their questions and take action if necessary.

Here's how a hotel's staff manual advises its staff to develop their listening skills.

1. ALWAYS listen to what customers are saying – however many times you've heard it before!
2. Look at them while they're talking – but don't stare.
3. Encourage them by nodding, smiling and making encouraging sounds.
4. If you're sitting down, lean forward slightly to show you're interested – but not so far you scare them off. Don't cross your arms and legs.
5. Make sure your tone of voice shows you're interested.

Feedback loop

Part of good communication is checking that you have been understood, and the feedback loop is a simple technique to do this. It allows the person giving information – the messenger – to confirm that a listener – the receiver – has understood what has been said from the feedback the listener gives. For example, a sales consultant in a travel agency will use feedback from a customer to confirm that the customer has understood the details of a holiday he or she is buying.

DISCUSSION POINT

Think about whether you as an individual communicate with people more effectively when you're on your own with them, or when you're part of a group.

■ How does your behaviour change?

■ When do you think it's more effective to communicate on a one-to-one basis, and when to a group of people?

Using the feedback loop can form part of an organisation's customer care policy.

MESSAGE

MESSANGER

RECEIVER

MESSAGE

Figure 15 Feedback loop

Communicating with individuals

A lot of the time staff and customers communicate one-to-one. Receptionists in sports centres and hotels talk to one person at a time. People selling tickets deal with customers one by one.

From the customer's point of view, being treated as an individual can make an enormous difference to the quality of communication. An elderly woman explains how staff at her favourite hotel always make her feel special:

❝ If I phone up to make a booking, or speak to staff face-to-face, they always make me feel I'm important. They treat me as an individual, and by the end of a conversation I always feel that there's a bit of a relationship. That's important when you're on your own like I am. By the end of a week's stay, I almost feel like they're friends. ❞

Communicating with groups

Some staff working in leisure and tourism have particular responsibilities for communicating with groups, for example:

■ tour guides who describe areas and attractions to parties of tourists
■ sports coaches who teach groups of people
■ museum staff who show displays to groups of schoolchildren.

All these people need to develop special skills in communicating with groups. A tour guide explains:

❝ When I'm showing round a party of 25 tourists, I have to make sure I communicate with all twenty-five at once. It's no good forming a good rapport with ten and not getting your message across to the other 15. I plan what I'm going to say carefully in advance, so that I'm confident and can answer questions they throw at me. I make sure I speak clearly and loudly, and check regularly that everyone can hear. Sometimes I write key words down on small cards, to remind me of all the information I want to tell the group. ❞

ACTIVITY

Prepare a short talk for a group of students visiting your area. The talk should give information on two local visitor attractions, describing their history, and what they offer visitors today. Prepare your talk carefully, and practise giving it in front of a mirror to get a better idea of what the group will see as you communicate.

Give your talk to other students in your group, and listen to their feedback on how you could have communicated better. When other students present their talks give constructive comments.

Customer service in practice

How do organisations go about putting their ideas about customer service into practice?

SPRINGBOARD HEALTH AND FITNESS CLUB

Springboard Health and Fitness Club is a gym offering workout facilities. The customer service manager describes how the organisation looks after its customers:

Our aim is to give everyone who joins the gym an individual service tailored to their needs.

The first thing we do is talk to the customer to find out what they want to get out of their gym sessions. Then we assess their fitness level. This involves asking about their health history – and noting any condition that might affect an exercise regime, taking their blood pressure, weighing them and measuring their height and their fat-to-muscle ratio, and finally checking their aerobic capacity and flexibility. We use all this information to devise an exercise programme to fit their aims, needs and fitness level. This can take a few days.

Next we take the customer into the gym area and go through the exercise programme with them. We explain exactly what each exercise will do for them, how they can expect to feel, how to use the equipment, what rate of progress they can expect, and so on.

Assessment of our customers' needs is an ongoing thing. We reassess them every two months and adjust their programme in line with the progress they've made and any different needs they may have.

We find people of all types and ages want to improve their fitness – people who work long hours in stressful jobs, retired people, people caring for babies and young children – so we are open 7 a.m. to 9 p.m. on weekdays and 9 a.m. to 8 p.m. at weekends. And we have a crèche every weekday morning. We also take care of our customers safety and security needs. All the equipment and training areas are maintained to the highest safety standards. All our facilities are kept clean and safe. We always have two trained instructors in the gym to keep an eye on people and advise them. We also provide lockers for customers' belongings – these are in the changing rooms, close to the showers and hairdriers. All customers are members and have membership cards as proof of identity. All staff wear badges showing their names and job titles. We give all members a booklet describing our health and safety procedures when they join, and there are also health and safety notices prominently displayed throughout the building and by each piece of gym equipment.

All members of staff can provide full information about our facilities and the products and services we offer. We have brochures, information leaflets and notices in the reception area. In addition to looking after the specific fitness training needs of our customers, we also offer advice and help on more general aspects of health and fitness. We have displays of information on nutrition and health education, free leaflets and brochures – and from time to time we arrange for health and fitness specialists to give talks.

Most of our contact with customers is direct, face-to-face. We all do a lot of talking and a lot of listening. We also talk to customers by phone and we have a membership newsletter which goes out every three months. We keep details of our members on a computer database. Apart from ensuring up-to-date and easily accessible information about our customers, it also helps us to speed up our administration tasks like subscription renewal reminders. All the customer details are treated with complete confidentiality.

Apart from keeping our customers informed, we also use our communication skills to keep them happy. Some people find the idea of exercise a bit daunting. They might be afraid of making fools of themselves or not progressing fast enough. We look out for the verbal and non-verbal signals that might suggest a customer is feeling uncomfortable and take great care to reassure them and help them feel they can use the gym with confidence.

Customer care theories can get to sound a bit complicated. But basically it's all a matter of common sense, common courtesy and good communication. We all prefer to be talked to in a polite and friendly way and treated as if we're valued. And that's what customer care is really – making an effort, taking the trouble, showing consideration. What you stand to gain from it far outweighs what it can cost you if you don't do it. If customers like what you've got on offer, they'll keep coming back for more. And they'll recommend you to other people. A lot of our new customers come to us because they've heard about us from existing customers. And happy customers make the staff's job more enjoyable which in turn makes them want to please the customers more. Unhappy customers don't come back – end of story and end of business. **99**

Key questions

1 Why is customer service important to leisure and tourism organisations?
2 What are the three aspects of customer service?
3 Can you think of four customer needs that should be met?
4 How might a dissatisfied customer's action affect a leisure and tourism organisation?
5 How does good customer service benefit the organisation and its employees as well as the customer?
6 Can you list six ways in which good customer service benefits everyone concerned?
7 How does good customer service help an organisation to achieve its goals?
8 Why does good customer service help employees feel satisfied in their work?
9 What are the five different types of communications used by leisure and tourism organisations?
10 What are the three basic rules when dealing with customers?

Assignment

A new hotel is writing a guide for staff which:
■ explains the importance of good customer service
■ shows how they should put it into practice.

The hotel is located in a seaside resort. It aims to attract tourist trade in summer and business conferences in winter. As well as the usual hotel amenities it has facilities to please both sets of customers, including:
■ an indoor swimming pool
■ a gym
■ two restaurants
■ conference rooms fitted with up-to-date communications and presentation equipment.

These facilities are run by separate organisations under contract to the hotel.

Write the guide, in two parts.

Part 1 explains:
■ what customer service is
■ what good customer service achieves for a leisure and tourism organisation
■ why customer service will be important for the hotel and its customers
■ the types of communication used in customer service.

Part 2 contains practical guidelines on how staff should put good customer service into practice. Write your guidelines for:
■ staff working in the hotel itself
■ staff working in one of the facilities under contract to the hotel.

ELEMENT **3.2**

Information and customer service

Excellent customer service often means providing the right information for customers when they ask for it – or even before they ask. In this element you will see what sort of things front-line staff need to know about so they can answer customers' questions. You'll also see where they can get all this information from, including computer databases and on-line services as well as brochures, timetables and other printed information. Finding out information is one thing, presenting it to customers is another. So you'll also look at different ways of giving information clearly.

> 66 *I produce posters and leaflets for our parents and children classes. They tell people about our classes and answer some of the common questions they may have. They take the pressure off having to answer questions all the time and leaflets also give people something to take away with them. Often, when you answer people's questions you find that they haven't absorbed any of what you've said, so it's good to be able to give them something they can take away.* 99

receptionist in a leisure centre

> 66 *We rely on our brochures mainly for the information we give to customers and we also have information manuals as well. We always ask customers to check their details, too. We might use a database sometimes to get information about which countries it is possible to visit at certain times of the year.* 99

travel consultant in a travel agency

> 66 *The information we provide to customers is in three forms: a guide book, a garden leaflet which shows a large plan of the garden, and a welcome leaflet. The welcome leaflet is a kind of orientation guide which shows you where you are on the property and promotes the facilities on site.* 99

administrator of a National Trust property

> 66 *The skills you need in my job are good communication skills, including being able to write press material. You need to have a sense of what makes good news so that you know how to interest the press in what you're doing. What I like most about my work is the community aspect. You get to speak to so many different kinds of people. I also like the public nature of it – being so involved with the community: there's a lot of life to it.* 99

press and publicity officer at an entertainments venue

The value of knowledge

Everyone working in leisure and tourism has their own area of special knowledge and expertise. You wouldn't expect a swimming pool attendant to know as much about prices and group discounts as a receptionist, or a receptionist to be an expert on pool safety. But as well as their own specialist subjects, all employees need a broad range of knowledge about their organisation and industry, so that they can:

■ meet customer needs
■ provide accurate information
■ save customers' time and money.

Meeting customer needs

Part of providing good customer service. At different times, leisure and tourism customers turn to staff for help, advice and information. Staff can meet these needs if they have the right level of knowledge and understanding. For example:

■ a gym instructor can only help someone to use equipment if she knows how to use it herself
■ a travel agent can only advise a holidaymaker on what insurance to buy if he has information on the different products on the market
■ a box office clerk can only tell a theatre-goer when a performance finishes if the information is close to hand.

Employees with a broad range of knowledge will be able to answer more questions, and meet more customer needs, than those who have a narrow, specialist field of knowledge. So:

■ the gym instructor should also be able to answer the customer's questions about a recent fitness scare
■ the travel agent should be able to explain to the holidaymaker exactly how different types of insurance work
■ the box office clerk should be able to answer the theatre-goer's questions about forthcoming plays.

Providing accurate information

Information has to be correct. Customers expect staff to provide accurate information and good advice. Giving people wrong or incomplete information is worse than giving them none at all.

If employees aren't sure of their facts, they need to ask. Making mistakes can:

■ waste customers' time and money
■ be frustrating and upsetting
■ endanger customers' safety and security.

But if employees give accurate information, customers are likely to:

■ make the most of a facility
■ feel their money has been well spent
■ come away satisfied by the experience
■ return to the facility, bringing friends and family with them.

DISCUSSION POINT

Think about going to an aerobics class for the first time.

■ What help, advice and information might you need?

■ What knowledge would an aerobics instructor need in order to answer all your questions and meet your needs?

Saving resources

Employees with a broad range of knowledge can meet customers' needs for information and advice quickly and efficiently. So it saves them time and money:

- time spent finding out about, or looking for information on, facilities and products that customers might want to know about
- money – spending time on the phone making enquiries, or having to travel around to find out basic information adds to costs indirectly.

Some jobs in leisure and tourism – for example, in travel agencies – aim to save customers money by finding them the best deals on products. In these cases, a well-informed employee can make direct savings for customers. A customer who recently planned a trip to visit relatives in another part of the UK explains how the knowledge of staff at his local railway station helped to save time and money:

66 *I went to the station to find out about train tickets for the family to go to Aberdeen. When I arrived there was a queue. I expected a long wait, but staff dealt with enquiries quickly and my turn came round sooner than I expected. The woman I spoke to was very helpful and told me about the costs of different tickets. She suggested that we bought a family railcard, which would mean the children could travel at a reduced rate. She also suggested we took a different route to the one I'd planned, as it would knock over an hour off our journey. I came away feeling that I'd saved both time and money.* 99

Knowing about the organisation

Leisure and tourism employees should know about:

- their organisation's products – so they can answer customers' questions about features and advise them what to buy or use
- the prices of products – so they can advise customers on the best buys
- health, safety and security procedures – so they can ensure customers are safe when using the facility
- the organisation's structure – so they understand the team they work in, and know who to turn to for help and support.

Knowing about the industry

It's also helpful for leisure and tourism employees to have a wider understanding of the industry as a whole. For example:

- a travel agent should know about trends in holiday sales across the tourism industry
- a fitness instructor should know about new equipment coming on to the market
- a hotelier should know about different types of reservations systems available.

A college-leaver has just started her first job, working on the reception desk of a hotel. Her manager has emphasised the importance of having a good broad knowledge of the hotel and catering industry, so that she can talk to customers knowledgeably and offer them good advice.

How would you advise the new receptionist to find out this information about the industry? Make a list of:

■ publications she could read
■ people she could talk to.

Choose a leisure and tourism facility in your area which is used by visitors to the area. List the type of questions about the region that visitors to the facility might ask. Using information from your local tourist information centre, put together a short checklist summarising the knowledge of regional context which it would be helpful for employees to know.

Employees who have a broad range of knowledge of the industry are likely to suggest new methods and opportunities, bringing benefits to their organisation. They also bring benefits to the customer by:

■ providing accurate information across a wide range of subject areas
■ helping to ensure the equipment and products available to customers are up to date and appropriate
■ providing good advice on what products to buy and use, taking into account long-term developments in the industry.

Knowing the regional context

Most people in leisure and tourism work in a particular geographical area. They should know about the region they work in, so they can answer customers' questions about facilities in the area.

A hotel receptionist explains the different questions she regularly has to face:

66 *People want you to know about the area. They see you as a leisure and tourism expert, and they want advice and information about all sorts of things. In the last hour, I've been asked what's the best museum in the area, where to hire a car in town, if you can see the area well by bus, where's a good Chinese restaurant and what is there for children to do around here! It's just as well I've got a good general knowledge of the area. We've also put together a stock of leaflets and brochures to hand out.* 99

Knowing the national and international contexts

Some facilities are regularly visited by people from across the UK and overseas – theme parks, national monuments and national parks. People working in these facilities may need to know about:

■ transport links and travel distances
■ the geography of the UK
■ facilities in other parts of the country.

Large facilities usually stock brochures and leaflets covering different parts of the UK, as well as their own region.

A broad knowledge of national and international contexts is particularly important for tourist information centres, which deal with customers from all over the world.

THURROCK TOURIST INFORMATION CENTRE

Staff at Thurrock Tourist Information Centre focus on helping local people and visitors enjoy the area. They need an enormous range of information at their fingertips. They have links with other tourist information centres in the area, so they can share information. They also have detailed information on leisure and tourism in their region, including travel, entertainment, accommodation, catering and visitor attractions.

Staff at the centre can:

■ provide information on national accommodation and attractions

■ sell maps and guides to all areas of Britain and other parts of Europe

■ organise cross-Channel travel

■ offer a foreign currency exchange service.

A family from abroad whose hired car broke down at the motorway service area near the Dartford Tunnel, where the tourist information centre is located, describe the help they got from staff:

66 *Our car broke down at the motorway service area late on a Bank Holiday afternoon, on our way to Canterbury. Our first thought was to phone the car hire company, but when we went to the information centre to get some change they immediately contacted the car hire company, and got a replacement car for the next day. They also found accommodation for us that night, which was lucky because I've never seen so many tourists as in Canterbury! While we were waiting, we discovered some leaflets full of interesting things to do during our trip to Canterbury.* 99

Knowledge about the organisation

Leisure and tourism employees are representatives of the organisation they work for. They need to know about:

- the products available
- prices of products
- health, safety and security at the organisation
- the organisational structure.

This knowledge helps them to answer customer's questions and do their jobs efficiently.

Products

A good knowledge of the range of products offered by an organisation is vital because products are the things customers buy or use – anything from holidays and meals, to sports coaching and playground facilities.

So that they can give customers information and advice on products, employees need to know about:

- the range of products available from the organisation – holidays on the market, meals on the menu, films being shown at a cinema
- the features of these products – what different resorts are like, the ingredients used in meals, whether films are thrillers or romances
- who products are suitable for – holiday packages for young people, meals for vegetarians, films for children.

With this type of information, staff can advise customers what to buy or use based on what's available and the customers' needs.

A fitness adviser at a sports centre explains why it is important for her to have good knowledge of the different fitness products available at the centre:

66 *When people come wanting advice on fitness training, I carry out a fitness assessment on them and ask about their aims. I use my knowledge of the different courses and sessions we run to advise them what they should go for. I need to know about the trainers who lead each session, the level of fitness it demands, the type of exercise it involves and what the session is aiming to achieve. I also need practical knowledge of timings and length of sessions, so customers can see how they fit in with their schedules.* 99

Prices

Most people want value for money and information on the prices of products. Leisure and tourism employees need to have information on prices to hand, so that they can answer questions quickly and correctly.

If a facility offers a limited range of products – for example, tickets for the cinema or a football match – employees can memorise the prices. In many cases that's impossible – for example, a travel agent has thousands of holidays on offer at any one time, and couldn't possibly remember the prices of all of them. But it's important to have a general idea of the price range of different holiday destinations and tour operators so they can give customers the right sort of help. Then they can look for the detailed information if a customer asks.

DISCUSSION POINT

Think of a time when an employee gave you the wrong information about products and their prices. What were the results of their mistake?

Health, safety and security

Customers and employees have a right to expect that facilities are safe and secure. Leisure and tourism organisations invest a lot of time and money in achieving this. For example:

- facilities such as sports stadiums, cinemas and hotels have detailed procedures for evacuation in the case of fire, and all staff are trained on what to do in an emergency
- catering facilities ensure safe storage and handling of food
- facilities which use equipment and machinery, such as theme parks and playgrounds, run constant checks to ensure they are safe to use
- activity centres and sports centres make sure that potentially dangerous sporting activities are well supervised.

All employees – the managing director as much as junior members of staff – are responsible for the health, safety and security of themselves and their customers. So they all need to know procedures and practice in their organisation.

Health and Safety at Work Act 1974

This is a law which:

- says that it is the responsibility of both employers and employees to make sure working practices are safe
- says employers must make the workplace as safe as possible, and provide safety equipment where needed
- aims to control the storage and use of dangerous chemicals
- aims to control the emission of noxious or offensive substances from the workplace.

SUN VALLEY	
SAFETY MANUAL	RESORT MANAGER
12.	IDENTIFY HEALTH RISKS TO STAFF AND GUESTS, E.G.SUNSTROKE, SWIMMING POOL, FOOD POISONING ETC.
13.	MAKE A LIST OF HEALTH RISKS AND PREVENTION.
14.	MAKE SURE ALL STAFF ARE FULLY TRAINED AND BRIEFED ON HEALTH RISKS AND KNOW THE CORRECT PREVENTATIVE AND EMERGENCY PROCEDURES.
15.	KEEP TRAINING RECORDS.
16.	FIND OUT WHO THE LOCAL DOCTOR IS AND KEEP HIS NUMBER ON YOU.
17.	TRAIN ALL STAFF IN KITCHEN HYGIENE AND MAINTAIN STANDARDS
	page 3

Most leisure and tourism organisations produce their own health and safety guidelines for staff, explaining how to make sure they and customers are safe at all times.

Many facilities run regular training sessions on health and safety, to give their staff up-to-date information on procedures and what to do in the case of accidents and emergencies. Some also have a health and safety committee which meets regularly to:

■ discuss health, safety and security on the site
■ suggest how to improve procedures.

SAFETY AND SECURITY AT THORPE PARK

Safety of both customers and staff at Thorpe Park is a high priority. Each employee is given a copy of 'Terms and Conditions of Employment', which includes information on safety procedures. It states that all staff must:

■ take care when using and maintaining machinery

■ keep work areas clean, tidy and free of hazards

■ keep to fire and bomb procedures.

All staff undergo a training programme which stresses the importance of individual responsibility for health, safety and security. This covers lost property procedures, and a pass which enables them to move freely around the park.

Organisational structure

Every organisation – from a multinational hotel chain to a restaurant – has its own structure. Some have charts which show the different jobs in an organisation and the relationship between them. The structure for a large organisation will be complex, with many different departments and levels within them.

Employees should know the structure of their organisation, so that they:

■ can understand their role in the team
■ know who to ask for information and advice
■ know who to refer different problems to.

All of these contribute to good customer service, as they improve the efficiency and effectiveness of staff.

ACTIVITY

Find out more about the health, safety and security arrangements at your work placement. Collect as much information as you can about procedures in place, including guidelines for employees and information given to customers. Make sure you cover the relevant areas, such as:

■ health and safety at work

■ fire precautions

■ first aid and accident reporting

■ food hygiene.

Using your findings, write a short leaflet giving basic information on the procedures in place to ensure health, safety and security on the premises.

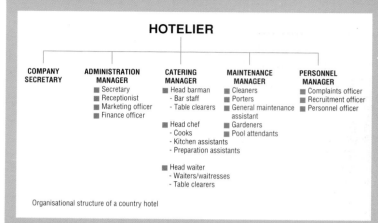

DISCUSSION POINT

HOTELIER

COMPANY SECRETARY

ADMINISTRATION MANAGER
- Secretary
- Receptionist
- Marketing officer
- Finance officer

CATERING MANAGER
- Head barman
  - Bar staff
  - Table clearers
- Head chef
  - Cooks
  - Kitchen assistants
  - Preparation assistants
- Head waiter
  - Waiters/waitresses
  - Table clearers

MAINTENANCE MANAGER
- Cleaners
- Porters
- General maintenance assistant
- Gardeners
- Pool attendants

PERSONNEL MANAGER
- Complaints officer
- Recruitment officer
- Personnel officer

Organisational structure of a country hotel

A kitchen assistant has just started work at a hotel with the organisational structure shown in this chart.

- Who manages the work of the kitchen team?

- Who is in the catering manager's team?

- If a customer wanted to send a fax, who would the assistant ask?

- If a customer wanted to make a complaint, who would the assistant contact?

- If a tap was dripping, who would the assistant go to?

Sources of information

People working in leisure and tourism need a wide range of information to provide good customer service. Where do they get the information from?

Computers

As with other industries, leisure and tourism has benefited greatly from the use of computers to store, record and access information.

Databases

Databases are used to store large amounts of information. Facts and figures which would have filled filing cabinets in the past can now be:

■ stored in electronic form – on floppy disc, hard disc or networks

■ found and updated quickly

■ sorted in different ways – for example, by surname or area.

Databases help leisure and tourism organisations provide a good service to customers because they are a source of instant information. A travel agent describes how important databases are in her work:

❝ *We need access to information to give customers a good service. Using computers has made us much more efficient. I had a customer in just now who enquired about a particular holiday. I accessed our database to find out information about destinations, the availability of products, fares and prices. Then I made a reservation for him immediately on the computer and printed out details of the booking for him to take away.* **❞**

Even small leisure and tourism organisations often have databases with details of their customers' names, addresses and interests. They use them to mail out information about forthcoming events which might be of interest, or to promote particular products.

DISCUSSION POINT

Think of other situations in which leisure and tourism organisations use a database as a source of information.

Electronic mail systems

Electronic mail (also known as e-mail) is a way of sending information from computer to computer over telephone lines.

To use e-mail, you need:

■ a computer

■ a modem – a device that turns data from the computer into a form suitable for sending down the telephone lines

■ a telephone line

■ an e-mail service – a host computer that receives messages, holds them, and then sends them on to the destination computer.

Telecommunications

Telecommunications means any long-distance communication carried out using electronic equipment.

Having a good telecommunications system is an important part of providing good customer service in leisure and tourism. It enables staff and customers to exchange information efficiently throughout the UK and the world.

Leisure and tourism organisations regularly use:

- telephones – for convenient, instant contact with customers
- faxes – to send written information quickly, such as confirmation of bookings
- Prestel/Teletext – to dial up information, make bookings and exchange messages (Prestel and Teletext use ordinary telephone lines to connect information stored on a computer with TV sets and computers)
- telex – to send printed messages over the telephone system using teleprinters.

Regional publications

Every region of the UK has its own publications which give information on things to see and do in the local area. These are given to customers by tourist information centres, hotels, restaurants, visitor attractions and other facilities.

The diagram below shows the different types of regional publications available, and the information they contain.

ACTIVITY

Visit a large leisure and tourism facility in your area. Find out how it uses computer-based sources of information to provide good customer service. Produce a chart to show:

- the different types of computer and telecommunications systems used
- the type of information they provide or record.

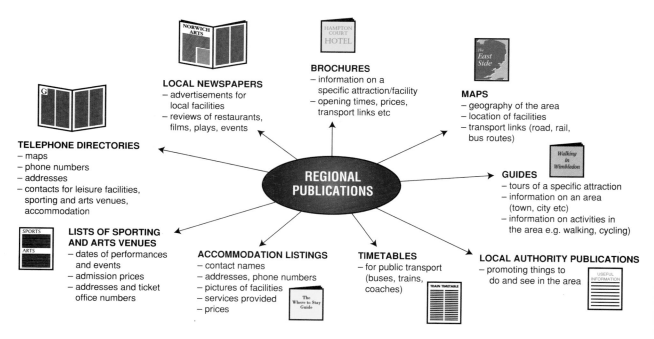

LOCAL NEWSPAPERS
– advertisements for local facilities
– reviews of restaurants, films, plays, events

BROCHURES
– information on a specific attraction/facility
– opening times, prices, transport links etc

MAPS
– geography of the area
– location of facilities
– transport links (road, rail, bus routes)

TELEPHONE DIRECTORIES
– maps
– phone numbers
– addresses
– contacts for leisure facilities, sporting and arts venues, accommodation

GUIDES
– tours of a specific attraction
– information on an area (town, city etc)
– information on activities in the area e.g. walking, cycling)

REGIONAL PUBLICATIONS

LISTS OF SPORTING AND ARTS VENUES
– dates of performances and events
– admission prices
– addresses and ticket office numbers

ACCOMMODATION LISTINGS
– contact names
– addresses, phone numbers
– pictures of facilities
– services provided
– prices

TIMETABLES
– for public transport (buses, trains, coaches)

LOCAL AUTHORITY PUBLICATIONS
– promoting things to do and see in the area

ACTIVITY

Identify one publication which fits into each of the categories shown on the diagram. Produce a chart listing:

■ the names of the publications

■ the types of information they contain

■ when you think customers would find them useful.

National publications

National publications provide useful information for customers on things to see and do. As these publications are available across the UK, they tend to focus on major attractions and events, or on holidays which will appeal to people nation-wide.

Some national publications are on sale in bookshops and newsagents. Others are distributed free of charge at tourist information centres and leisure and tourism facilities.

The diagram below shows the different types of national publications available, and the information they contain.

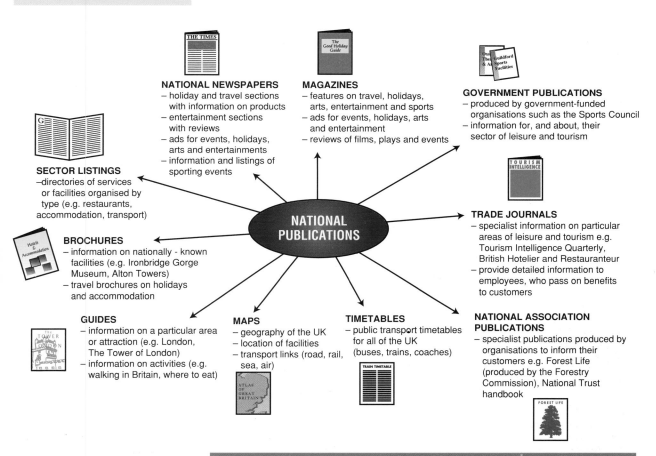

NATIONAL NEWSPAPERS
– holiday and travel sections with information on products
– entertainment sections with reviews
– ads for events, holidays, arts and entertainments
– information and listings of sporting events

MAGAZINES
– features on travel, holidays, arts, entertainment and sports
– ads for events, holidays, arts and entertainment
– reviews of films, plays and events

GOVERNMENT PUBLICATIONS
– produced by government-funded organisations such as the Sports Council
– information for, and about, their sector of leisure and tourism

SECTOR LISTINGS
–directories of services or facilities organised by type (e.g. restaurants, accommodation, transport)

BROCHURES
– information on nationally - known facilities (e.g. Ironbridge Gorge Museum, Alton Towers)
– travel brochures on holidays and accommodation

GUIDES
– information on a particular area or attraction (e.g. London, The Tower of London)
– information on activities (e.g. walking in Britain, where to eat)

MAPS
– geography of the UK
– location of facilities
– transport links (road, rail, sea, air)

TIMETABLES
– public transport timetables for all of the UK (buses, trains, coaches)

TRADE JOURNALS
– specialist information on particular areas of leisure and tourism e.g. Tourism Intelligence Quarterly, British Hotelier and Restauranteur
– provide detailed information to employees, who pass on benefits to customers

NATIONAL ASSOCIATION PUBLICATIONS
– specialist publications produced by organisations to inform their customers e.g. Forest Life (produced by the Forestry Commission), National Trust handbook

NATIONAL PUBLICATIONS

ACTIVITY

Ask your local tourist information centre if you can look at the weekly log recording enquiries. Produce a table analysing the information requested in one day. Then:

■ tick the information which could be found in a national publication

■ give the title of the relevant publication.

Giving information to customers

Giving clear information to customers is a skill which people who work in leisure and tourism need. Communication – written or spoken – is required in many situations. Some basic rules apply:

- use simple language and understandable terms
- make sure information is correct
- speak clearly
- check to see that customers have understood
- use diagrams if it helps
- write down information where appropriate.

Language

People mostly communicate using language. Leisure and tourism employees who use language well will communicate clearly with their customers.

The customer services manager at a large hotel explains the advice she gives her staff on how to use language well:

66 *I tell staff to use simple language and not to choose long, impressive-sounding words for the sake of it. For example, I tell them to say 'last' not 'ultimate', 'end' not 'conclusion' and 'buy' not 'purchase'. I also tell them not to use words unless they're sure what they mean. They're advised to steer clear of jargon. I say that words which are familiar to them and other people in the hotel business may mean nothing to visitors. When they have to write information down, I tell staff to keep sentences short. If a customer has to read a sentence twice, there's something wrong with it.* 99

Correct information

Giving people incorrect information can be worse than giving them none at all – it can waste customers' time and money, and even put their safety and security at risk. So it's worth getting it right.

To give the correct information, leisure and tourism employees should know:

- the main sources of information they can use
- where records and files are kept, and understand how to use them
- the structure of their organisation, so they can check any facts they're unclear about with the right person.

Speaking clearly

Clear spoken communication doesn't just depend on what you say, it's also how you say it.

A museum in London, which specialises in guided tours for visitors, gives its staff these guidelines on how to speak clearly.

ACTIVITY

Here are four phrases from letters sent to customers. Rewrite them so they are easier to understand.

Herewith enclosed please find your tickets for the performance

We hope to be of assistance to you in the future

May we be allowed to pass on our heartiest felicitations on the occasion of your marriage

Please accept the enclosed voucher for a complimentary beverage at our establishment

---

DISCUSSION POINT

Think about the information you use in your GNVQ assignments.

- How do you check that it's correct?
- Do you think any of these techniques would be helpful if you were working in a leisure and tourism organisation?

1. Speed – if you speak too fast, it's hard for people to follow what you say. If you speak too slowly, people become bored and distracted.
2. Loudness – this depends where you are, and how close you are to the customers you're talking to. You can talk more quietly if you're in a small room with one person than if you're in a large gallery with a group of people. If you talk too loudly, it can give the impression that you think the other person is stupid. If you're too quiet, they won't be able to hear you.
3. Tone. The tone of your voice can give away whether you're feeling enthusiastic, happy, sad, angry and so on. Don't give away feelings which would be better kept to yourself.
4. Pitch. If your voice is too high or low it can be hard to listen to.
5. Words. Think about which words you want to emphasise – be aware of what you're saying as you say it.

ACTIVITY

Using a cassette recorder, make tapes of yourself reading a short piece from a leaflet or brochure. Try experimenting with:

■ loudness

■ speed

■ tone

■ pitch

■ emphasising different words.

Once you think you've got it right, play the tape to friends and ask them to give you feedback.

Checking understanding

However clearly you communicate, there will be times when people misinterpret or misunderstand what you say. If they think customers may have misunderstood, staff should always check that there is no confusion. Misunderstandings can lead to mistakes and frustration.

But checking customers' understanding without seeming rude and patronising can be difficult.

DISCUSSION POINT

A gym instructor has just explained to a new customer how to use a rowing machine, but isn't sure that her customer has understood all the equipment settings clearly. Which of these would be the best way for her to find out?

■ 'You're not catching on very fast here – you don't get it, do you?'

■ 'Have you got any questions? Would you like me to go over something again?'

■ 'Right, now let's see if you can explain it to me.'

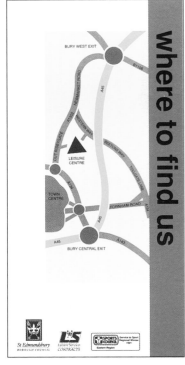

Some information is almost impossible to communicate without using diagrams

Using diagrams

Sometimes a picture is worth a thousand words. For example:

■ a map is often better than a complicated list of directions

■ diagrams and drawings can help non-English speakers

■ a table plan is easier to understand than a long list of names and numbers

■ pie charts, graphs and bar charts give a better instant impression of figures than a page of statistics

■ a diagram can often show more clearly than words how a piece of equipment works.

ACTIVITY

Show someone the way:

■ from where you are now to a nearby leisure and tourism facility

■ from the facility to the main road out of town.

Working with a partner:

■ explain each route in speech

■ write down directions

■ draw a simple map to show the route.

From the results of this experiment, when do you think it is most appropriate to use diagrams?

Writing it down

Writing down information for customers can help when:

■ the information is complicated and would be hard to explain in speech

■ there's a message to pass on – for example, a telephone message

■ a customer wants to keep information as a reminder – for example, directions or train times

■ a customer has impaired hearing.

The administration manager at a large city centre hotel explains the tips she gives her staff on writing down information:

66 *We hold a lot of conferences at the hotel so there are often many business people staying. They're always getting messages so our staff have to be on their toes to pass on the information quickly. Even if it's only a brief message, I tell staff to use headed paper or a compliment slip, write clearly and check the spelling of people's names. Every time they put something down on paper, they're putting the hotel's reputation on the line.* 99

Customers who don't speak English

Some facilities cater for a large number of non-English speaking customers. They should bear in mind language needs when providing information to customers:

- should brochures, leaflets and tour guides be printed in more than one language?
- should taped messages and announcements – for example, in airports – be translated?
- should signs be produced in more than one language – particularly those relating to health, safety and security?
- should they employ multilingual staff to meet customers' needs?

Speaking and listening can be especially difficult. Employees who deal regularly with non-English speaking customers should be trained in how to break down the communication barrier. It helps if you:

- speak clearly and slowly
- don't shout or speak too loud
- stay patient if the customer doesn't understand.

CARING FOR JAPANESE CUSTOMERS

Recognising the importance of attracting visitors from Japan, many leisure and tourism facilities across the UK are now providing information in Japanese. For example:

- The Bank of England Museum has a cassette guide in Japanese for a 45-minute tour.
- Leeds Castle in Kent publishes a guidebook in Japanese.
- The World of Beatrix Potter in the Lake District has a Japanese commentary.
- In Haworth, West Yorkshire, signs in Japanese guide visitors to attractions.
- The National Railway Museum, the Jorvik Viking Centre and the Museum of Automata all have brochures in Japanese.
- Major London department stores such as Harvey Nichols, Harrods, Selfridges and Liberty's have Japanese-speaking staff to help visitors.

Customers from different cultural backgrounds

Customers from different cultural backgrounds can have particular needs. For example, a guide showing a group of visitors from the Middle East around a tourist attraction may need to consider:

- the use of certain English words during a presentation – some words may offend overseas visitors so should be avoided
- what refreshments are available – these need to cater for cultural differences
- ways of addressing individuals' religious differences.

Customers of different ages

Many staff in facilities communicate with customers of widely differing ages, from young children through to the very elderly. When giving information to different age groups, they should consider:

■ the customers' level of understanding – children may have a smaller vocabulary than adults

■ whether the customer has any special physical requirements – some elderly people may be hard of hearing

■ whether there is any particular information which would be of interest to the customer – for example, special prices for children and pensioners, classes for over-50s.

But it's not good to make any assumptions about someone's needs based solely on their age. Employees should judge each customer's case individually. An elderly person describes the frustrations of being pigeon-holed:

66 *People see I'm in my seventies, and instantly assume I must be deaf and half-awake. They shout at me, try not to use long words, and generally treat me like a child. I'm sick and tired of it. I feel like wearing a badge saying 'Yes, I'm over 70, but treat me as a normal human being!'* 99

Customers with specific needs

A few customers are likely to have specific communication needs because of:

■ visual impairment

■ mobility problems

■ hearing impairment

■ difficulties with reading and writing, or using numbers.

When they recognise that customers have specific needs, employees should:

■ choose an appropriate means of communication – spoken or written

■ think about any special information they need, such as disabled facilities.

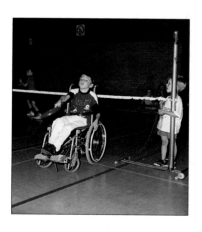

A woman with disabilities planning a visit to a theme park explains how important it is for staff to give her clear information:

66 *I always get good information about disabled facilities before going anywhere. Recently I planned a trip out with my children. I phoned up in advance to find out if my wheelchair could be accommodated. The girl in customer service was extremely helpful. She explained that there were ramps at all steps and disabled toilets around the site – she sent me a map so I knew where they were. She told me that staff were experienced in dealing with people with disabilities and would be able to provide any support I needed. I was delighted to be given such clear, accurate information in advance.* 99

Business visitors

Business visitors have particular needs:

- for information on business-related services, such as faxing, international dialling, typing – most hotels with regular business guests leave this information in hotel rooms, but staff should also be able to answer face-to-face queries quickly and efficiently
- for speed – business people are often pressed for time, so employees need to communicate with them efficiently and pass on messages promptly
- for accuracy – if an employee takes down a business-related message incorrectly, it could be serious.

UNIT

3

ELEMENT **3.2**

DISCUSSION POINT

Most companies make arrangements for travel and accommodation through a business travel department, so travel agents rarely communicate directly with business people.

- What problems might this create?
- How could they be overcome?

People visiting friends and relatives

Travel agencies offer many services to people visiting friends and relatives. Usually, VFR (visit, friends and relatives) customers only need transport as they are likely to be staying with their friends or relatives. They might also need general information about their tickets and journey, such as connection times and facilities. Whereas customers, say, interested in package holidays buy both transport and accommodation.

Specific information needs

Different customers have different information needs. To provide effective customer service, staff in leisure and tourism organisations need to recognise these needs and provide the right information.

Here is how one organisation – a country house hotel – identifies and meets the information needs of all its customers. The text on the next four pages is taken from the staff handbook, given to all staff to help them perform their jobs efficiently and effectively.

Binstead Park Hotel

At Binstead Park Hotel we pride ourselves on giving accurate, clear information as part of our overall high standard of customer service. Through interviews with staff and guests, we know that our visitors need information on:

- our products – different accommodation packages, facilities
- costs
- safety and security
- timings – times of breakfast and dinner, bar opening times
- directions
- specific requirements – disabled facilities, language support.

We have identified five key groups of guests who have particular information needs:

- visitors who don't speak English
- children
- elderly people
- business guests
- guests with disabilities or mobility problems.

Our products

You may work on reception or in the kitchen, you may handle telephone enquiries or have day-to-day contact with guests. Wherever you work at Binstead Park you need to know about the different products we offer so you can answer questions quickly and accurately.

Products you should know about include:

- different types of rooms available – doubles, singles, suites
- different accommodation packages available – mid-week breaks, romantic retreats, businessman's stopover, fitness fortnights
- catering services – in the restaurant, in the bars
- room services – catering, laundry, newspaper delivery, cleaning
- sports facilities – swimming pool, sauna, jacuzzi, gym
- the grounds – where to walk, spots to sit and relax.

Most of this information is included in the hotel's brochure. This is translated into German, French and Japanese. When preparing rooms, you

BINSTEAD CARVERY

Open at 12 noon for
buffet lunches
and
6.30 pm for
full 4 course dinner
(last orders 10pm)

should make sure that the appropriate translation of the brochure is available. A notice in reception lists staff with particular language skills – try them if guests need more information.

Although we don't have children staying very often, when we do, remember to explain the children's menu and games room down by the pool. Older people may be more interested in the pianist in the bar on Thursdays, and the fitness classes for over 60s. Just make sure that you know about all the products we offer, and match them up to the guests you meet.

Business people have a particular need for information on the business services we offer – faxing, secretarial services, message recording and presentation facilities. If you're likely to have contact with business guests, make sure you're completely up to date with what we offer. It's especially important to give our business guests the information they need quickly and efficiently.

Costs

At some point, all of you are likely to be asked information on costs by guests at the hotel. People might want to know the cost of:

- rooms and different accommodation packages
- meals and drinks
- business services
- telephone calls... and much more.

Binstead Park Hotel

M E N U
A La Carte

Starters

Cream of asparagus soup	£3.50
Crown of Galia melon filled with slices of fresh pear drizzled with port	£6.50
Smoked Scottish salmon with green peppercorns and balsamic vinegar	£6.95
Smoked duck set on a bed of lettuce, served with orange vinaigrette	£7.50
Mediterranean prawns with segments of fresh grapefruit and a trio of sauces	£6.95
Warm chicken liver and bacon salad	£5.95
Mushrooms à la crème served in a pastry chest	£5.95

Main Course

Fillet of chicken stuffed with finely chopped mushroom, onion and garlic served with a sweet red pepper sauce	£14.50
Medallions of oak smoked fillet of beef with a rich port wine sauce	£16.50
Monkfish mornay served with saffron rice	£16.50
Roast breast of pheasant with a country vegetable pot and roast potatoes	£15.50
Fillet of Dover sole with lobster bathed in a champagne cream	£17.50
Rosettes of lamb served in a rosemary, garlic and red wine jus	£15.50
Covent Garden tart with hollandaise.	£11.95

All main courses are served with either seasonal vegetables or a salad of your choice.
(Except the roast pheasant which is served as described)

Dessert £3.95

Ask your waitress to bring the dessert trolley.

Coffee and petit fours.

Always check information if you're not sure. Remember that we offer concessions on accommodation packages for children, and special mid-week breaks for pensioners. Make sure business guests are aware of the costs of the business services they use. Non-English speaking guests may be confused by numbers, so you could write down prices as well as saying them.

Safety and security

We don't take any risks when it comes to the safety and security of our guests.

It's of vital importance that everyone who visits the hotel is able to understand information related to safety and security. Warning signs around the hotel are printed in four languages. If you take a booking for a customer with a different language need, contact the customer services manager.

Children may be particularly at risk in the pool area. Cartoon posters giving guidelines on pool safety are displayed around the pool, but you may need to explain the safety rules to children if they are misbehaving.

Notices giving details of fire evacuation procedures are displayed around the hotel. Make sure that elderly guests or people with mobility problems are clear on the procedures for evacuating the building, and feel they would be able to reach emergency exits safely.

Finally, information is included in the welcome pack in each room on leaving valuable items in the hotel safe.

Timings

While staying at the hotel, all guests will need information on:

- when breakfast is served
- restaurant and bar opening hours
- when room service is available
- the collection times for laundry
- when they are expected to vacate their room.

All of this information is included in the hotel's brochure. Times for specific fitness classes are included as a loose sheet in the welcome pack, as these change regularly. You may want to point out the times of special children's sessions and over 60s classes to our younger and older guests.

Business guests will need to know when different business services are available. Ask at reception to find out the availability of secretarial staff on a week-by-week basis. For visitors who need to know the times of local public transport, timetables are available at reception.

Directions

Occasionally, you may be asked for directions either to another part of the

---

Binstead Park Hotel

POOL SAFETY

Do not bring drinks into the pool area.

Do not run around the pool side.

Do not dive into the pool except in the diving area.

Do not leave young children or non-swimmers unattended.

The pool is 1 metre deep at the shallow end and 2 metres deep at the deep end.

The pool is open from 7.00am till 10.00pm.

The benefit of loyal customers is the repeat business they bring. Everybody wins:

- customers returning to a facility build up a good relationship with the employees who are selling products
- employees grow to understand the customers' needs better, and are able to sell them the right products again and again
- customers benefit from being assured of satisfaction when buying products
- the organisation benefits because customers are spending more money.

Financial benefits

Sales have a direct relationship to income and profit. The more products an organisations sells, the more money it makes.

The sales director of a chain of pubs outlines the financial benefits of selling as part of customer service:

66 *In a business like ours, good customer service is good selling, and good selling brings profit. When we train bar managers, we emphasise that the customer is king. I tell them: 'Get your customer service right, and your sales figures will be right too'. Regular customers are all-important. Staff build up good relationships with local people, they come in several times a week, and spend money on food and drink. The more they spend, the better it is f or business.* 99

Increased business

Organisations which provide good customer service and sell their products well benefit from:

- increased usage – sports centres have fully-booked courts
- increased occupancy – hotels have fully-booked rooms
- increased sales – takings from the bar go up.

As the diagram below shows, the benefits of selling as part of customer service are all closely interlinked.

DISCUSSION POINT

The quality of selling affects whether people use shops, facilities and organisations again. Think of times when:

- you've been impressed by the customer service you've received, and have decided to go back
- the sales approach of staff annoyed you so much that you've never gone back.

ACTIVITY

Talk to the manager of a leisure and tourism facility about the importance of selling as part of customer service. Do they see a direct relationship between customer satisfaction, repeat business, financial benefit and increased business? Draw a chart to show your findings.

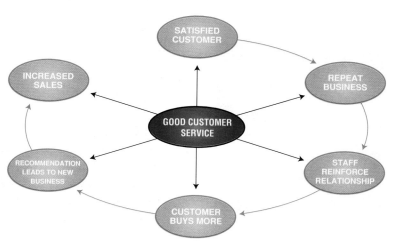

Section 3.3.2   # Sales situations

The leisure and tourism industry in the UK is broad, ranging from play schemes for toddlers to holidays for the elderly. All of these facilities need to attract and keep customers. Employees and customers get involved in a wide range of sales situations.

Retail outlets

Retail means selling products directly to the public, through shops, facilities and other outlets.

As well as selling their own products and services, many leisure and tourism facilities have retail outlets which sell other products to the public.
For example:

- stately homes and museums have shops selling gifts and souvenirs
- theme parks have outlets selling food, ranging from à la carte meals to burgers and pizzas
- big sports centres have shops selling sports equipment and clothing.

❝ *I work in a shop attached to a museum. We sell souvenirs, gifts, books and other products related to the museum. People normally come into the shop after they've been around the museum, so they already know what they're interested in. They come in here and browse. I have to know the stock well so that if people have a specific request I can help them. Basically, we just try to be on hand to provide a friendly, efficient service when we're needed.* **❞**

> ### DISCUSSION POINT
>
> Think about the shop attached to the museum.
>
> - What benefits would good sales in the shop bring to the museum?
> - If you were managing the shop, how would you try to improve customer service and increase sales?

Travel agencies

One of the most visible retailers of the leisure and tourism industry. Every high street has at least one travel agent, selling a wide range of leisure and tourism products – round the world trips to weekend breaks within the UK.

❝ *I work for an independent travel agency based in the south-west of England. I sell holiday packages and arrange one-off flights, train tickets, holiday insurance, coach trips, that sort of thing. Basically we try and cater for all our customers' travel-related needs. Our main aim is to provide good customer service and build up a strong reputation in the local community. Our manager is keen that we create the right impression through our personal appearance and*

ACTIVITY

Visit two travel agencies in your area, and watch the way staff greet and help customers.

- Does it seem as if their main aim is to sell?
- Or do they seem to be providing a customer service, resulting in holiday sales?

the way we treat customers. As soon as someone walks through the door, we try to make sure there's a member of staff on hand to help them. Although we're employed to sell travel products, I feel as if my job is more to do with pleasing customers – but then, I suppose if our customers are satisfied, we'll get the results our manager's looking for. 99

Bars

Bars – including pubs, night clubs, and hotel bars – aim to establish a regular clientele by providing good customer service. They do it by:
- selling drinks – both alcoholic and non-alcoholic
- creating an enjoyable environment
- selling food
- providing entertainment.

66 *I work shifts in the bar, covering either early or late evenings. At the start of the shift, I make sure the place is OK for customers to come to – clean tables, floors, ashtrays, all that. When people come in you've got to be friendly and chatty. You try and build up a good rapport with customers – if they feel they've got friends at the bar, they'll come back. So we don't really feel like salespeople at all, even though we're here to sell drinks and food.* 99

DISCUSSION POINT

Can you think of any problems which might arise from people who work in bars and other facilities getting too friendly with the people they're selling to?

Restaurants

There's an enormous number of restaurants in the UK, from roadside caterers and fast food outlets to à la carte restaurants in five-star hotels. All provide the same type of customer service, and involve similar sales situations.

66 *I've been here for three years now, and I've got quite skilled at being a waiter. People eat in the hotel restaurant in the first place because they're staying in the hotel and it's convenient. Our job is to show them that they've done the right thing, so they'll come again in the future. We try to provide a polite and prompt service. I can also offer advice on different menu options and drinks.* 99

ACTIVITY

Talk to someone you know who has worked as a waiter or waitress in a restaurant. Did they feel like they were selling products to customers?

Accommodation

The accommodation sector of the leisure and tourism industry in the UK is wide-ranging and competitive, covering everything from caravan parks and self-catering accommodation to guest houses and hotels. In order to attract and keep customers, many staff who work in the accommodation sector are involved in selling either directly, or through the services they provide.

66 *I'm involved in selling all the time. When I book people into rooms I also sell them services – like asking if they'll be eating in the restaurant. I also do promotional selling by sending out brochures and leaflets to people who have stayed with us in the past. The personal selling is mostly about providing good customer service – I'm helpful and welcoming, and I try to give customers the information and advice they need to choose the right services. The promotional mailings are more like traditional selling – trying to win new customers, and keep old ones. When reservations are up, I find it very satisfying.* **99**

Selling memberships

Some leisure and tourism organisations aim to get a regular income by selling memberships. Examples are:

■ a sports club or gym, giving members the right to use facilities not open to the general public

■ a special interest club, such as a theatre-going group, which organises trips and gives members reductions on events and bookings.

Memberships are usually sold on an annual basis, so customers spend a relatively large amount of money at once. Selling memberships involves both personal selling and promotional activities.

66 *Part of my job is to try and get new members. I'm on the front desk some of the time, where I'm in direct contact with the public. We get people coming in to enquire about joining, so I give them information on memberships, what the club offers, prices, and so on. I ask them if they want to wander round, have a look at the bar and gym – people want to join a club where they can get some exercise and have a good time. Sometimes I organise advertising campaigns and send out mailings to people who were members in the past.* **99**

Selling trips and excursions

People regularly spend time away from their home, or their holiday base, to see visitor attractions. Selling trips and excursions involves the same high standards of customer service as selling a holiday, and many travel agents sell them in addition to holidays. They are also sold directly by the coach operators who provide transport, and by resort representatives whose job is to ensure customers enjoy their holidays as much as possible.

❝ *I'm a resort representative on a small Greek island. My job involves welcoming guests, giving them information on the island, and solving any problems they have during their stay. I also arrange activities and sell pre-arranged excursions. For example, we take visitors shopping to the island's capital city, to some ruins on the other side of the island, and on a boat trip round the bays. People really enjoy these trips, so I'm happy to encourage them to take them – my aim is to ensure holidaymakers have as good a time as possible, so I don't sell them anything they don't enjoy. I see the trips and excursions as just part of the overall customer service we provide.* ❞

Direct selling of leisure and tourism products and services

Direct selling is when an organisation sells its own product direct to the customer, rather than selling through someone else – for example, a tour operator might sell its products directly, or through a travel agent.

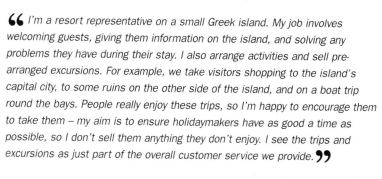

DISCUSSION POINT

Think about the advantages and disadvantages of booking a holiday through a travel agent rather than directly with a tour operator.

Section 3.3.3

Sales techniques

Who would you trust to sell you the right product?

There are close links between customer service and selling in the leisure and tourism industry. Employees who provide good customer service:

■ are polite, efficient and friendly
■ communicate well with customers
■ are able to provide information and products to meet their needs.

These are all qualities which make a good salesperson.

There are also some specific sales techniques which can improve people's ability to sell – and their success:

■ creating positive first impressions
■ using open and closed questions
■ starting a conversation
■ handling complaints
■ telephone sales
■ keeping records.

First impressions

First impressions are very important in selling. Just one look at a leisure and tourism employee can make a customer decide whether or not to buy a product from them.

It's important for leisure and tourism employees working directly with the public to remember that customers are constantly making instant judgements on them – for better or worse. A staff handbook gives this advice to staff about first impressions.

> You're all at the front line. Don't forget that customers judge the quality of our products by your manner and appearance. When you're working on a front desk, always follow these guidelines.
>
> 1. Make sure you are neat and tidy at all times. We issue you with uniforms so you create a smart first impression; wear them properly! If your hair is long, don't let it flop all over your face as customers like to be able to see your eyes.
>
> 2. Look up when a customer walks in. Smile and look interested.
>
> 3. If you're talking to a colleague, break off your conversation so you can greet the customer – don't leave customers waiting while you sit and have a chat.
>
> 4. Make eye contact with the customer, but don't stare.
>
> 5. Think about your body language. Lean forward slightly in your seat to show you're interested. Don't cross your arms – it puts people off. Whatever you do, don't yawn.

A customer describes how he feels when an employee doesn't create a good first impression:

❝ *Last week I went into our local sports centre for some information on five-a-side football sessions and to renew my membership. There were two older people on the front desk, talking about where they were going on holiday. They looked up as I approached, then just looked away again and carried on their conversation. I felt as if I was interrupting them. They weren't wearing uniforms and I wasn't even sure if they worked for the centre. In the end I had to break into their conversation to ask for help.* ❞

Open and closed questions

Open questions can't be answered by a simple 'Yes' or 'No'. They ask for information from a customer, and make a good starting point for a general conversation.

Open questions often start with:

■ What?
■ When?
■ Where?
■ How?
■ Who?

Closed questions can be answered by 'Yes' or 'No'. Because there's a fifty per cent chance of getting the answer 'No', asking a closed question often results in a very short conversation.

Open questions are a more effective way of getting information from a customer and engaging them in conversation. Closed questions are good for checking points of information and confirming details.

Starting a conversation

Conversations with customers in a sales situation are to:

■ find out more about what the customer wants and needs
■ establish a friendly relationship with the customer
■ describe the organisation's products and how they can help the customer.

Understanding open and closed questions is vital when starting a conversation.

> On her first day working in a gift shop at a stately home, an employee was struggling to start conversations with customers. Here's her first attempt:
>
> Employee: 'Can I help you?'
>
> Customer: 'No, thank you.'
>
> By the end of the day, she had realised that she needed to ask open questions to gain the customer's attention and start a conversation:
>
> Employee: 'How can I help you?'
>
> Customer: 'Well, I'm looking for a present for my aunt. . .'

As well as starting the conversation by asking an open question, employees should use body language to communicate well as they talk:

■ nodding to show interest and attention
■ keeping a relaxed posture and expression
■ smiling and looking at the customer.

This is called creating rapport.

ACTIVITY

Which of these are open or closed questions?

■ Can I help you?

■ How can I help you?

■ What products are you interested in?

■ Where did you hear about us?

■ Are you happy with the product you're using at the moment?

Handling complaints

People in the UK are often unwilling to complain. Instead they take their business elsewhere rather than make a fuss. Employees need to know how to respond when a customer does complain. If situations are handled well, it can make all the difference between losing customers for good, or winning back their loyalty.

The best way to handle complaints is to avoid them in the first place. The most common reasons for customer complaints are:

■ they are unhappy with a product or quality of service – customers who are given bad service when buying a product are more likely to buy something which doesn't meet their needs

■ they have been kept waiting – the longer customers have to wait for service and attention, the more likely they are to complain. If waits are likely, organisations can help to relieve frustration by providing entertainment such as TVs or video screens

■ they have been patronised – employees must take care not to adopt a superior attitude, or to assume that customers don't know what they're talking about.

If customers do complain, employees should be patient, considerate and offer practical solutions.

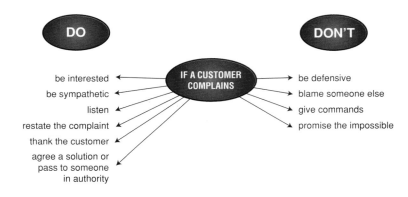

Identifying customer needs for selected situations

Whenever leisure and tourism employees start working in a new situation, the first thing they have to do is identify their customers' needs.

Whether they are working in a restaurant or a rugby club, the basic principles of customer care are always the same – be polite, friendly, efficient, interested and helpful. But meeting specific customer needs means a different thing in every facility. So employees identify these needs in order to provide the service customers expect.

Catering staff at one big theme park change their jobs every three months, so that they gain experience of different aspects of the organisation and don't get bored. A detailed training programme is in place to help staff move from job to job, as their personnel manager explains:

66 *We employ a large number of catering staff. On the theme park site there is scope for gaining experience of many aspects of the catering industry. We have a three-monthly rota for catering jobs, so as well as providing training in the skills needed for each new job, we train staff to get to know the different needs of customers. Someone coming into the restaurant for a three-course meal is expecting a very different product and service from the customer who stops off at a hot dog stall between rides.* 99

This facility put together a chart, identifying customers' needs in different catering outlets on the site. Staff are given this when they change jobs, so they have a clear idea in advance of how to meet customers' needs.

ACTIVITY

Do some research to identify the different customer needs which might have to be met by:

■ a hotel porter

■ a lifeguard at a swimming pool

■ a box office attendant at a cinema or theatre.

If possible, talk to people doing these jobs to find out information on who their customers are, and their needs for:

■ products

■ help

■ advice

■ information

■ safety and security.

Present your findings in a chart like the one shown above.

Food outlet	Customers' needs
The Pizza Parlour	*Main customers:* families, young people Sit-down service, but fast and efficient. Average length of stay is 30 minutes. Customers want basic information on different types of pizzas, extra toppings, drinks available, vegetarian options, etc. Atmosphere is hectic; customers expect speed and excitement. Need knowledge of rides in the area, to direct customers.
The Rider's Rest	*Main customers:* older people Relaxed sit-down service. Average length of stay is one and a half hours. Mainly used by people who want a retreat from the bustle of the park. They're looking for calm, polite service; knowledge of the menu and wine list; and a clean and pleasant environment.
Hot-dog stand	*Main customers:* children, young people Fast food service given from a stand near the meeting point at the entrance. Customers are passing, and grab food on the way – quick service is essential. Only product knowledge needed is of different trimmings. But staff working on the stand get asked for directions all the time, so it's vital that they have a good knowledge of the whole site.

Identifying the information required

One of the main customer needs in leisure and tourism facilities is for information such as:

- details of products and prices
- opening times
- public transport.

Types of information

To give good customer service, staff should identify the different types of information customers are likely to need. Then they can make sure in advance that they will be able to answer questions and give accurate advice.

Before starting her first job as an assistant in a sports centre, a college-leaver put together a chart identifying the main types of information customers might ask her for.

TIMES
- opening times
- times of courses and classes
- times of bar/restaurant opening
- opening times of crèche

PRICES
- of swimming
- badminton court hire
- squash court hire
- using gym
- of classes/courses
- of coaching
- of membership
- concessions for children, OAPs, unemployed

EXPLANATIONS OF PROBLEMS
For example:
- closure because of redecoration/ technical faults
- limits on numbers in pool/classes

(I will add to this as I gain experience of the job)

WHAT INFORMATION MIGHT CUSTOMERS NEED?

UNRELATED INFORMATION
- local transport
- directions to other facilities
- directions to shops

SOLUTIONS TO PROBLEMS
For example:
- lost locker keys
  – call maintenance
- fully-booked courts
  – suggest alternative time
- full swimming pool
  – suggest customers take tickets for next session

(I will add to this as I gain experience of the job)

DETAILS ABOUT PRODUCTS
- squash courts
- badminton courts
- gym facilities
- swimming pool
- catering facilities
- crèche facilities
- courses/classes available
- coaching available
- classes for different age groups

ACTIVITY

Choose a leisure and tourism facility in your area. Visit the facility and make notes on the types of information you think customers might need. Leaflets, brochures and watching staff and customers will give you useful information.

Using your research findings, produce a diagram like the one above, listing the different information customers might need in the six categories shown.

66 *I read the centre's leaflets and brochures to get familiar with products, times and prices. Then I walked around the area so I would be able to help customers needing information on local transport and facilities. On my first day at work I talked to colleagues to check information I wasn't sure about. Gradually, as I gained experience, I updated my lists explaining solutions to problems.* 99

Information required by particular customers

All customers may need the different types of information in the diagram on the previous page. Some customers have their own, more specific information needs. Staff should:

■ be aware of these customers

■ know the types of information which might help them.

A week into his job, the new sports centre assistant realised that he had to be clearer about the special types of information needed by particular customers. During a busy weekday, he listed these different types of customers who visited the centre:

■ individuals

■ groups

■ people from different age groups

■ people from different cultural backgrounds

■ people from different linguistic backgrounds

■ people with specific needs.

He drew another diagram, identifying the particular information needs of each of these types of customer.

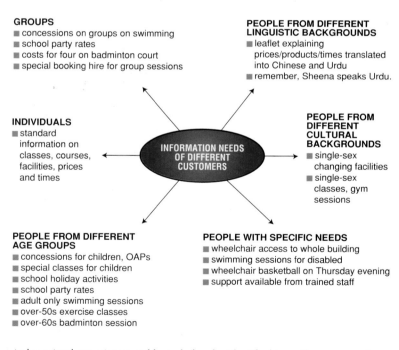

GROUPS
■ concessions on groups on swimming
■ school party rates
■ costs for four on badminton court
■ special booking hire for group sessions

PEOPLE FROM DIFFERENT LINGUISTIC BACKGROUNDS
■ leaflet explaining prices/products/times translated into Chinese and Urdu
■ remember, Sheena speaks Urdu.

INDIVIDUALS
■ standard information on classes, courses, facilities, prices and times

PEOPLE FROM DIFFERENT CULTURAL BACKGROUNDS
■ single-sex changing facilities
■ single-sex classes, gym sessions

INFORMATION NEEDS OF DIFFERENT CUSTOMERS

PEOPLE FROM DIFFERENT AGE GROUPS
■ concessions for children, OAPs
■ special classes for children
■ school holiday activities
■ school party rates
■ adult only swimming sessions
■ over-50s exercise classes
■ over-60s badminton session

PEOPLE WITH SPECIFIC NEEDS
■ wheelchair access to whole building
■ swimming sessions for disabled
■ wheelchair basketball on Thursday evening
■ support available from trained staff

As he gained experience and knowledge, he identified two other groups of customers with particular information needs:

■ satisfied customers

■ dissatisfied customers.

223

66 *Satisfied customers find that the centre provides the activities and classes they want. They think we give good customer care, and are keen to return in the future. They want information on membership fees, regular classes, coaching and new activities starting up in the future. Dissatisfied customers feel the centre doesn't provide the products they wanted. They are unhappy with some aspect of the service we provide. If people complain, or asked for information on who to complain to, there's a standard procedure we have to follow for handling complaints.* **99**

ACTIVITY

Using the same leisure and tourism facility as you looked at in the last activity, identify different types of customer who use the facility and their particular information needs.

Using your research findings, produce a second diagram showing the different types of customers who use the facility and their specific information needs.

THE NATIONAL MARITIME MUSEUM

The National Maritime Museum offers special facilities for different types of customer, including groups, different age groups, non-English speakers, and those with special needs. Staff are ready to provide information for:

■ groups – group rates, special low prices for schools and youth organisations, the special booking unit for groups; special programmes of events aimed at families

■ different age groups – concessions for senior citizens and children; special workshops for children

■ non-English speakers – leaflets available in different languages; tour guides that speak French or German

■ people with special needs – sign language tours for the deaf; touch tours for the visually impaired; wheelchair access and lifts.

Demonstrating customer service

Providing effective customer service depends on:

- caring for customers
- meeting their needs – for help, advice, information, products, and safety and security
- satisfying customers.

Caring for customers

Customers are taken care of whenever they come into contact with staff. The details of customer care differ between facilities. But there are rules which apply to all.

To do all this, staff need training in communication skills, listening skills, telephone skills, body language, and handling complaints.

A busy ten-pin bowling alley prides itself on providing good-quality customer care at all times. One of its staff, who works on the till and issues bowling shoes, explains:

66 *Every day I come into work half an hour before we open, and make sure my area has been left neat and tidy from the night before. When the first customers arrive, I welcome them with a smile and try to meet their needs as well as I can. Lots of young people come bowling – I've come to know many of them quite well, so we have a chat and laugh as I serve them. Over the years I've worked out how to be friendly without spending too long with any one customer – the most annoying thing if you're a customer is to be kept waiting. Occasionally we get a difficult customer, but I just stay calm and polite, let the customer have his say, and get help from the manager if I need to.* 99

Meeting customer needs

At different times, customers may need:

- products
- help
- advice
- information
- safety and security.

All leisure and tourism employees should identify and understand these needs, and know how to meet them as closely as possible.

This conversation took place between a new sports centre assistant and an elderly customer who came into the centre.

Employee: Hello. Let me reach that leaflet down for you. Are you looking for any information in particular?

Customer: Oh, hello, yes. I wonder if you could tell me whether you offer any special classes for older people?

Golden rules of customer care

- Make sure facilities are clean, tidy and create a good impression.
- Make sure staff are neat, smart and welcoming.
- Always pay customers attention – don't leave them waiting.
- Always be friendly, polite and interested in what customers say.
- Provide the information and products customers need efficiently and promptly.
- Don't patronise customers.

ACTIVITY

List the ways in which this employee provides good customer care. Then put them into practice yourself in a role-play with one other person.

Choose one of the following situations:

■ someone serving customers in a bar

■ a hotel receptionist greeting guests

■ a sales assistant in a gift shop helping customers.

Take it in turns to be employee and customer. Show how the employee:

■ prepares to serve customers

■ provides customer care to one customer.

Employee: Yes, we do. On Mondays, Wednesdays and Fridays at 2.30 there are keep fit classes for people over 50, and on Thursday mornings there's a badminton session for over-60s.

Customer: I'm wondering if they'd be suitable for me.

Employee: Well, all the classes are very friendly, and the instructors make sure everyone exercises at their own pace. We don't want anyone to overdo it, or damage their health in any way.

Customer: That sounds like the type of thing I'm looking for. Would you recommend one more than the others?

Employee: Not really, just whichever's most convenient for you. They're all taught by the same instructor, so it doesn't really matter which day you choose to come.

Customer: Good. Can I book myself in for next Wednesday's session?

Employee: Yes, of course. Let me take down your details.

ACTIVITY

From the conversation above, identify how the sports centre and its staff meet customers' needs for:

■ particular products

■ help

■ advice

■ information

■ safety and security.

Then get together with another person and role-play a situation showing how employees can meet customer needs. Examples of situations are:

■ a travel agent booking a holiday for a customer

■ a waiter serving customers in a restaurant

■ a resort representative welcoming and giving information to holidaymakers.

Achieving customer satisfaction

If leisure and tourism employees combine good customer care with meeting customer needs, their customers are likely to be satisfied.

Here the elderly woman explains how she felt after her conversation with the sports centre assistant:

66 *Well, I was really pleased. The young woman who helped me was friendly and polite, and she gave me the information I needed. She booked me in then and there for a fitness class, and I'm sure it's exactly what I was looking for.* 99

Keeping accurate records

It's part of customer service for organisations to keep records of:

■ customers

■ sales

■ cash.

They do this by keeping different documents, produced by hand and on computer.

Customer details

Recording details of their customers helps leisure and tourism organisations to:

■ identify the different types of people who use a facility

■ see what products they are likely to want and need

■ identify new target markets for promotional campaigns

■ build up a database of customers to use for direct mailing.

LONDON TRANSPORT MUSEUM

The London Transport Museum keeps simple records of its customers through its ticket system. When customers buy a ticket, it identifies whether they are:

London Transport Museum

■ adults

■ children under 5

■ children and young people between the ages of 5 and 15

■ students

■ families

■ old age pensioners

■ registered disabled

■ unemployed

■ London Transport staff

■ museum friends/corporate members or staff.

This helps the Museum to see what proportion of its customers fall into each category, and identify new target markets for promotional campaigns.

Organisations like hotels and sports clubs also keep detailed information on their customers – for example, their name, address, telephone and fax number, occupation, particular interests. They use these details to try to attract repeat business by mailing brochures and leaflets promoting particular events.

Personal details kept on computer for future quick checking in and mailshot →

Details for help with target marketing in promotions and mailshot →

For safety and security →

Customer history tells us what sort of break and price bracket these quests fall into – which helps with mailshot and future promotions →

A) For customer convenience. Already on file helping with quick and easy payment.
B) For hotel security against bad debtors
Helpful not to make the same mistake twice →

CUSTOMER DETAILS

NAME: MR B. FARREL
ADDRESS: 2 HONEYWOOD RD
               MUNFORD THETFORD
PHONE: 01589 333125
OCCUPATION: SALES REP
AGE: 33
MARITAL
STATUS: MARRIED
CHILDREN: 3
CAR REG: M859 22Q

HISTORY:

1. 24.12.93 – 1.1.94 'CHRISTMAS BREAK' £760.00 PER ROOM, ALL INCLUSIVE PACKAGE 2 ADULTS, 2 CHILDREN.
2. 1.4.95 ONE NIGHT £110 FOR ROOM, NOT INCLUSIVE

CREDIT CARD NO: 4039 7920 7991 9134

COMMENTS / COMPLAINTS

ACTIVITY

Carry out a survey to find out what type of customers use a leisure and tourism facility. With the manager's permission, collect basic information on the customers who visit:

- their age
- what area they live in
- what they're interested in at the facility.

Use this information to create a set of customer records showing these details.

ACTIVITY

How does a leisure and tourism organisation you know about keep records of sales made? Talk to the staff who work there to find out more information about their recording system and the sales details they collect. Spend some time standing alongside the staff who take the money, and write down details of the sales made. If the canteen uses a computerised till, ask if you can compare the records to see whether you collected the information correctly.

Using your findings, design a manual system for recording sales details. What are the disadvantages of collecting this type of information manually?

Sales details

Many facilities now have computerised tills, which produce till records with copies of the receipts given to customers. These show details of the date, time, amount spent, method of payment and products bought. The computerised system at the London Transport Museum provides a daily, weekly, monthly and annual print-out of sales.

Booking information

Many leisure and tourism organisations keep booking information to make sure they don't double-book facilities or overstretch themselves. For example:

- a hotel keeps booking information so it doesn't double-book rooms
- a sports centre keeps booking information so it doesn't double-book courts
- a restaurant keeps booking information so it knows when people are due to arrive and how busy it will be at particular times of the evening.

Some facilities keep computerised records of bookings, others still prefer to keep booking information manually. Written records can be left by the phone or on the front desk to give employees an instant impression of how busy the facility will be at different times. These can then be updated quickly and easily, either when taking bookings over the phone, or face-to-face.

Date of booking →

Number of people dining; important for table planning and also a good indication of the number of staff required both in the kitchen and in the restaurant.

Name of guest. (It is common for staff and particularly the restaurant manager to acquaint themselves with guests' names within a hotel as a more personal touch of service.)

Time of guests' arrival in restaurant – very important for the restaurant manager and his staff to make sure the table is ready on time.

The room number lets us know whether the guest is a resident or not, and if so, which room to charge the meal to – very important for the reception staff who make up the bills.

Which table the guests will be seated at. Important for waiting staff to know and if the guest is not a resident it's important for reception staff who make up the bills.

This tells us whether the value of a resident guest's meal is included in the room, weekend or package price so the restaurant manager knows not to pass charges through to reception.

KINGS BRIDGE HOTEL
RESTAURANT DIARY
DATE: *15th DECEMBER 1995*

TIME	NAME	NO.	ROOM NO.	TABLE NO.	FIXED MENU
8pm	FOSTER	2	34	5	✓
8pm	KINGSLEY	5	-	12	-
8:30pm	CARLTON	2	21	10	✓
9pm	GREEN	4	13	9	✓
9:15pm	TAYLOR	2	-	2	-
9:30pm	COBBOLD	6	4	11	✓
9:45pm	STERLING	4	24	19	✓
10pm	HARVEY	2	-	7	-
10:15pm	KNIGHT	2	17	15	-
	TOTAL	29			5

Ticket details

It's important for leisure and tourism organisations to keep records of tickets issued because they:

- are proof of payment received
- allow the customer to enter the facility or receive product or service
- help the organisation monitor sales of their range of products or services.

Cash details

Most leisure and tourism organisations take in cash, as well as other forms of payment, for their sales and keep regular records – usually daily or weekly – of monies received. For example, a travel agency will cash up at the end of each day's trading and record the amount taken before banking the money. This record of sales will be measured against budgets and achievement targets to monitor how well the agency is performing.

Evaluating and summarising performance

Sometimes organisations need to stand back and evaluate the customer service their staff provide. Only by judging whether they are succeeding or failing can organisations make changes and improve customer service in the future.

For exactly the same reasons, individual employees should evaluate their own performance in providing customer service, in order to:

■ check if they are achieving customer satisfaction – attracting new customers, and keeping existing ones
■ identify areas for improvement
■ identify any extra training they need.

Dominique, a Leisure and Tourism GNVQ student who had just completed a week's work experience in a bed and breakfast facility, produced this summary evaluating her own performance.

For my recent work experience, I provided customer service to guests in a family-run bed and breakfast with seven rooms. My work involved greeting people and showing them to their rooms, giving them information and advice, serving breakfast, and preparing rooms. My customer service aims at the outset of the work experience were:

• to provide good customer care
• to meet customers' needs for help, advice, information, products, and safety and security
• to achieve customer satisfaction.

This is my evaluation of the work experience.

How did I care for customers?

Providing customer care at all times was an important part of my job. The manager told me to wear a black skirt and white shirt, so I always looked neat and tidy to give a good first impression. I was friendly and cheerful to customers, and the manager told me how nice it was to have a happy face around. I worked hard to make sure rooms were clean and tidy when guests arrived, and put fresh flowers in them so they had a homely feel.

At first I felt a bit nervous when talking to customers, and I think some of them may have realised this. But because I made sure I smiled and was friendly, I think it was OK. The one area I think I could have improved was on the telephone – I felt quite uncomfortable about what to say. If I did this type of work again, I'd ask for some training in telephone skills.

How did I meet customers' needs?

During my week at the bed and breakfast, I met a wide

range of customer needs. I answered telephone enquiries, gave customers information on prices and facilities, and booked rooms. I helped customers carry luggage to their rooms, and showed them how to use the heating and showers. Some guests asked my advice on what to do in the area, and I used my local knowledge to give them ideas. I also gave them copies of the leaflets that are kept in reception. Most often, people wanted information on the bed and breakfast itself - when breakfast was served, where the lounge was, whether we served evening meals, etc. I made sure I knew all of this information in advance, so I didn't have to keep asking the manager.

I didn't really meet customers' needs for safety and security properly. Posters explaining fire evacuation procedures are pinned on the back of each door, but I didn't make a special effort to point them out to people. When I was talking to the manager at the end of my placement, she said this would have been a good idea. Because I didn't do the evening shift, I wasn't responsible for locking up at the end of the day.

Did I make the customers satisfied?

Overall, I think most of the customers were satisfied with the standard of customer care I provided, and felt I had met their needs. This is quite hard to evaluate, but most seemed happy at the end of their stay. Several gave me a tip when I helped them carrying their bags, and when they left one couple asked the manager where I was so they could thank me specially.

I asked the manager how I could evaluate customer satisfaction, and she said that three of the groups I served had already booked return trips. So I think this is a pretty good measure of how satisfied they were with the customer service they received.

Only one person complained to me - someone who had ordered an ensuite room and I showed to a standard room. He was angry when he saw he didn't have his own bathroom, and started complaining to me. I wasn't sure what had happened or what to do, so I went and got the manager to sort it out. I really didn't know what to do when someone complained, and I think this is something I need to work on in the future.

ACTIVITY

Evaluate your own performance in providing customer service in a leisure and tourism facility, looking at:

- how you cared for customers
- how you met their needs
- whether you achieved customer satisfaction.

Summarise your evaluation findings, following the structure shown in this report.

Key questions

1 Why is it important to identify customer needs in different situations?
2 Can you think of three different types of information that most customers at leisure and tourism facilities might need?
3 Can you list five or six different types of customers who might require specific information?
4 Can you list the possible information needs of one of those types of customers?
5 What are the three ways you can demonstrate customer service?
6 What are the six golden rules of customer care?
7 Why should leisure and tourism organisations keep accurate records?
8 What are the four ways in which recording details about customers helps leisure and tourism organisations?
9 Can you think of three reasons for keeping information about bookings?
10 Can you give three reasons why employees should evaluate their own performance?

Assignment

Your tutor will arrange for you to provide customer service in three different situations. Keep a brief note yourself of what happens each time you provide the service. Using a wordprocessor, design a form on which you can note down:

■ basic information about the customer(s) – whether they are individuals or groups, their approximate age, whether they had special needs
■ how you identified each customer's (or group of customers') needs
■ what type of information they required
■ what advice you gave them
■ how you helped them
■ what records you kept – about the customer(s), about sales, bookings or tickets.

Complete a form as soon as you can after you have finished with the customer(s). Your tutor or another assessor will be observing you as you provide the service. The completed forms should help to remind you and your assessor what you actually did.

Use the forms to write an evaluation summarising how you provided service to customers (or you could record your summary on cassette). Describe:

■ who the customers were
■ what needs they had
■ how you met their needs – by providing information, advice or help
■ whether they were satisfied by the service you provided – and how you know.

UNIT **4**

Element 4.1
Planning an event

Element 4.2
Your role in the team

Element 4.3
Evaluating an event

Running an event

ELEMENT **4.1**

Planning an event

This element shows you what needs to be done when you're planning an event. If you've looked at Element 2.2, you will already have an idea of what the planning process involves.

But planning an event is a bigger job than planning a promotional campaign and there are many more things to think about. What resources are needed? What will the team do if there's an emergency or something unexpected happens? How can you make sure people work together well? You'll find answers to questions like these, and many more. And you'll see how a team plan for the event is put together.

❝ We are very democratic in the way we plan things. Before a tour we meet together and agree the weeks that we have free. We start by organising the bigger concerts at the main venues, then we fill in with smaller ones in between. We plan the music together. We sit down at some time during the season and say what we would like to perform. When we are planning individual concerts we pick items from this list. With a new piece we try it first at small venues so we're well practised for the bigger ones. We definitely choose the programme for the audience. Some audiences will be interested in the more outrageous stuff, some prefer more traditional things. ❞

leader of a band

❝ The first thing I do is to plan the performers involved in the event. It's necessary to do this about nine months in advance as we need to book artists before someone else does. Good ones are always in demand. Then there are all the details of organising the equipment and venues. Venues have to be booked at the same time as the events. Then we arrange for the sub-contractors – they provide things like box office, sound, lighting, stage building and chair shifting. I have the first meeting with one individual from each sub-contractor six or nine months before the festival. We all meet at least two or three times before the event, each time discussing more and more of the detail as it becomes available. We build up to a full technical schedule at the same time – who does what and where, what is needed where and when. We usually have about four drafts of the schedule – the final one is ready about one week before the festival. During the event itself I meet with the key technical people every other day. We check the schedule for the next two days and cover any late changes. I find that meeting every day is too much! ❞

organiser of a major festival

❝ I have overall responsibility and organised everything the first year. Now there is a team of six. All have expertise: one's an accountant, one has computer knowledge and skills, the local rowing club provide a couple of their top people to advise and one person from the club organises qualified umpires and marshals. Everyone's roles are quite clearly defined. We have at least three planning meetings and landmarks that have to be reached by certain dates. ❞

organiser of a regatta

The planning process

DECIDING THE OBJECTIVES OF THE EVENT

■ What do we want to achieve?

For more information see page 236

COMING UP WITH AN IDEA FOR THE EVENT

■ What shall we do to achieve our objectives?
■ Who will our customers be?
■ What activities shall we organise?
■ When should the event take place?
■ How will people get there?

For more information see page 240

CALCULATING RESPONSES

■ What do we need in terms of money?
■ time?
■ people?
■ materials?
■ equipment?
■ information?

For more information see page 242

IDENTIFYING CONSTRAINTS

■ What problems might we face?

For more information see page 246

AGREEING CONTINGENCY ACTIONS

■ What will we do if things go wrong?

For more information see page 250

IDENTIFYING ROLES

■ Who should do what?

For more information see page 255

What do a village whist drive, the Olympic Games, a fireworks display and a music festival have in common?

They are all leisure and tourism events – one-off happenings which aim to:
■ give people enjoyment
■ attract customers and sales
■ promote a product, service or organisation.

Events like these don't just happen. Organising them takes money, effort, time and commitment. The diagram on the left shows the different planning stages leisure and tourism organisations go through in order to ensure their event is a success.

All the headings on the diagram will be dealt with in more detail in the next six sections.

ACTIVITY

Part of your work in this unit will be to plan and run an event with other people.

Produce a poster, based on the diagram, to act as a reminder of the planning stages. Use illustrations to make your poster striking. Add any extra information you think might be useful for the event you are planning.

Objectives of an event

Leisure and tourism organisations arrange events for many different reasons – for example, to:

- increase the number of customers using a facility
- increase sales and profitability
- promote a product
- promote a service
- promote the organisation.

They are often closely linked. For example, a new night-club which organises a free evening for people living in the local area will hope to:

- let people in the area know they exist
- get their good will
- attract future customers.

Increasing customer take-up

One of the main reasons for organising one-off events is to increase the number of customers using a facility.

Events like an open day, festival or workshop attract new people to the facility. If they are impressed by what they see and do at the event, they are likely to return to the facility and become regular customers.

The manager of a sports centre explains how staff at the centre organised an event to increase the number of customers using squash and badminton facilities:

66 *Someone suggested at a staff meeting that we should run a free 'Sunday Funday' for people living nearby, to try and make them realise that squash and badminton are fun as well as good exercise. We didn't take any normal bookings for the day and posted leaflets through letterboxes in the area. To encourage people to come who might not bother for just squash and badminton, we also offered free swimming. It was a good day. Two months later we compared court bookings before and after the event – they were up by 25%.* 99

DISCUSSION POINT

What other organisations, apart from sports centres, might organise events in order to increase customer take-up?

Improving sales and profitability

Almost all leisure and tourism events are run to increase sales and improve the profitability of the organisation. It may not be the main objective of the event – for example, the main aim of the sports centre which organised the Sunday Funday was to attract new customers. But by doing this, more squash and badminton courts were booked, and the centre made more money.

UNIT

4

ELEMENT **4.1**

Travel companies work particularly hard to increase their sales. Time-share organisations – which sell customers a share in a holiday home – regularly use events as a way to achieve this. Potential customers are invited to a hotel, where they are given free drinks and a meal. Then representatives from the company show videos and give presentations on the benefits of time-shares. It can be an effective way to increase sales. The event brings together a captive audience, people are sometimes impressed by the VIP treatment and may be more receptive to what the organisation is trying to sell.

Promoting products and services

If leisure and tourism organisations want to promote a particular product or service, they might do it by organising an event. For example:

■ a bar has a Happy Hour during which its new range of cocktails is sold at half price

■ a museum organises an open day for schools, at which it promotes its range of educational services

■ a football club puts on a special family day at the ground, to show off its facilities for families

■ a resort representative organises a drinks party for newly-arrived holidaymakers, to promote trips and tours on offer.

Events are particularly useful for promoting new products and letting more customers know about them. A country house hotel started organising special wedding packages, and decided to organise an event to promote its new products and services for brides. The hotel's marketing manager explains:

❝ *We've always been used as a venue for wedding receptions. Recently we branched out into special wedding packages. As before we provide reception, catering and rooms for the guests. We also help the family to organise the cake, flowers, place-names, photography and video, and the evening's entertainment. Last month we put on a special 'wedding fayre', with a fashion show, beauty advisers, hairdressers, and so on. Over two hundred people came on the day. Our staff were on hand to talk to visitors about the wedding package, hand out leaflets, and give regular presentations. The result – seven firm bookings, plus more enquiries.* ❞

As in this case, leisure and tourism organisations often use events to promote products and services when they have something new to offer.

Promoting the organisation

Events can be a good way to promote the whole organisation, as well as specific products. Leisure and tourism organisations sometimes want to raise their profile in the community. Arranging events can help to get their name better known. For example:

■ a new Saturday craft fair wanted to make shoppers aware of its existence, so it hired a local theatre group to run a street theatre show in the town centre, with free performances for families

■ a pub manager, worried that a theme bar opening nearby might take away trade, organised a celebrity cricket match and barbecue for families to promote its image as a family pub.

Charity events, or events helping the local community, can be a particularly effective way for leisure and tourism organisations to raise their profile and improve their image in the community. For example, some facilities organise a free Christmas party for local children, raising their profile and winning supporters in the process.

THE GNVQ SPECIAL EVENTS TEAM

A team of students at a college set up an events committee to organise social events for other students. It went well at first, but after a while people stopped coming to the events. The committee members decided to grab their attention by running an extra-special event near the start of term, to attract new students. One of them explains:

66 *We all know there seems to be much less interest. The new lot of students don't seem to have picked up on the events, and always go into the town centre instead. We've tried advertising, but people don't pay much attention to posters around college. We've come to the conclusion that the only way to get people to notice us is to make a big splash – to run an event that grabs people's imaginations.* 99

Together, the committee talked through the main objectives of the campaign. They decided that low attendance was caused because not enough students knew about the events programme. After a long discussion, they agreed that the main objectives of the special event were to:

■ promote the programme for the term

■ increase awareness among other students in the college, especially those in their first year

■ improve attendance, sales and profitability.

ACTIVITY

Think about the event you and your team are planning in this unit. Look through the different objectives explained in this section, then:

■ agree what you are trying to achieve

■ rank the objectives in order of importance

■ write them down so you can refer to them as you plan, put into practice, and then evaluate the event.

Selecting an event

The first thing an event planning team does is to decide its objectives. Then it has to come up with an idea for the event itself.

Leisure and tourism organisations arrange an enormous variety of different events – for example:

- sports days
- competitions
- carnivals
- exhibitions
- parties
- fairs and fêtes
- open days
- workshops

. . . and many, many more.

The planning team has the difficult task of deciding what type of event would be the best way to achieve the agreed objectives.

CASE STUDY

The manager of one facility realised that she needed to take action when a competitor opened up nearby. She decided that the best way to remind people of the special service offered by her organisation was to run a one-off event. She explains how she went about planning the event with her team of staff:

❝ As soon as I knew that we faced serious competition, I realised that we had to do something. I found out – don't ask me how! – that our competitors were going to run an advertising campaign. So I decided we should organise a one-off event just before their campaign was due to start. I got the staff together and explained to them that I wanted us to organise an event as a team. They were enthusiastic and agreed to put in extra time. We agreed that the main objective of the event was to promote our organisation and the services we offer, emphasising the personal touch which makes it stand out from the competition. ❞

The team came up with a long list of ideas:

- a beach party night
- a themed evening's entertainment, with music and food from three continents
- a 1970s day, with people dressed in 1970s clothes, 1970s music, food and drink on sale at 1970s prices
- a cheese and wine party
- a raffle with prizes
- a video presentation
- a treasure hunt

. . . and plenty of others.

CHEESE & WINE PARTY

AT THE PRIORY

Friday 15th December
8.00pm

In the end, the team agreed to go for a themed evening with a number of prizes to be won in a free raffle. They advertised the event in local papers and by leafleting in town. All staff dressed up in costumes, special food and drink was on offer, and everyone who came through the door got a free raffle ticket. And the result?

66 *We all think the event was a success. We got to know more people in the community, who now see us as a friendly, local organisation. Over a hundred people came to the evening – we've had some of them in since. A reporter came from the local paper, so we got a picture and feature on the front page.* 99

ACTIVITY

In your own planning team, run a 'brainstorming' session to come up with your own list of events. What event do you think has the best chance of achieving your objectives?

Calculating resources

Finding out what resources are needed for an event is the next stage in the planning process. The idea has to be realistic – if the planning team finds out that it doesn't have enough resources, it has to rethink.

So what types of resources are needed for leisure and tourism events?

Figure 16 Resources needed for leisure and tourism

Finance

However small or large the event, some money will be needed to finance it. The cost of an event varies with its size:

■ a village fête will need a small amount of money for refreshments, prizes, programmes, and any extra equipment needed

■ staging the Olympic Games involves the investment of millions of pounds, often through sponsorship.

Whatever the scale of the event, the planning team should work out:

■ how much money is needed for it

■ where the money will come from.

One member of a college group which staged a barbecue for children at a local special school explains how they arranged funding:

❝ *We worked out our costs carefully in advance. All the cooking would be done by volunteers, but we had to supply food, drinks, and entertainment – a bouncy castle and a clown. When we added up these costs, we realised our original budget wasn't going to be enough. So we approached local companies for funding – one of the best offers was from a local restaurant, which supplied 100 burgers and 50 hot-dog sausages free of charge. With support like this, we were able to go ahead with the event without spending more than we'd budgeted for.* **❞**

DISCUSSION POINT

What different types of financial support might leisure and tourism organisations be able to get for events?

Time

When planning an event, never underestimate the amount of time needed to do it well. If you're rushed, planning stages are missed and mistakes are more likely to happen. Many teams establish a timetable at an early stage, so that they:

- have enough time for every planning stage
- set a realistic date for the event.

One planning team in a school started by producing a rough timetable for its event.

Date	What to do
29 April–29 May	Plan timetable of events, and advertise in school to get volunteers. Produce posters, send notices round classrooms and announcements in assembly. Book loudspeaker equipment hire from local leisure centre. Make sure other equipment will be available on the day, hire anything needed. Prepare the programme.
22 May–29 May	Organise helpers for different events on the actual day. Organise staff and students to do catering, programme sales etc.
29 May–22 June	Agree final programme for day.
13 June	Send programmes to be printed.
27 June	Collect printed programmes. Buy refreshments.
29 June	Events start at 2.00 p.m. People involved in setting up equipment/catering need to be available from 12.00 p.m., and then until 6.00 p.m. to clear up at the end of the day.

Although the actual date of the event was fixed, the team didn't stick rigidly to other dates on the timetable. But it showed them that they needed two months to organise the event, and gave them a good idea of what needed to be done by when.

People

The most important resource of all. Planning teams should check that:

- enough people are available to plan and stage the event
- they have the right skills – specialist skills (such as sports coaching, childcare, catering, first aid), organisational skills and teamwork skills.
- they have enough time.

Here's what the manager of a pub found out when he tried to organise a charity football match with the wrong people:

66 *We planned a football match on the green outside the pub to make money for charity. We decided to use just the pub staff to organise and run the event – that was the big mistake. One of the bar staff was in charge of organising equipment but organisation never was her strong point, and we ended up*

hunting round for a ball and goalposts the day before. On the day, my chef was referee, but it turned out his knowledge of the rules was a bit loose. Because he was refereeing, I ended up doing the barbecue. The result was chaos on the pitch, and a lot of charred burgers and sausages. **99**

Materials and equipment

Some leisure and tourism events need materials and equipment to run smoothly. For example:

- a local tennis tournament will need courts in good condition, balls, nets, umpires' chairs, seating for spectators, food and drinks, tickets, a cash box for takings, posters advertising the event, programmes showing matches for the day, and so on.
- a children's Christmas party in a restaurant will need food, drinks, menus, party hats, balloons, Christmas decorations, prizes for games, and so on.

Planning teams should list the materials and equipment they need for the event at an early stage. This gives them time to:

- find and book items
- borrow or hire equipment
- get materials produced and printed – it can take several weeks to organise the design and printing of programmes and leaflets.

Information

Sometimes organisations plan events which aren't directly related to their specialist area – for example:

- a hotel organises a bridal fayre
- a sports club organises a Christmas disco for members
- a pub organises a charity football match.

People on the planning team may not have all the knowledge they need to run the event. They will have to get the information they need from other sources.

DISCUSSION POINT

Where would you be able to get the information needed to run the three events listed above?

NETBALL 2000

A local leisure centre wanted to increase the number of teenage girls who used the facility. They decided to run a one-day event called Netball 2000, to encourage girls to use the courts more regularly.

With objectives and event already decided, the planning group concentrated on what they would need to put the event into action. Here's a summary of a team meeting half-way through the planning stages:

Resource	What we need
Finance	Money for refreshments, prizes, paying a tournament referee, new whistles and netballs, printing posters etc. Total cost of this is estimated at £400. We have already approached a local sportswear company about providing sponsorship, and it's interested.
Time	We've drawn up an action plan, and have decided we need three months to organise the event properly. The date of the event has been set as 27 March.
People	Centre staff have the skills we need, but most of them will be busy in other parts of the centre on the day. Sports staff from a local school have agreed to umpire some of the matches, and we will book a tournament umpire from the county netball association. One of the receptionists has agreed to be official timer, record results, and register teams. The bar staff will carry out catering.
Materials/equipment	Netball equipment needed – 20 netballs, eight sets of bibs (four matches will be played at a time), four whistles, netball posts, five stopwatches, board for recording results.
	Catering equipment needed – crockery and cutlery for up to 150 people, tea urn, tea, milk, sugar, orange squash, biscuits, cake, crisps, oranges.
	Posters advertising the tournament, and entry forms.
	Prizes for winning teams.
Information	The county netball association will give us information on running a netball tournament, and the tournament umpire will advise us on the day.

Identifying constraints

UNIT

4

ELEMENT **4.1**

A **constraint** puts limits on what you can do.

Plans for an event have to be realistic. It's good to be ambitious, as long as you don't end up with plans that are impossible to put into practice. That's why leisure and tourism organisations planning an event try to think in advance of any constraints which might limit what they can do.

Staff availability and skills

It's difficult and risky to run an event without the right people.

Staff availability

- Will staff have enough time to plan their roles in the event carefully?
- Will they have time to take part in the event on the day?
- If their work on the event is in addition to their normal responsibilities, are staff happy to put in the extra time?
- Or will they end up rushing things and making mistakes?

Staff skills

- Do staff have the planning skills needed to organise the event?
- Do they have the specialist skills needed to put the event into practice?
- If staff don't have the skills, can they be trained in time?
- Or will the organisation need to enlist the help of outside experts?
- Can it afford to do this?

DISCUSSION POINT

A facility is organising a summer party, including a barbecue, a crèche for children and a disco. Staff have been freed from other duties for the evening, so that they can take part in the event.

- What skills would the staff need in order to ensure the success of the event?
- What might be the results if they went ahead without the necessary skills?

Opening times

The opening hours of a facility where an event is to be staged can limit the timing for the event. Many facilities – such as pubs, restaurants and sports centres – have fixed hours of opening which they may not be able to vary because of:

- staffing
- the needs of their usual customers
- legal reasons.

Others may be able to extend normal opening hours for a one-off event.

Facility capacity is the maximum number of people a facility can hold.

Facility capacity

Facilities have a maximum capacity determined by:

■ the size of the venue and how many people they can comfortably hold

■ fire regulations

■ regulations on Safe Practice for the Management of Outdoor Events, produced by the Health and Safety Executive.

At an early stage in the planning process, teams need to do one of these two things:

■ choose where to hold the event, find out the facility capacity, and fix the number of people who can attend

■ decide how many people they want to attend, and find a facility which has a large enough capacity.

Customer transport times

Timing can be affected by how customers travel to and from the event. If people are likely to use public transport, the planning team needs to make sure that the timing of the event is convenient.

ACTIVITY

Research possible venues in your area for an 18th birthday party with:

■ 150 guests

■ disco

■ buffet food

■ a bar.

Check the facility capacities to make sure they can hold enough people and provide these services. Also work out the costs.

CAMBRIDGE - NEWMARKET - BURY ST EDMUNDS								X11

Mondays to Saturdays (Except Bank Holidays)

SERVICE X11 LIMITED STOP SERVICE — STOPS AT THE FOLLOWING ADDITIONAL STOPS: Newmarket Rd./ Napier St., Newmarket Rd./ Ivett & Reeds, Newmarket Rd./ Airport, Bottisham Beechwood Ave., Stetchworth Toll, Newmarket High St., Kentford Landwades.

	S						M-F	S
Cambridge Drummer Street (Bay 11)	0800	0845	1000	1200	1400	1600	1750	1805
Bottisham Bell	0816	0901	1016	1216	1416	1616	1806	1821
Newmarket Rookery	0830	0915	1030	1230	1430	1630	1820	1835
Newmarket Rookery	0832	0917	1032	1232	1432	1632		
Kentford Cock	0839	0924	1039	1239	1439	1639		
Bury St Edmunds St Andrew's St North	0855	0940	1055	1255	1455	1655		

CODES:
M-F = Mondays to Fridays Only.
S = Saturdays Only.
All X11 journeys serve both Newmarket Rookery and the High Street.
For additional journeys between Newmarket and Cambridge via Burwell, Reach and the Swaffhams see service 111 timetable.

Equipment

Some events need a large amount of equipment. Planning teams should find out:

■ what they can use from their own organisation's stock of equipment
■ what they can borrow or hire from the venue where the event is to be held
■ what specialist equipment they need to get from other facilities and organisations.

Finding, borrowing and hiring equipment needs to happen in advance, so that teams can make other arrangements if they can't get what they need. They should also make sure someone is on hand with the skills to use the equipment – organisers mustn't just assume that equipment is easy to use.

Health, safety and security

Every event needs to consider the health, safety and security of the staff running the event, and the customers attending it. By law, people who organise an event have a 'duty of care' – which means a responsibility to look after – the health, safety and security of everyone involved.

Health, safety and security tips

■ Find out if there are any particular health and safety risks involved, such as sports events, fireworks, children's play areas.
■ Make any special security arrangements needed.
■ If food and drinks are being served, observe food hygiene regulations.
■ Make sure everyone knows fire precautions and evacuation procedures.
■ Remind staff and visitors about the safe use of equipment.
■ Arrange for medical advice and back up to be on hand – are trained staff needed? do you have the support of voluntary organisations such as St John's Ambulance?

NETBALL 2000

Once they had worked out what resources they needed, the planning team for Netball 2000 thought about the constraints which were likely to affect their event. Here's what one of them said:

66 *The first thing we considered was who would staff the event and what skills they have. Some staff at the leisure centre were qualified umpires, but there weren't enough for the tournament. So we asked for volunteers from a local school and arranged with the county netball association to send a tournament umpire.*

There wasn't a problem with opening times, as we decided to hold the tournament on a Saturday. But we had to restrict the number of teams in each age group because there were only four courts. The seating capacity was 100, so we printed 100 tickets for spectators. Buses run past the centre regularly on Saturdays, so public transport was fine. We borrowed enough stopwatches from staff and the school.

St John's Ambulance agreed to provide medical back-up at the event, and some facility staff were on hand as trained first-aiders. Lockers were available to keep possessions secure, and security staff on the door made sure that only ticket-holders were allowed in. 99

ACTIVITY

When your planning team has listed the different resources you need for your event, think about any constraints which might affect it. Look at:

■ the availability and skills of people to plan and run the event

■ opening times of the facility where your event is to be held

■ capacity of the facility

■ public transport times

■ the availability of equipment, and people to use it

■ health, safety and security concerns and regulations.

Section 4.1.6

Contingency actions

Contingency actions are there in case something happens which wasn't planned, or something goes wrong – emergencies or unplanned disruptions.

Part of running a leisure and tourism event is dealing with any problems that occur. It's important but unpredictable. When they're planning the event, teams need to think in advance about:

- emergencies which might occur – fire, accidents to customers, participants or staff
- disruptions – caused by the weather, or by a change in the number of participants.

Once they have foreseen possible problems, the team needs to decide how it will deal with them. This is called agreeing contingency actions.

Fire precautions

These basic guidelines should be followed by all facilities planning an event:

- practise a fire drill, so all staff know how to evacuate the building in case of fire
- restrict the number of people allowed in the venue – never allow more people in than the number allowed by law or the fire officer
- make sure fire escapes are clearly signposted and not obstructed
- have people on hand who are trained in fire safety.

Fire

Fire is a serious risk at leisure and tourism events. Any event which brings together a large number of people into a confined space carries a risk of fire. It's the responsibility of the organisers to make sure that precautions and systems are in place in case a fire does break out.

The Fire Precautions Act of 1971 requires some leisure and tourism facilities to get a fire certificate from the local fire authority before they can stage events. To be sure of safety, the planning team should contact its local fire officer for more information on fire regulations and safety.

ACTIVITY
Contact your local fire officer, and:

- arrange for someone to talk to the planning group about fire safety at events
- check the fire and safety regulations at your event.

Make sure everyone in the group knows about the fire precautions for your event.

Accidents

Event organisers are responsible for:

■ making sure the facility is safe
■ providing first aid if accidents occur to customers, staff or participants in the
event.

Planning teams need to think in advance about the type of accidents that
might happen, and make sure procedures and expertise are on hand to deal
with them. They may have to:

■ arrange training for staff in first aid
■ organise for a voluntary first-aid organisation, such as St John's Ambulance
or the Red Cross, to be on hand in case of accidents
■ notify the emergency services beforehand, in the case of a large event.

Caused by weather

How many times have you been to an event disrupted by the weather? Mid-
summer garden parties washed out by a downpour, football matches
abandoned because of frost. It's all part of living in Britain – but a great
inconvenience if you're organising an event.

Planning teams organising an outdoor event in the UK always need to be
aware of the possibility of disruption because of the weather. They should
think of:

■ what to do if the weather is bad, and people stay away
■ whether the event could be moved inside in the case of rain or high winds
■ under what conditions to postpone or cancel the event.

Numbers of participants

As part of the planning process, teams estimate the number of people they
expect to participate in their event. They should also think what to do if more
people come than expected – or fewer.

A sports centre organising a fun run in aid of its local hospital explained how its plans were disrupted:

66 *People were asked just to turn up on the day – there was no pre-registration or anything. We expected anything between 300 and 500 people, so we had three separate starting times. We even talked about how we would cope if more than that number arrived. After a week of fine weather, we woke up on the day to pouring rain. People gradually arrived, but by the start time it was clear we'd wildly overestimated the number. We had 50 participants, so we quickly merged the three runs into one. There was a mountain of sandwiches left at the end. We should definitely have planned more carefully for any number of people turning up.* 99

NETBALL 2000

The planning team made detailed plans in case of emergencies and disruptions. Here are the meeting notes recording the points they considered and discussed.

Possible emergencies and disruptions

1 Fire

The centre has its own emergency plans for fire which we have to keep to. Jo and Lorna are going down there before the event to take part in a fire drill and check where emergency exits are. Lorna wrote to the local fire officer, who sent some information on fire safety at events.

2 Accidents

The centre will provide trained first aiders to be on hand during the netball tournament. We're also arranging for St John's Ambulance to be there.

3 Weather

If it's raining, the tournament can be held on the inside courts (the centre has kept one hall free in case). But because there would be fewer courts, we'd have to reduce the length of matches. We've worked out a proper timetable for if the event takes place either outdoors or indoors.

4 Number of participants

We'll know how many participants to expect in advance because they all need to fill in an entry form to enter (by 4 March). If teams don't turn up on the day, we can easily reduce the number of matches each team has to play. We won't have a problem with more teams turning up than we expect as teams have to enter in advance. There's a limited number of spectator tickets available on the day, as most were sold in advance through schools and we have a limited seating capacity.

Roles for team members

Almost all leisure and tourism events are planned by more than one person. It's a team effort and good teamwork can make all the difference to the success of the event.

These two diagrams show:
- what makes a good team
- the different roles that individuals can play in the team.

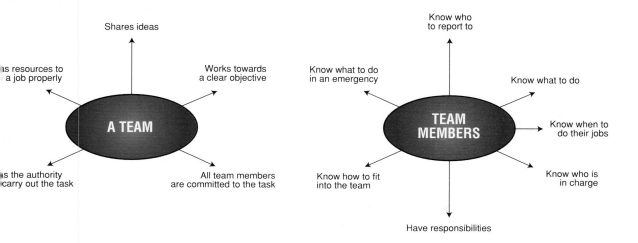

Individuals in the team have to know:
- what they are responsible for – their functions
- who is in charge
- how their role relates to those of other people – the interrelationship with others in the team.

Functions

Most teams have a leader who is responsible for:
- getting the team to work well together
- overseeing progress towards achieving the event's objectives.

A team leader describes her role:

66 *I'm well organised myself, and I'm also good at organising other people. That's why I was chosen as a team leader. I'd say that the most important thing is to be an effective communicator – there's a lot of communication with people in the team and with outside organisations. It helps to be enthusiastic yourself, and you have to pass on your enthusiasm to the rest of the team. It's hard work too.* **99**

253

Team roles

- secretary – takes notes of meetings, keeps a record of decisions, writes letters etc.
- treasurer – looks after the finances
- equipment manager – makes sure equipment and materials are available and working for the event
- promotion manager – markets the event to potential participants
- catering manager – organises the food and drink

ACTIVITY

In your planning team, agree:

- the different roles needed
- who should do what
- an organisational chart for the team.

If the team is small, your chart will probably be quite simple. But it still provides a useful overview of people's roles.

Other team members take on different roles. Some are listed on the left.

When agreeing roles, teams should think about people's particular skills, experience and personality. Shy, artistic people might not make good equipment managers, who have to deal with a lot of outside organisations and be firm about requirements. But they might use their creative skills to produce brilliant promotional material.

ACTIVITY

Ask each person in your planning team to:

- list their skills and experience
- think of a role they would like to have in the team.

Then decide who should do what in your team.

Interrelationship with others

Everyone in a team has to know their own responsibilities. They should also try to understand how their responsibilities relate to other people's roles. For example:

- a catering manager will need to turn to the treasurer for advice on the budget for food and drink
- a promotional manager will need to ask the team leader for information on the overall timing of the event.

Many planning teams find it useful to draw a chart showing:

- the structure of the team
- lines of authority
- who different people report to.

It's particularly useful to have a chart if the team is large.

NETBALL 2000

A team of twelve people worked on planning and organising Netball 2000. At an early planning meeting, they decided that jobs should be divided between these roles:

- team leader
- treasurer
- secretary
- catering manager, and two assistants
- promotion manager, and one assistant
- equipment manager, and one assistant
- tournament manager
- health and safety manager.

| TREASURER | **TEAM LEADER** | SECRETARY |
| Graham Mullard | Jo Muhmud | Tim Noel |

CATERING MANAGER	PROMOTION MANAGER	EQUIPMENT MANAGER	TOURNAMENT MANAGER	HEALTH & SAFETY MANAGER
Chloe Robinson	Richard Smith	Petra Shilling	Ruth Karniol	Lorna Roberts
CATERING ASSISTANTS	PROMOTION ASSISTANT	EQUIPMENT ASSISTANT		
June Patel Chris Jones	Maria Borrowdale	Vince Kermode		

They talked about who should take on what job, bearing in mind their skills, experience, personal qualities and preferences. The result was this organisational chart.

Producing a team plan

When the team organising a leisure and tourism event has worked through all the planning stages, it's ready to produce a team plan. This summarises all the decisions the team has made about:

- the objectives of the event
- what the event will be
- what resources are needed
- constraints which might affect the event
- contingency actions to take in case of emergencies or disruptions
- the role of each team member.

A team plan is useful as a reminder of the original aims of the event and how the team agreed to put it into practice.

NETBALL 2000

After a series of planning meetings, the Netball 2000 team put together a plan summarising what they intended to do. The report was agreed by all the team members, wordprocessed and distributed to all members by the group's secretary, Tim Noel.

Team plan – Netball 2000

Objectives of the event

❝ We decided that the main objective of the event is to increase the number of teenage girls using facilities at the centre (increase customer take-up).

In doing this, the centre also wants to raise its profile among young people, and increase sales by attracting new customers.

The actual event

The actual event, Netball 2000, will be a netball tournament for 14- to 18-year-olds. As well as participants, up to 100 spectators are expected, including parents, friends, and supporters from local schools. The tournament will be held on four outdoor courts at the leisure centre unless it is raining, in which case we will move inside to three indoor courts. Matches will be played in two age groups, 14 to 16 and 16 to 18. The two teams with the most points in each age group will then compete in the final.

The tournament will be held on Saturday 27 March at the leisure centre. The first matches will begin at 2 p.m., and the finishing time for the tournament will be 5 p.m. Several schools have already told us that they will transport teams to the tournament on school minibuses. Other people will either travel to the event by car (there is plenty of parking at the centre) or by bus (buses stop regularly outside the centre).

Resources

Graham (treasurer) has estimated we need £400 to cover the cost of new netballs, whistles, refreshments, prizes and paying a tournament referee. We may be able to save some money by borrowing rather than buying a lot of this equipment. A local sports company is interested in providing some sponsorship.

We have decided we need three months to organise the event. PE staff from a local school have agreed to umpire some of the matches, and to train members of our team as umpires. We will book a tournament umpire from the county netball association. Bar staff will prepare refreshments. One of the reception staff will be official timer at the tournament and record results.

We need the following equipment:

- *20 netballs (8 new match balls; 12 practice balls borrowed from school)*
- *netball pumps*
- *eight sets of bibs (borrowed from school, if possible)*
- *four whistles (new)*
- *netball posts (already in centre)*
- *five stopwatches (already in centre)*
- *blackboard for recording results (already from centre)*
- *crockery and cutlery (already in centre)*
- *tea urn, tea, milk, sugar, orange squash, biscuits, cake, crisps, oranges*
- *posters advertising the tournament, and entry forms*
- *prizes for winning teams.*

The county netball association is giving us information on areas of running a tournament we're not sure about.

Constraints

The centre has trained umpires, but some staff have to work in other parts of the centre on the day so won't be available. PE teachers from the school are training members of our team to umpire. We've had to restrict the number of teams in each age group because there are only four courts, and can only have 100 spectators because of seating capacity. There may be some problems borrowing equipment (we've already found out the centre doesn't have enough stopwatches). But we should be able to borrow things from the school instead.

Contingencies

The main contingency is if the weather is bad. If it's raining, we won't be able to play on the outdoor courts, and will have to hold the tournament inside instead. As there are only three courts inside, we're going to have to reduce the length of matches so we can still finish the tournament by 5 p.m. We've worked out exact timings for this, and don't think it will be too much of a problem.

We will follow the centre's fire precautions in case there's a fire, and have been in touch with the local fire officer to inform him of the event. We know where the fire exits are if the event's held indoors, and Lorna (health and safety) has been to a fire drill so knows evacuation procedures. St John's Ambulance will be at the tournament in case of accidents, and there will also be trained first aiders from the centre. If we get less people than we expect on the day, we can easily reorganise the programme so teams still get a good range of matches.

Team roles

The team roles have been allocated as follows:

- *team leader – Jo Mahmud*
- *treasurer – Graham Mullard*
- *secretary – Tim Noel*
- *catering manager – Chloe Robinson*
- *catering assistants – June Patel, Chris Jones*
- *promotion manager – Richard Smith*
- *promotion assistant – Maria Borrowdale*
- *equipment manager – Peta Shilling*
- *equipment assistant – Vince Kermode*
- *tournament manager – Ruth Karniol*
- *health and safety manager – Lorna Roberts.*

Will it work?

In terms of the resources available, yes. We are going to get sponsorship from a local company, so money isn't a problem. We've allowed three months to organise the event, which is plenty of time. We've checked that we're going to be able to borrow or buy all the materials and equipment needed within budget and in the timescale. And we've found out that we can get all the information we need from the netball association.

In terms of existing constraints, yes. As we've already said, there aren't many constraints on the event. Those there are, concerning staffing, numbers and equipment, we've managed to solve. **99**

ACTIVITY

Following the same structure used by the team planning Netball 2000, produce a team plan for the event your team has planned. Make sure everyone in the team has their own copy to refer back to as they carry out the event.

Key questions

1 Can you think of five objectives an event might have?
2 Can you draw up a list of six or seven ideas for an event?
3 What are the six key resources needed for any event?
4 Why is it important to identify any constraints?
5 What should you remember about health, safety and security?
6 What are the two main reasons that make planning contingency action necessary?
7 What are the three things individuals in a team have to know about their roles?
8 Why can it be helpful to draw a chart of who's doing what in a team?
9 What six decisions should be summarised in a team plan?

Assignment

The activities in this section ask you to go through the stages of planning an event with others in your team. Before you start the activities, get together as a team and decide how you are going to keep a record of your planning.

You could:

■ arrange to record the meetings on cassette, or video recorder
■ keep notes of all meetings
■ create a display of anything you produce as part of the planning process – things like organisational charts, posters and other publicity
■ ask someone from outside the team, such as your tutor, to sit in the meetings and observe what happens – they should make notes and sign them afterwards.

As you go through the planning process, remember to check that you have kept a record in one of these ways (or any other ways you can think of). At the end, get all your records together and make a list saying:

■ what each record shows
■ how you contributed to the planning session it records.

Keep the list as evidence for your portfolio.

" We have checklists which we give to people running activities to ensure that they are meeting health and safety requirements. We also ensure that everyone is aware of the fire exits in a venue – and in fact we only use venues that have already been cleared. "

entertainments officer in a local authority

" We each take a role in the management of the band during tours. One of us is the business manager, another does the accounts and any artwork needed – posters for example. Someone else does most of the administration and as the leader I do the accounts and have the public relations role. I write all the letters – I write a first draft and then circulate it to all the other members of the band. Wherever we are in the tour we operate as a team – it's the only way to get things done. "

leader of a band

Your role in the team

In this element you will see how team members carry out their roles during the event itself. Some things can't be predicted and people may need to react fast and change roles in the middle of an event. You'll also see how important it is to follow guidelines for health, safety and security. The idea of keeping a log to record what happens to you during the event is introduced. You should think about what sort of record you will keep during the event you are running with other members of your team.

259

Contributing to a team event

Everyone in a team wants their event to succeed. So they should all contribute to the event according to their:

■ function – what they are responsible for doing

■ interrelationship with others – who they work with, and how they work together.

Functions

Early in the planning stage, a role is agreed for each team member, so that they each know their particular responsibilities and tasks. For example:

■ the treasurer keeps a careful watch on money, making sure the event doesn't go over budget and cause financial problems to the organisation

■ the equipment manager sees that all the equipment needed is available and ready for use on the day

■ the promotion manager markets the event so enough people turn up on the day.

It is up to individuals to make sure they do their jobs properly. Whoever's the team leader also:

■ oversees the teamwork

■ encourages members to pull their weight

■ motivates them to play an active role.

The team leader responsible for coordinating a museum open day explains how an event can fall apart if people don't contribute as expected:

> 66 *I was responsible for a team of six people organising workshops. We held regular planning meetings and everything seemed to be going smoothly. Two days before the event, one of the workshop organisers came to me and said he hadn't got round to preparing properly. He was in a panic because he realised he hadn't left enough time. Fortunately, by calling everyone else away from their normal jobs and putting in long hours, we managed to salvage the situation. As team leader, I learnt an important lesson about keeping watch over team progress.* 99

DISCUSSION POINT

Ask yourselves these two questions at your next planning team meeting.

■ What might happen if team members don't contribute as agreed?

■ How are you going to make sure that this doesn't happen?

Interrelationship with others

Working together means following the agreed:

■ team structure

■ lines of authority – who is responsible for different areas of work

■ reporting structures – who each team member should inform of what they're doing.

If individuals act independently without consulting other team members and reporting to those in charge, confusion and mistakes can occur. The team planning Netball 2000 soon discovered the importance of cooperating as a whole team. Team leader, Jo Mahmud, describes some of the early teamwork problems experienced by the team:

66 *We agreed roles at the start, but obviously some people were happier about what they ended up doing than others. It was clear who was in charge, but one or two of the team didn't seem to accept it. Vince, the equipment assistant, went and bought four new whistles without telling his manager and then asked the treasurer for the money. The treasurer had already given money for whistles to Peta, the equipment manager. Luckily, Peta was able to take the whistles she'd bought back to the shop and get a refund. Maria, the promotion assistant, didn't get on at all with her manager, and refused to accept that she had to report to him. In the end, we held a meeting to discuss problems people had with their roles, which helped to clear the air. Richard said he could handle promotions on his own, so Maria moved over to help the tournament manager.* 99

ACTIVITY

When you know your role in your event planning team, write down:

■ exactly what your function is

■ your place in the team structure

■ who is in charge of what you do

■ who you should report to, so that everyone knows what is happening.

Look back at your notes as you prepare for and run the event to make sure that you are doing your job properly and that the rest of the team is well informed about what you are doing.

Using resources effectively

All leisure and tourism events work within some limits in terms of resources.

Resource limits

- the amount of money available to spend – your budget
- the amount of time available to plan, prepare for and stage an event
- the number of people available to help, and the skills they have
- the materials and equipment available for use
- the information on hand to help

To make their event a success, teams make the most of the resources they have.

Finance

Every team should have someone – a treasurer – to look after the money side of things and make sure financial resources are used properly.

Using finance effectively

- Monitor the budget for the event – the budget is the amount you have to spend on the event.
- Work with team members to calculate what resources are needed.
- Estimate how much of the budget should be spent on different aspects of the event.
- Make sure team members know how much they can spend on items.
- Pay bills, or give money to team members to buy items.
- Keep records of all money spent, and income generated by the event.
- Balance the books at the end of the event.

ACTIVITY

In your planning team, work out:

- what you will need to buy for the event
- how much these things cost
- the total amount you have to spend
- where the money will come from to pay the costs – if the costs are too high you may have to think again about the event
- your budget – the total income and costs.

QUARTERLY EVENTS BUDGET	JAN	FEB	MAR	TOTAL
Income:				
Sale of entrance tickets	1600	1320	1685	4605
Sale of raffle tickets	300	232	337	869
Fund donation	250	180	300	730
TOTAL	2150	1732	2322	6204
Expenditure:				
Catering	600	550	480	1630
Entertainments	300	300	300	900
Hire of hall	200	200	200	600
Promotion				
Leaflets and posters	300	260	138	698
Tickets	150	130	130	410
TOTAL	1550	1440	1248	4238
PROFIT	**600**	**292**	**1074**	**1966 (Total profit)**

Time

Planning helps to make the best use of time. At an early planning meeting, event teams should:

- fix a date when the event will take place
- agree an action plan with a timescale for different stages and activities – it's best to do this by working back from the date of the event and deciding how to make the best use of the time available.

NETBALL 2000

The leisure centre wanted the tournament to take place at the end of March, and the planning team began working on the project in mid-December. Working back from the timing suggested, and allowing for Christmas, this gave them three months to plan and prepare for the event.

Working back from 27 March, they produced a rough action plan to help them make the most of the time available. Richard Smith, the promotion manager, produced a timetable of his own, to make sure he made the best use of the time available for marketing.

Timing	What I should be doing
Over Christmas	Plan how to promote the event to schools, youth groups and other teenage girls in the community. Decide what promotional materials we need and how to produce them.
January	Write, design and agree promotional materials and entry forms with the rest of the team. Aim of these will be to encourage teams to enter. Get them reproduced and ready for distribution by the end of the month.
February	Distribute promotional materials advertising the competition and how to enter. If entries don't come in quickly, think of other ways to push the tournament. Start preparing materials advertising the event to spectators.
March	All entries should be in by 4 March. Then distribute materials advertising the event to spectators.
27 March	The event itself! Hopefully see promotion has been a big success by the number of people who turn up.

His outline plan helped Richard to make good use of the three months. It also meant that he didn't end up producing materials at the last minute, or rushing and making mistakes.

People

As well as their own team members, some planning teams get extra help from other people to run the event:

■ experts who provide specialist help

■ volunteers who've agreed to lend a hand on the day.

Whoever they are, people are a valuable resource. Teams should make sure that they make the most of people's skills and availability.

A youth club leader explains how they went about using people effectively when planning a sponsored swim:

66 *The idea was that ten youth club members would swim legs in rotation for twelve hours to raise money for the club. Because the event was so long, we had to get volunteers to help staff at the swimming pool. We made sure a qualified lifesaver was there all the time, which meant checking with the pool manager on the availability of staff. Volunteers filled in a sheet saying when they were free to help. I set up two-hour shifts with two volunteers on each shift, one to give the swimmers refreshments, and the other to provide general back-up.* **99**

Materials and equipment

Making the most of materials and equipment calls for good organisational skills, persistence and detective work.

A member of hotel maintenance staff who is responsible for organising the equipment and materials for events ranging from auctions to wedding receptions, explains:

66 *Well, you need a good eye for noticing things which might be useful one day. I've been called on to find the strangest things for events. Once I was asked to borrow a horse-drawn carriage for a Cinderella themed party – just as well they didn't ask for it to look like a pumpkin! You do need to be a bit practical and resourceful. It's no good getting hold of gadgets if you don't know how to use them, or know someone else who can. One mistake I made was to hire a lighting system for a disco, thinking I could work it on my own. An hour before it started, I was frantically phoning round electricians to get them to show me how to use it.* **99**

Information

Each team member needs the facts and figures specific to their role if they are to do their particular job well. Some information will be passed on by the team leader or other team members at the planning stage, but sometimes more information is needed once you've started preparing for an event. A promotions assistant in a provincial theatre explains how a programme to relaunch the theatre was affected by a lack of information:

66 *Our children's events and popular musicals were always well attended, and we knew we could attract those kinds of audiences. The plan was to broaden our repertoire, and increase our audience, by staging more classical drama and light comedy. This was quite a risky venture for us, but the management thought it would pay off. We carried out some research before planning the detail of the forthcoming season. We checked what other small and large theatres in the region were planning to put on and we contacted the local and regional cinema chains, and the independents too to find out what they'd be showing. With all this information we felt confident we could put together a season of plays that would be winners, and set about all the pre-production work.*

What we didn't know was that we'd have a lot more competition than we'd bargained for. One of the more popular pubs in the centre of town started a theatre upstairs staging avant garde productions which proved quite a draw. Then we found out that the local sports stadium had organised a series of rock concerts that would clash with our programme dates. And finally we were leafleted by the local college – they were announcing their autumn term drama series and we knew this would attract a lot of interest. 99

ACTIVITY

Are you making the best possible use of the resources available to you in your role in planning an event? Make notes on how you are using:

■ money

■ time

■ people

■ materials and equipment

■ information.

Think again about your plans. Is there any way you could use resources more effectively?

Health, safety and security

Organisations have a duty of care to both their employees and customers. If people's health and safety are put at risk during an event, it could be dangerous and might have serious repercussions for the organisation. People have a right to feel secure when attending an event. So systems are needed to ensure the security of property and people at a facility, and of information collected for an event.

Teams running events should consider:

- health, safety and security during the planning process
- their own, and their colleagues, health and safety during the event
- the health and safety of customers during the event
- the security of the facility during the event
- the security of information collected for the event.

Health and safety of the team

The Health and Safety at Work Act (1974) gives employees responsibility for their own, and their colleagues, health and safety. To observe the Act, people involved in a leisure and tourism event should:

- take care to avoid injury to themselves and others
- make sure they don't move or misuse anything provided to protect their health and safety
- help to ensure the requirements of the Act are put into practice throughout the event.

What this means in practice depends on their role.

Health and safety in practice

- Wear protective clothing and encourage other team members to do the same.
- Check equipment is in a good condition before using it.
- Don't touch anything which looks like it might be faulty, and warn other team members about it.
- Keep the work area tidy, and put up signs to warn others of slippery floors, obstacles and other hazards.
- Make sure fire escapes and emergency exits are kept clear.
- Be prepared for possible accidents, so you can react quickly and efficiently.
- Report any hazards or accidents that do occur immediately.

Look carefully at this photograph.

■ What are the potential health and safety risks to people working in this environment?

■ What could they do to avoid danger?

Health and safety of customers

Customers should be able to enjoy themselves at leisure and tourism events without any risk to their health and safety. It's the responsibility of the event team to make sure they can do this.

Every team member needs to be aware of health and safety at all times, and take precautions to protect the well-being of customers. Every team should also have one person who takes particular responsibility for the health and safety of customers.

NETBALL 2000

Lorna Roberts, health and safety manager for the team planning Netball 2000, surveyed the leisure centre facilities carefully before the event. She made this list of potential health and safety risks to spectators and participants.

Potential risks

■ damaged equipment – wobbly netball posts

■ damaged seating

■ not enough qualified first aiders on hand

■ not enough St John's Ambulance people available

■ slippery ground in the case of rain

■ dirty toilets, showers and changing rooms, with slippery floors

■ fire escapes and emergency exits blocked

■ bad food hygiene for refreshments

She had to check the first four points in advance and then on the day of the event, she spent time checking each of these possible hazards, and took action to solve any problems.

DISCUSSION POINT

Look at the photograph carefully.

■ What are the potential health and safety risks to customers at a venue like this?

■ What precautions should be taken to avoid accidents and emergencies?

Security risks

- The physical security of people from violence and abuse. Security guards and police (at large events) can help to prevent attacks occurring. Many local facilities now have their own security guards.

- Security of property. Security guards patrolling a facility can help to prevent vandalism. Closed-circuit television (CCTV) can also be a useful way to monitor security across a facility.

- Security of possessions and equipment from theft. Many facilities provide lockers for customers' personal belongings, and take care to lock away any equipment which might be stolen. Security guards and CCTV can deter thieves.

- Security of money taken on the door. Takings should be locked away securely in a till or cash box.

DISCUSSION POINT

Think of other leisure and tourism events where security is a major concern. What do facilities do to prevent security risks?

Security of facility

Teams running leisure and tourism events need to be aware of the risks to security that arise when there's a crowd of people in a small space.

When taking part in an event, team members should:
- make sure security arrangements are in place for customers
- keep an eye out for trouble
- know what action to take.

Some leisure and tourism events have such a serious security problem that it puts people off attending.

SECURITY AT FOOTBALL MATCHES

One of the main aims of staff working at football matches is to ensure the security of everyone in the ground. Following a long history of crowd trouble at football matches in the UK, police and football authorities have introduced crowd control measures for the security of spectators.

The government has passed laws which make it an offence to throw objects, chant abuse, or run on to the playing area. There are also controls on alcohol at football grounds and transport to and from grounds. Convicted football hooligans can be barred from going to football matches and travelling abroad to attend matches.

These measures are enforced by police, the National Criminal Intelligence Service Football Unit, and the staff at clubs, who want to ensure the security of their fans. Closed-circuit television (CCTV) has helped police in spotting and stopping trouble.

Security of information

When planning a leisure and tourism event, teams collect a large amount of information about customers, staff and organisations. In the past, all of this information would have been kept on paper, leaving it at risk from fire and theft, and making it easy to lose. Today, most of this type of information is held on a computer. Event teams can make back-up copies quickly and easily and store them on floppy discs.

The administration manager at a hotel which specialises in organising business conferences explains why it is important to make information secure:

66 *I'm extremely careful about the security of information. If we lost our records of customers and events it could cost the business thousands of pounds. Then there's confidentiality. We hold a lot of information about different companies and individuals, and we owe it to our customers to make sure we keep this information secure. All the conference-related information is stored on one computer, and anyone using it has to have their own password to get into the database. Every day, the information on the hard disc is backed up on floppy discs, which are stored in a fire-proof safe in the manager's office.* **99**

ACTIVITY

Are you contributing fully to ensuring the health, safety and security of your team event? Make notes on what you are doing to ensure:

- your own health and safety, and that of your colleagues
- the health and safety of customers
- the security of the facility
- the security of information.

Cooperating with others

Cooperating means working together towards a shared goal.

Team members have to work well with other people – their colleagues and their customers – to help a leisure and tourism event meet its goals.

Cooperating with colleagues

Teamwork is a skill that everyone uses when planning and running a leisure and tourism event. The team plan sets out people's roles and the team structure for an event. Team members have to work together in line with this structure and their roles in it.

This diagram shows some of the ways that colleagues cooperate with each other.

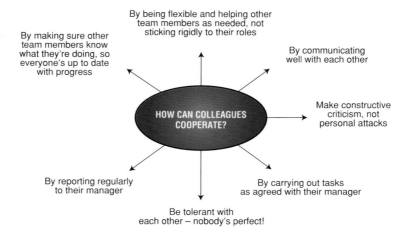

By being flexible and helping other team members as needed, not sticking rigidly to their roles

By making sure other team members know what they're doing, so everyone's up to date with progress

By communicating well with each other

HOW CAN COLLEAGUES COOPERATE?

Make constructive criticism, not personal attacks

By reporting regularly to their manager

By carrying out tasks as agreed with their manager

Be tolerant with each other – nobody's perfect!

Regular team meetings can help team members communicate and work together. It's one of the responsibilities of the team leader to spot situations where team colleagues aren't cooperating, and to try to resolve any misunderstandings or conflicts.

DISCUSSION POINT

A member of a team planning an event at a school gave this description of how she worked with other team members:

❝ The group I was in was a complete nightmare. Laura was supposed to be my manager – what a joke! She can only just manage to get up in the morning. I didn't pay her any attention. Planning meetings were held after school, but I missed some and didn't get round to telling the rest of the group what I was doing. When I did, they all went mad at me because I hadn't done the right thing. Well, honestly, what could they expect? ❞

How could the team leader have improved cooperation in this group?

Cooperating with customers

Almost all members of a leisure and tourism event team will have some contact with customers during the course of the event. The way staff relate to customers can make a big impression – not only of the event, but also of the organisation which managed it and the facility where it was held.

So it's important that team members should cooperate with customers and help them to enjoy the event. The diagram shows some of the ways they can do this.

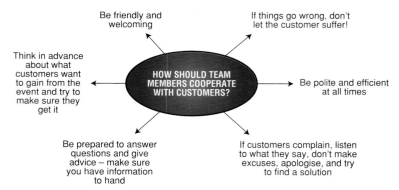

Be friendly and welcoming

If things go wrong, don't let the customer suffer!

Think in advance about what customers want to gain from the event and try to make sure they get it

HOW SHOULD TEAM MEMBERS COOPERATE WITH CUSTOMERS?

Be polite and efficient at all times

Be prepared to answer questions and give advice – make sure you have information to hand

If customers complain, listen to what they say, don't make excuses, apologise, and try to find a solution

The main thing is to put the customer first. After all, the event has been organised for their benefit.

ACTIVITY

How good are you at cooperating with other people? Make notes about:

■ times when you cooperated particularly well with team colleagues and customers

■ times when you didn't cooperate so well.

NETBALL 2000

One of the team, Chris Jones, took on the role of catering assistant for Netball 2000. Here he describes how his part in the team involved cooperating with other team members and customers:

❝ I worked closely with Chloe, the bar manager, who told me what I was responsible for. There were two of us as catering assistants, so we didn't have much to do in the early stages. When the promotions assistant said she was snowed under, I went and helped her out with posters and entry forms for a while. On the day, the three of us responsible for catering worked really well together. A couple of times things got a bit tense, but we managed to have a laugh and came out the other side feeling OK.

On the day I had a lot of contact with customers when they came for refreshments. We'd practised serving, so it was all quite efficient. Three or four customers asked for directions to telephones and lavatories so the maps we'd done in advance were useful. Once or twice people complained about the wait they'd had for refreshments. I apologised and explained we'd been really busy – they seemed to go away happy. ❞

Changes to an agreed role

In a good team, everyone agrees their roles in an event early on. But things don't always go quite as planned.

Part of working as a team is being flexible enough to change roles occasionally. For example, if the people doing the catering are rushed off their feet and the person responsible for marketing has nothing to do, it makes sense for the marketing person to help out with refreshments.

Team members can make changes to agreed roles in two ways:
- by taking the initiative themselves
- by getting instructions from a manager or the team leader.

Taking the initiative

During an event, team members may notice that things aren't going exactly to plan. For example:
- it's taking longer than expected to put out equipment, and customers are already starting to arrive
- catering staff can't cope with the number of customers queueing up for lunch
- the person taking money on the door is having trouble because there isn't enough change
- someone is needed to take an injured competitor to the first aid room.

In any of these situations, team members might take the initiative and help out where needed. If they do, they should tell their team leader where they are going and why. If they're busy in their agreed roles, it might be better to tell the team leader, who will try to find someone else with more time to spare.

Getting instructions

The team leader is responsible for overseeing the smooth running of the event and making sure that the work is divided fairly. If some team members are overworked and others have time to spare, a good team leader will ask people to change roles and help out. If a team member is absent on the day, it's the team leader's job to reorganise roles and explain the new arrangements to the rest of the team.

If they are told to change roles, team members should accept the instructions without a fuss and carry out their new roles as efficiently as they can. The organiser of a one-off conference at a hotel explains:

66 *Everybody knew what they were supposed to do in advance. But we hadn't planned for the fact that delegates to the conference would come in a rush. When we opened, people on the registration desk just couldn't cope. I left a skeleton staff of two people in the hall to show delegates where to go and told the other staff to help at the desk. When it became clear that more people were beginning to drift into the hall and make for their seats, I asked the staff who'd been in the hall originally to come back again and help direct the delegates in the right direction.* 99

DISCUSSION POINT

Think about these situations for a moment. If you were a team member:
- what would you want to do?
- what might stop you doing it?

DISCUSSION POINT

Can you think of other reasons why there might be changes to agreed roles during an event?

DISCUSSION POINT

In your planning team, discuss possible situations when you might need to make changes to agreed roles during the event you are organising. Agree procedures for:
- taking the initiative in changing roles
- giving and receiving instructions to change roles.

273

Reacting to disruptions

THE WALDEGRAVE SPORTS CENTRE

GRAND OPENING

Saturday 9th December
at 2.00pm
By the star of track and field:
**Winfield
Christopher**

Some events go smoothly. But it's quite likely that there will be some disruptions. Disruptions can cause annoyance and discomfort to customers – and the team must react fast. Team members will be more flexible and alert if they know in advance:

■ the different disruptions that might affect events
■ what changes might need to be made as a result
■ how to inform others of these changes.

Changes of plan

Things don't always run to plan, and plans are not meant to be fixed in concrete. It might be necessary for team members to change roles, timings or the services they provide.

Changes

To roles

If some team members are absent or very busy, others may need to change roles temporarily. If roles are changed, the team leader must tell all team members so they know what their new roles are and who they are working with. Customers don't need to be informed – if teamwork is good, they need never know there was a problem.

To timings

Bad weather, fewer participants than expected, or activities which overrun may all change the original timings. Team leaders should tell team members about any changes, so everyone is working to the same timetable. Customers should also be told, so they know when to expect different events. If changes are known about early enough, a correction slip can be put inside programmes. A public address system can be used to communicate last-minute changes to customers.

To services

Faulty equipment or absent team members may mean changes to services. Team leaders should make sure all team members know what the changes are and why, so they can answer customer enquiries and handle any complaints.

Emergencies

Sometimes emergencies happen at events. It's particularly important for team members to react promptly. Procedures should be established in advance so that the whole team knows what to do in the case of:

■ fire – calling the emergency services, showing people to the fire exits, following evacuation procedures, closing doors, going to meeting points.
■ accidents – getting help from a first aider, asking a voluntary medical organisation for help (e.g. Red Cross, St John's Ambulance), calling the emergency services in the case of a serious accident.

The team member responsible for health and safety should:

- make sure systems are in place to deal with emergencies
- circulate information to the rest of the team in advance.

Anticipated disruptions

Some disruptions can be predicted in advance, including:

- changes caused by bad weather
- changes caused by an unexpected number of participants (either more than expected, or fewer than expected).

Event teams should have contingency plans in place to deal with them, so they can react promptly and minimise inconvenience to customers.

Disruptions can result in changes to timings and services. These must be communicated quickly and clearly to customers, so they know what to do and expect. The organiser of a street festival describes how the event team reacted when disruptions occurred:

66 *We knew from the start that the festival needed good weather – a bad risk in this country. We'd decided that if it rained we'd get the sound systems under cover in the stalls first, and we also had a few big rolls of polythene to protect them. When we saw that the weather was going to change for the worse we changed the timings of some of the activities. The master of ceremonies or whatever you call him put out regular messages on the PA system explaining the new timings, and apart from getting wet people had a good time all the same. The weather didn't win.* 99

NETBALL 2000

The Netball 2000 team had to cope with several disruptions to the event. They'd expected some of them, and there were others they hadn't foreseen. Ruth Karniol, the tournament manager, describes what happened:

66 *As we'd half expected from the forecast, it was pretty awful weather on the day of the tournament – rain and sleet. Obviously it would have been dangerous and miserable playing outdoors so we moved the tournament inside. Because there were fewer courts inside, the timing of matches had to change. We'd planned all the changed timings in advance, so on the morning of the tournament we went through the programmes and changed them neatly by hand. We also put up posters around the sports hall explaining the changes.*

Peta, the equipment manager, phoned me early in the morning and explained she was ill and wouldn't be able to come. I spoke to Jo, our team leader, and we quickly reorganised people's roles so that equipment would be taken care of. As soon as the team arrived at the leisure centre at 10 a.m., we held a meeting and Jo told everyone about the changes.

During the afternoon, everything seemed to run amazingly smoothly. People helped out where they were needed and everybody communicated well. One girl sprained her ankle while playing, but we took her straight to the representative from St John's Ambulance, who dealt with the injury quickly. 99

ACTIVITY

Are you ready to react promptly to any disruptions to your event? In your planning team:

- write a list of anticipated disruptions

- make sure everyone's clear about changes which may have to be made

- work out how you will inform each other and your customers of any changes that need to be made to team roles, timings and services provided.

Keeping a log of your contribution

A **log** is a record of things done – it's like a diary of an event.

If team members want to show the role they played in an event, they can keep a log of their contribution from the planning stages through to the actual event itself. A log could contain many different types of information.

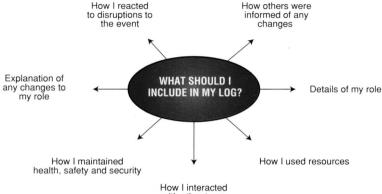

How I reacted to disruptions to the event

How others were informed of any changes

Explanation of any changes to my role

WHAT SHOULD I INCLUDE IN MY LOG?

Details of my role

How I maintained health, safety and security

How I used resources

How I interacted with other team members and customers

NETBALL 2000

Some team members involved in organising the Netball 2000 event kept a log in the form of a diary. Here's one, kept by Chloe Robinson, catering manager for the event.

15 Dec: *The centre manager has asked us to run a netball tournament for teenage girls to attract more people to our facilities. There's a team of 12 of us working on the project. Today we talked about the objectives of the event, what we would do, and what roles people should play. Because I'm experienced and well organised, I am going to be the catering manager. This means I am responsible for buying, preparing and selling food and drink for the event. The aim is to break even – we don't have to make a profit. I've got two assistants – June and Chris.*

8 Jan: *At today's planning meeting we talked more about our roles, and I drew up an organisational chart for the team. June and Chris report to me, and I report directly to the team leader, Jo. We agreed to have a planning meeting once a fortnight to say how we are getting on with our jobs.*

20 Jan: *Reported on the action plan I have drawn up for catering activities. This was our main resource meeting, and we discussed who would do what, the skills we all have and what equipment we need. We also thought what we might do in an emergency.*

3 Feb:	Graham gave us a budget for the event and told me how much we had to spend on food and drink. There was a general discussion about what should go into our team plan.
17 Feb:	We reviewed the team plan, and I suggested some changes to the resources – not enough people to help on the publicity, I thought. Tim is going to incorporate the changes and then circulate a new copy.
3 March:	Planning meeting about health and safety standards. We decided to stick to simple ready-made foods and not do any cooking ourselves on the day.
7 March:	Got price list from the wholesaler, and started listing the things we need to buy.
9 March:	Called a catering team meeting to look at the price list and see if we could bring the costs down a bit as I was £40 over budget. Then we decided how much to charge for each item. I asked Graham what he thought, and he agreed with the prices we suggested.
10 March:	Went to the wholesaler with June and bought the first batch of food and drink – things that keep like tea, sugar, crisps, sweets and biscuits.
14 March:	Got Chris to check that there was enough crockery and cutlery. Reminded June to check the equipment.
17 March:	Regular planning meeting. Three of us wrote security notices on the word processor and laminated them. I brought up the issue of spectator safety. Lorna had found out that spectators had to sit at least 5 feet away from the court edge to prevent accidents.
19 March:	We got back 100 programmes from the photocopier. Richard and I folded them. They look really good. We decided that if it rains and we move the tournament indoors we'll correct timings by hand – hope it doesn't happen!
25 March:	Went with June to the wholesalers to buy the last food and drink for the event – things that had to wait until the last minute.
26 March:	Final planning meeting. Jo went through the schedule for tomorrow in detail, and we all talked through what we expected to be doing when. We agreed to meet at the leisure centre at 10 a.m.

27 March: Woke up this morning and it's sleeting outside – we're going to have to move the event indoors.

10 a.m.   Arrived at the centre. Most of the team were already there. We held a meeting, and decided officially to hold Netball 2000 indoors. Jo divided responsibilities out between the team. Some people helped to move equipment inside and set up the courts. Four of us went to work changing the times on 100 programmes. We'd already decided the new timings, so we just had to correct them so spectators knew when different matches would be played.

11 a.m.   Started checking all the catering equipment was working and in order. Asked Chris and June to lay out crockery and cutlery on a trestle table behind the counter so it would be easy to use. Told Chris to make a price list on a blackboard outside the serving hatch.

12 noon   Jo came round to check how we were getting on. I explained what we'd been doing, and she said to let her know if we needed any more help. June spilt a kettle full of water when filling the tea urn – mopped it up straightaway, so no one would slip on it. Lorna, health and safety officer, came round to check that everything was in good order.

1 p.m.   Started to get the food ready. I made sure the three of us were wearing aprons and tied my hair back. We laid out biscuits, cut cake, made squash, and got boxes of crisps and sweets ready to sell. Graham brought a float so we could give people change. I was worried about the security aspect, and he came back with a lockable cash box. We decided to keep a float of £10 at all times, and put the rest away in the box.

1.30 p.m.   Served our first customer! She thanked us and said it looked like we were going to do a good job.

2.00 p.m.   A steady stream of customers. We coped quite well, serving them food and drink, taking money and being friendly and cheerful. Several asked us questions, such as directions to the toilets and when different matches were due on court. We were able to help most of them even though we were busy.

Go through Chloe's log carefully and write down:

- what her role was
- what resources there were and how she used them
- how health, safety and security standards were maintained
- how Chloe interacted with other team members and customers
- if there were any changes agreed to her role
- how she reacted to and dealt with disruptions to the event
- how she let others know of any changes that affected them.

3.00 p.m.	The tournament interval, and we've been rushed off our feet. We managed to stay calm and not panic, and served everyone as quickly as we could. Jo came by to see how we were getting on, and sent Tim and Maria over to help. I showed them quickly what to do, and they fitted in well.
4.00 p.m.	Business slack, as everyone settled down to watch the final. I saw one girl come out of the changing rooms limping, and asked if she was OK. She told me that she'd hurt her ankle, and as we weren't busy I told June and Chris where I was going, and took her to the St John's Ambulance people myself.
4.30 p.m.	Started clearing up the equipment and cleaning the kitchen area. We packed up the dishwashers and set them running. We made sure everything was spotless so it was ready for the next people to use it.
5.00 p.m.	Tournament ended. Graham came round to pick up the cash box, and counted our takings – £379.30, just enough to cover the costs.
5.30 p.m.	Some of the team were still clearing up the seating and court areas, so I lent a hand.
6.00 p.m.	Went home.

Key questions

1 What are the two ways in which all team members should contribute to a team event?
2 How can the team leader support other members?
3 Why is it important to use resources effectively?
4 What are the five health, safety and security concerns that should be considered when running an event?
5 Can you think of six or seven ways in which team members can cooperate with colleagues?
6 Can you think of five or six ways in which team members can cooperate with customers?
7 What are two ways in which team members might make changes to agreed roles?
8 What are three changes to plan that can cause disruption at an event?
9 Why keep a log of the event?

Assignment

An important part of your work on this unit is taking part in running an event. To keep a record of what happened, fill in a log like Chloe's in the last section to record your contributions to the event.

Your log should include details of:
■ your role in the event
■ how you used resources
■ how you maintained health, safety and security
■ how you interacted with other team members and customers
■ any changes that were made to your agreed role
■ how you reacted to any disruptions to the event
■ how others were informed of changes affecting them.

ELEMENT **4.3**

Evaluating an event

When it's all over, team members involved in an event think about what worked well – and what didn't. Evaluation helps to improve things next time round. In this element you'll look at how teams set criteria for evaluating the success of an event and how they get feedback from each other and other people involved, including customers. You'll see how each team member contributes to the overall evaluation. You'll also look at the types of recommendations that can be made to improve future events.

> 66 We evaluate the success of our work by looking at criteria, such as how many children we are helping and how many areas our programme is covering. We have to cost each event to establish our year-to-year performance. 99
>
> *entertainments officer for a local authority*

> 66 After a concert we always discuss how it went – in particular what went wrong. Most of the discussion is on the musical side, but we do discuss the acoustics of the venue, the helpfulness of the staff and other things like the temperature. Sometimes we make a decision not to go back to a venue. 99
>
> *leader of a band*

> 66 We have a 'wash-up' meeting on the day after the event where we pick up litter, then meet. We count the money, check that all the bills will be paid, and set a meeting for evaluating how it went. Every one of the key people evaluates what they did and decides which bits need to be changed for next year. For example, this year we were short of landing stages, so next year we will try to make sure that enough are left out! 99
>
> *organiser of a regatta*

Criteria for evaluating the event

Evaluating an event means agreeing what worked and didn't work, and assessing whether the event was a success or a failure.

What is evaluated?

- whether the event achieved its objectives
- how well the team worked together
- the contribution of different team members
- how well resources were used
- whether health, safety and security were maintained
- how disruptions were handled
- how the event could have been improved
- what lessons can be learned for the future

Identifying evaluation criteria
HOW WILL WE JUDGE WHETHER THE EVENT WAS A SUCCESS?

Designing an evaluation form
HOW WILL WE RECORD OUR EVALUATION FINDINGS?

Collecting and recording evaluation feedback

Exchanging evaluation feedback within the team

Summarising the team's evaluation

Making and recording suggestions for improvements in the future

Evaluation can only be completed when the event is over. But it starts right at the beginning, when the planning team agrees the objectives for the event.

Evaluation criteria are the things against which the event is evaluated – they can be quantitative, such as the number of people attending, or qualitative, such as how much customers enjoyed the event.

Common criteria for evaluating events are listed in the box at the top of the page.

Did the event meet its objectives?

Probably the most important evaluation criteria. Objectives are agreed at the start of the planning process. After the event, teams look back and evaluate whether they have been met. It can't always be done immediately – for example, if one of the objectives was to increase the number of people using a facility by 15% in the next two months, the team won't be able to judge whether it has achieved this until two months after the end of the event.

If an event doesn't achieve its original objectives, it can't be a complete success. The marketing manager of a night-club explains:

66 *Most of our customers were under 20, so we decided to run an event to increase the number of customers we get over 21. We organised a Friday night 70s party, with free entrance to people who could prove they were over 21, a free drink to anyone dressed in 70s clothes and we played 70s and early 80s music. It seemed to work at the time – we had two hundred people through the doors, and three-quarters of them were over 21. But a month later, the number of over-21s using the club on a normal night hadn't gone up at all.* 99

Were resources used well?

Evaluation covers the team's use of:

- money – their budget
- time taken for planning, and on the day
- different people – their skills and availability
- materials and equipment
- information from sources outside the team.

Was health, safety and security maintained?

Teams planning leisure and tourism events have a duty of care to look after the health, safety and security of people and property. They should evaluate:

- the health and safety of the team and other people helping with the event
- the health and safety of customers
- security of the facility
- security of information.

Did the team cooperate?

Teamwork skills are developed through experience. Individuals can transfer what they learn through evaluating one team event to other teamwork situations in the future.

Evaluating how well the team worked together is especially important if the people in the team are likely to work together again. They could ask questions like:

- how flexible were we in helping out where needed?
- how well did the team structure work?
- were lines of authority followed?
- did the reporting process work well?

NETBALL 2000

On the Tuesday after the Netball 2000 tournament, Jo Mahmud, the team leader, called a first evaluation meeting. Team members were full of ideas on how to evaluate it. Working together, they produced a list of criteria for evaluating its success.

- Did we achieve our main objective of attracting more teenage girls to use the leisure centre's facilities?

- How well did we use resources, including finance, time, people and equipment?

- How well did we maintain health, safety and security throughout the tournament?

- How well did we work together as a team? Did we communicate well?

- Did team members fulfil their agreed roles?

- How well did we handle disruptions?

Did people stick to their agreed roles?

Flexibility and willingness to help is important, but people are assigned specific roles to make sure jobs get done. If they don't fulfil these roles, the event may fail. So it's useful for teams to evaluate how well different team members performed their agreed roles.

The leader of a team which planned an event in a residential home for the elderly describes what happened when staff didn't stick closely enough to what they were supposed to be doing:

66 *Ten of us were involved in planning and carrying out the event. There were specific things that needed doing. I thought we were all quite clear about who should be doing what. But things went wrong because people didn't stick to their roles. The person making tea and coffee got side-tracked to food, and the tea stewed. Three people were supposed to be taking food round, but they disappeared at the crucial time and some customers fell asleep waiting to be served.* **99**

Were disruptions handled well?

Almost all events will experience disruptions of some kind. Being able to handle them can make all the difference between the event's success or failure. At the end of an event, teams may find it useful to evaluate how well they:

- reacted to changes of plan
- responded to emergencies
- dealt with anticipated disruptions – bad weather, changes in numbers of participants
- informed customers and each other of any changes made.

ACTIVITY

After your leisure and tourism event, get the planning team together and agree what criteria you will use to evaluate the success of your event.

Evaluation forms

When a team has agreed the criteria for evaluating an event, each team member has to think about and record their ideas. An evaluation form helps everyone to do this in a similar way. It's a good idea to wordprocess the form and print out enough copies for everyone in the team, and anyone else involved in evaluating the event.

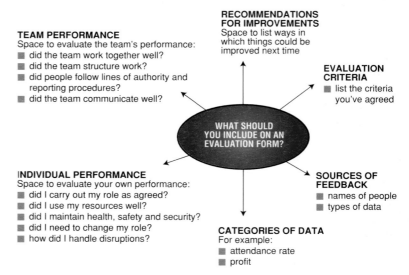

TEAM PERFORMANCE
Space to evaluate the team's performance:
■ did the team work together well?
■ did the team structure work?
■ did people follow lines of authority and reporting procedures?
■ did the team communicate well?

RECOMMENDATIONS FOR IMPROVEMENTS
Space to list ways in which things could be improved next time

EVALUATION CRITERIA
■ list the criteria you've agreed

WHAT SHOULD YOU INCLUDE ON AN EVALUATION FORM?

INDIVIDUAL PERFORMANCE
Space to evaluate your own performance:
■ did I carry out my role as agreed?
■ did I use my resources well?
■ did I maintain health, safety and security?
■ did I need to change my role?
■ how did I handle disruptions?

SOURCES OF FEEDBACK
■ names of people
■ types of data

CATEGORIES OF DATA
For example:
■ attendance rate
■ profit

The form should be laid out like a table, with plenty of room for people to write down ideas and comments, as in the example on the next page.

ACTIVITY

Design an evaluation form which you and others in your planning team can all use to evaluate the event.

Lay it out in the form of a table, with plenty of space for people to fill in ideas and comments. Remember that the form may also be used by other people not in your planning team, so it must be easy for them to understand as well. Wordprocess the form and distribute copies so everyone is filling in exactly the same document.

Evaluation criteria
Did the event meet its objectives?
Were resources used effectively?
Were health, safety and security maintained?
How well did the team cooperate and communicate?
Did people adhere to their agreed roles?
How well were disruptions handled?

Sources and data
What people have provided feedback?
What evaluation data is there?

Individual performance
Did you carry out your role as agreed?
Did you use resources well?
Did you maintain health, safety and security?
Did you need to change your role? Did you inform people?
Were there any disruptions? How did you handle them?

Team performance
Did the team work well together?
Did the team communicate well?
Did the team structure work?
Did people follow lines of authority and reporting procedures?
What were strengths and weaknesses of the team?

Recommendations for improvements
How could we improve the event if we ran it again in the future?

Gathering and recording feedback

It's good to have feedback from a wide range of sources. It helps to give a well-rounded view of the event, rather than a biased perspective.

Team members can collect feedback from different sources and record it on their evaluation forms. The main sources are:

- you
- customers
- colleagues
- your assessor
- other evaluation data.

Your own assessment

Because you were there, you are in a good position to provide your own assessment of the event. It's not easy to be objective, but you should try:

- to be honest about your own strengths and weaknesses
- not to let personal feelings interfere with your evaluation of other people's performance.

You may want to refer back to your log recording the event, to help you remember what you did and how it was achieved. Your memories of what customers and other team members said and did can be a good way to evaluate different aspects of the event.

Customers

They're on the receiving end, so they can provide some of the most useful feedback of all.

Customer feedback will need to be collected during, or straight after, the event, by:

- observing their reactions during the event – if you have a video camera recording the day you can look at the film later
- carrying out a survey, to find out what type of people have attended and their opinions on the event
- keeping records of feedback given in the form of comments and complaints.

A specialist event organiser explains the different methods for collecting feedback from customers:

66 *We collect feedback from customers formally and informally. Formal methods include face-to-face surveys during and after the event, and questionnaires which we ask people to fill in before they leave. Sometimes we have a prize draw to give people an added incentive to complete questionnaires. I'm a strong believer in the value of what customers do and say on the day. I'm often on hand myself, watching the way customers move about and react to activities. I also give staff feedback sheets to fill in during the day, and ask them to record any comments and complaints they get from customers.* 99

Colleagues

As well as assessing their own role, team members can provide feedback on each other's performances in planning and running an event. They can comment on:

- what role someone played as part of the team
- how well they communicated
- whether they fulfilled the responsibilities of their role.

It's important for colleagues to give objective feedback. Personal differences or friendships shouldn't affect the evaluation. Feedback from colleagues is only useful if it's honest and fair.

DISCUSSION POINT

Two members of a team evaluated their team leader's performance like this:

66 Simon was useless as team leader. He didn't turn up to all the meetings. He didn't tell us what to do properly, and I could never find him when I wanted him on the day of the event. He's too boring for anyone to pay attention to anyway. 99

66 Simon made a good team leader because he's serious. He was busy organising something else at the same time as the event, so he missed some meetings. But I thought we got on well without him anyway. He always tried his best to help us whenever he could be around. 99

- How useful do you think these two evaluations are?
- How could the evaluation of Simon's performance as team leader be made more useful?

Assessors

Assessors who observe the way events are planned and run are in a good position to provide feedback. They:

- watch progress on the event from early planning through to the final stages, and have a good overview of the whole thing
- aren't directly involved, so they can give a balanced view of what has happened
- know the constraints the team was working under.

ACTIVITY

Talk to the assessor who observed your event about how he or she would like to give the team feedback. Ask them if they will:

- fill in an evaluation form
- come and talk to your team about the event.

289

Evaluation data

These are facts and figures which may give the team useful information about what was achieved. Depending on the event, evaluation data might include:

■ attendance figures
■ information about the type of customers who came – how old they are, their sex, where they live, etc.
■ figures for profit (or loss)
■ information on how people travelled to the event
■ information on how people heard about the event.

The type of evaluation data which is useful will depend upon the evaluation criteria the team has identified. For example:

■ if the main objective is to make a profit, financial data will be important
■ if the aim is to attract new customers from outside the area, information on who came to the event will be useful.

Often, evaluation data can only be collected some time after the event.

NETBALL 2000

Jo Mahmud, the leader of the team planning and running Netball 2000, thought about the sources of information she wanted to use when filling in her evaluation form and wrote herself a list.

Sources of information

■ me – my own assessment of how the event went

■ feedback from customers – small-scale survey on the day, and customers' comments

■ my supervisor's comments – he came to two of the planning meetings and was there on the day

■ what other team members said to me during the day and in the pub that evening

■ any data we collected – number of spectators, number of participants, money taken

ACTIVITY

List the different sources – people and data – that you can use to get feedback on your event. Collect information from these sources, and record it on your evaluation form.

Exchanging feedback

Informal feedback

Team members take it in turns to give their personal views and comments on their performance, and on how the whole team performed. This sort of feedback identifies broad areas of success and failure.

Formal feedback

Team members summarise the information they have recorded on their evaluation form, and present it to the rest of the team, who then have a chance to respond.

When each person in the team has collected feedback and had time to think about their own views, the whole team should get together and share their thoughts.

Giving feedback

Team members can give feedback to each other in two main ways.

Informal feedback sessions tend to become too personal, so formal feedback is often more constructive.

DISCUSSION POINT

How will you make sure that any criticisms you make when giving feedback are constructive, not personal?

Responding to feedback

When a team member has given feedback to the rest of the team, there should be an opportunity for other people to respond. Before responding, team members should ask themselves:

- Is the praise deserved?
- Are the criticisms fair?
- What can I learn from what my colleague has said?

A team member describes what happened at their evaluation review.

❝ *I was quite on edge about it at first – I suppose you're always worried that someone's going to criticise you. But it turned out to be OK. We decided to stick to the format of our evaluation forms, and took it in turns to go through what we'd written and answer questions. At one point, Tim said he thought I could have taken the initiative a bit more. My immediate reaction was to be angry and defend myself. When he explained what he meant, I realised he was probably right.* **❞**

ACTIVITY

Organise an evaluation feedback session for the whole team. Ask an assessor or tutor along to help make the meeting constructive and not too personal. Make sure someone takes notes – they will be a useful summary of the overall findings of your team's evaluation.

Summarising the findings

Because events are planned and run by a team, the summary of the evaluation findings should reflect the team's view, rather than the view of any one team member.

As they've been working together, the team should have a common view of what happened, what went well and what improvements could be made next time. Having done the evaluation as a team, they should be able to agree on what the findings show – though there may be things they don't agree on and need to discuss further.

A summary of the findings must be:

■ brief

■ concise

■ to the point.

Clear headings will help and so will diagrams and tables – particularly with any financial information you want to summarise.

NETBALL 2000

The Netball 2000 team agreed these headings for their summary:

■ Event objectives

■ Evaluation methods we used

■ Evaluation criteria

- Main objective

- Resource objectives

- Health and safety objective

- Teamwork

- Team roles

- How we handled disruptions

■ Overall success rate

■ Recommended improvements.

Suggestions for improvements

The purpose of evaluation is to find out what succeeded and failed, and to learn lessons for the future. Organising an event gives team members useful experience. Thinking about how they would carry out similar events in the future helps them to make the most of what they have learned.

What type of improvements is it useful to consider?

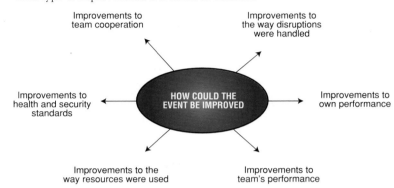

NETBALL 2000

Jo Mahmud, the team leader, spent a long time thinking how she would improve the event if she was involved in something similar in the future. After talking to her colleagues and her supervisor, she filled in the final section of her evaluation form.

Recommended improvements

How could we improve the event if we ran it again in the future?	1. Run the tournament at the end of April, chances of fair weather better then.
	2. Extend the event – run more heats with a greater number of teams competing over a weekend
	3. Each member of the planning and organising team to have a back-up person who could take over their role at short notice if needed.
	4. Include venue details on back of tickets – map of layout, parking, etc

ACTIVITY

Talk to the rest of the team and your assessor about how the event could have been improved. If you were to carry out a similar event in the future, what improvements would you make? Think about:

■ your own performance

■ the team's performance

■ team cooperation

■ the use of resources

■ health, safety and security standards

■ the way in which disruptions might be handled.

Make notes, then fill in the final section on your evaluation form. Keep a copy, so you can refer back to it when you take part in events in the future.

Key questions

1 What does evaluating an event mean?
2 What are evaluation criteria?
3 What eight things should be evaluated after an event?
4 Why is it helpful for everyone to use an evaluation form?
5 What should be included on an evaluation form?
6 What are the five main sources of feedback?
7 What are the two main ways in which team members can exchange feedback?
8 Whose views should be summarised in the findings after an event?
9 A summary of findings should be three things – what are those things?
10 Can you think of five or six ways in which suggestions for improvements could be useful for future events?

Assignment

Get together with the other people in your team. Design a form for evaluating the event. Use a wordprocessor or desktop publishing software to produce a final version. Your form should include:

■ the criteria you agree on for evaluating the event
■ sources of feedback on the event
■ data you are using to evaluating it – things like the number of people attending and the amount of profit made
■ space for each individual member of the team to summarise their own performance
■ space for an evaluation of the whole team's performance
■ your team's suggestions for improving the way events are run in future.

When you have produced the form, write a summary of your own performance. Then make time to meet as a team to fill in the rest of the form. Your tutor or another assessor will be observing the way you and other members of the team work together to design and complete the form. Don't forget that when you're taking part in discussions you should:

■ contribute at appropriate points – when you have something to say
■ say things clearly
■ check that other people understand what you are saying
■ check that you understand what they are saying
■ keep the discussion moving by asking questions and summarising points made by others.

Index